BETH MOORE

DAVID

Seeking a Heart Like His

LifeWay Press®
Nashville, Tennessee

ISBN 9781415869482
Item 005337219

Dewey Decimal classification: 220.07
Subject heading: BIBLE STUDY \ WOMEN—MINISTRY

Unless otherwise noted Scripture quotations are from the Holy
Bible, New International Version, © copyright 1973, 1978, 1984
by International Bible Society. Scripture quotations marked
NASB are from the New American Standard Bible. © The Lock-
man Foundation, 1960, 1962, 1963, 1968, 1971, 1972, 1973,
1975, 1977. Used by permission. Scripture quotations marked
NKJV are from the New King James Version. Copyright © 1979,
1980, 1982. Thomas Nelson, Inc., Publishers. Used by permission. Scripture quotations marked HCSB® are taken from the
Holman Christian Standard Bible, copyright © 1999, 2000,
2002, 2003 by Holman Bible Publishers. Used by permission.

To order additional copies of this resource, write to LifeWay Church
Resources Customer Service, One LifeWay Plaza, Nashville, TN
37234-0113; fax (615) 251-5933; phone toll free (800) 458-2772;
order online at *www.lifeway.com;* e-mail *orderentry@lifeway.com;* or
visit the LifeWay Christian Store serving you.

Printed in the United States of America

Leadership and Adult Publishing
LifeWay Christian Resources
One LifeWay Plaza
Nashville, TN 37234-0175

DEDICATION

To my beloved friend, Johnnie,

Because you've stuck with me for over 30 years.

Because you'd be the first one to recognize all my weaknesses but God forbid that anyone else criticize me in front of you.

Because you made raising children so much fun.

Because you wouldn't let me pack up and move back home with my parents when I was a young mom. Keith and I stuck it out many times because of you and David.

Because few people on earth have made me laugh any more than you.

Because God used you and the women's group you led to give me the opportunity to try my awkward hand at curriculum. It's still awkward.

And because when I fell into self-doubt over the revision of this particular Bible study, you said, "It's my favorite one. Do it."

And so, here it is, and partially because of you.

I thank God for you, Johnnie Haines. My life would have been so different had God not graced my path with the likes of you.

Thank you for loving me even when I wasn't very lovable.

About the Author

Beth Moore has written best-selling Bible studies on the Patriarchs, Esther, Moses, Paul, Isaiah, Daniel, John, and Jesus. *Breaking Free, Praying God's Word,* and *When Godly People Do Ungodly Things* have all focused on the battle Satan is waging against Christians. *Believing God, Loving Well,* and *Living Beyond Yourself* have focused on how Christians can live triumphantly in today's world. *Stepping Up* explores worship and invites us to reach a new level of relationship and intimacy with God.

Beth's ministry is grounded in and fueled by her service at her home fellowship, First Baptist Church, Houston, Texas. Beth believes that her calling is Bible literacy: guiding believers to love and live God's Word. *David: Seeking a Heart Like His* grew from her fervent desire that women know greater intimacy with God.

Beth has a passion for Christ, a passion for Bible study, and a passion to see Christians living the lives Christ intended. God bless you as you join Beth and explore the new and updated version of *David: Seeking a Heart Like His.*

Beth loves the Lord, loves to laugh, and loves to be with His people. Her life is full of activity, but one commitment remains constant: Counting all things but loss for the excellence of knowing Christ Jesus, the Lord (see Phil. 3:8).

CONTENTS

WEEK ONE
Summoned from the Sheepfold. 10

WEEK TWO
Sowing the Seeds of Jealousy. 34

WEEK THREE
Survival Skills and He Who Wills. 58

WEEK FOUR
Tragic Ends and Faithful Friends 82

WEEK FIVE
The Long-Awaited Throne 104

WEEK SIX
A Man After God's Own Heart. 126

WEEK SEVEN
The Wages of Sin 148

WEEK EIGHT
The Unrelenting Sword 170

WEEK NINE
Back Where He Belonged. 194

WEEK TEN
The Final Years and Settled Fears. 218

Endnotes 240

INTRODUCTION

Welcome to *David: Seeking a Heart Like His.* I'm thrilled you've chosen to take this journey through Scripture with me. We have quite an expedition before us as we tour the pastures, caves, and palace of one of the most well-known figures in history—King David.

We will quickly discover David's multifaceted personality. Our responses to his experiences will likely be as diverse as he was. He will make us laugh and cry. He will delight and disappoint us. He will make us want to be just like him at times and nothing like him at others.

David's life and times will cause us to have many responses, but boredom will likely not be one of them! He is sure to capture your interest, if you let him. And God is sure to change your heart, if you let Him.

Getting prepared for a study of David is somewhat like getting ready for a tornado. Gather the necessary supplies (a Bible, your member book, and a pen). Find a refuge where you can study, and hold on for dear life.

A Woman's Heart's basic theme is God in relationship to man. *David* gives us a glimpse of the opposite, man in relationship to God. These pages will highlight the best and the worst of humanity. David lived thousands of years ago, yet he dealt with many issues that plague God's people today. If you've ever had doubts, fought temptations, battled personal inconsistencies, fallen into sin, suffered losses, or anguished over family problems, this Bible study is for you. If you haven't, you may need to check your pulse.

David is an in-depth 11-session Bible study. It takes us through virtually every twist and turn of David's life as a shepherd, a refugee, and a king. Each week contains five daily lessons; each requires about 45 minutes to complete. Completing each day's assignment is crucial for you to benefit from the study. I hope you will not miss a single lesson.

Each week includes five Principal Questions marked with a color background like the following:

Your small group will discuss these each week.

Also, you will find Personal Discussion Questions identified with a color line above the activity like the following:

These will help you personally relate the events to your life. Your small group will address each of these, but you will never be expected to share anything personal in the group. Share only what you are comfortable talking about.

Please answer each lesson's questions whether or not you share your answers in your small group. Often your heart may overflow with the desire to share what God is doing through the study. Other times you may desire to keep God's very personal work between the two of you.

A Scripture called Today's Treasure introduces each daily lesson and represents the lesson's theme. You will be asked to complete reading assignments and various types of learning activities. You may find multiple choice questions, true/false activities, fill-in-the-blank statements, creative thinking exercises, or straightforward questions you will answer in your own words. You will also occasionally be asked to write a Scripture to emphasize what God's Word is saying to you.

At the close of each daily lesson I encourage you to ask two questions: In what ways do you believe God was speaking directly to you today? What is your response to Him? God wants to speak to you personally through His Word. We are not studying Scripture to increase our head knowledge. We want God to change our hearts and lives. Reflect on how God specifically spoke to you. Each time He speaks to you through the study, make a fresh commitment to Him. Your life will yield fruit from these truths forever if you will fully participate in each lesson.

You will notice *David* primarily employs the New International Version of the Bible. If you do not own this version, you will still be able to reap riches from God's Word and answer the questions in each lesson.

The most effective environment for studying *David*—like most in-depth Bible studies—is in a group. You are more likely to complete this study if you enjoy the benefits of a weekly discussion group. Members will meet for weekly accountability and discussion and watch video segments. In the video I share additional material to what you find in this workbook and conclude each week with additional truths and challenges. As you view each video segment, you will record information on the response sheet located at the end of each week's work.

God taught me about Himself and His servant David through this Bible study. He also taught me about myself. I now have a greater grasp of the woman I could be. I want to be a woman after God's own heart. I also have confronted my weaknesses and acknowledged vulnerable places in my life. The enemy will invariably strike these places and attempt to bring me defeat. I believe I have never been as aware of my capabilities, both good and bad.

I have made specific adjustments in my personal life as a direct result of God's direction studying the life of David. The process of this journey was often painful for me, but it never failed to be pertinent. This study takes courage, my friend. You will not be able to confront God's Word day after day and refuse to change. You will either shut the book or allow God to change you. Let Him do His perfect work so that every word will be used to mold you with A Heart Like His!

Beth

Our objective is to study the life of David. We will launch our journey with Scripture's first reference to him; then we will flash back momentarily to capture our historical context.

v 14 first whisper of David.

Read 1 Samuel 13:1-14.

Consider the following statements as starting points:

1. A person's __story__ never begins with his or her own. Two figures loom large in David's introduction: __Samuel__, Israel's last __judge__, and __Saul__, Israel's first __king__.

2. Our lives are often laboriously __intertwined__ with another we have neither __chosen__ nor fully __accepted__. The lives of Samuel and Saul were knotted by two simple words: "__asked for__."

1 Sam 1:20

   • The name *Samuel* is a compound of the Hebrew words for __shem__ *name*
   (*shem*) and __God__ (*el*), and means he over whom the name of God has been said. In Hebrew the name also __sounds__ very similar to the verb *ask* (*sha'al*).

because hunter }
bow hunter } sounds the same
different meaning

• The Hebrew name Saul (*sha'ul*) is drawn from this very same word and literally means ___asked___ ___for___. Ralph W. Klein presents Samuel as the one "who had been asked ('___Sauled___') of God (v. 20) and who had been dedicated ('___Sauled___') back to God (v. 28)."[1] (See 1 Sam. 1.)

Samuel
Saul

8:5

Israel not called to be like all the other nations.

• First Samuel 8:1-10 again has the play on words between the people's request and the word *Saul*.[2]

• In 1 Samuel 13:12 "Sought the ... favor" means "to ___soften___ by caressing: to ___appease___, flatter."[3]

butter-up hng. to get something.

A true leader does not only lead, but loves.

3. A ___position___ that exceeds ___passion___ often settles with ___appeasement___.

difference between appeasing God + pleasing God.

1 Sam 11:6-8

10:17-19
what
y god, they "asked for "
12:12-15 be faithful to God.
...ion of leadership - Moses, Joshua - a speech given.
...12 not farewell speech.

1. Ralph Klein, *Word Biblical Commentary*, Vol.10 (Waco: Word Books, 1983), 9.
2. Ibid., 76.
3. Robert L. Hubbard Jr., gen. ed., "The First Book of Samuel" in *New International Commentary on the New Testament* (Grand Rapids, MI: Eerdmans Publishing Company), 346.

Chron. 16:9.

Summoned from the Sheepfold

Day 1

A Father Unlike His Son

Day 2

An Arrogant King

Day 3

Straight to the Heart

Day 4

Chords of Comfort

Day 5

One Smooth Stone

DAY 1

A Father Unlike His Son

TODAY'S TREASURE

"Nothing can hinder the Lord from saving, whether by many or by few."

1 Samuel 14:6

Our study of David begins with Scripture's first mention of him and ends with his last breath. We begin shortly after the birth of the Hebrew monarchy. The Israelites were beginning to reap what they had sown in their demand for a king like other nations had. We will meet several important figures in Hebrew history who tremendously impacted David's life.

From our first glimpses of David, you will begin to wonder how one person could be so utterly typical in some ways and so completely atypical in others. The question will bless us and haunt us throughout the next 10 weeks. Our first unit is the study of David's youth and the relationships that would shape his future. Anticipate all God wants to teach you this week.

Try to approach the week without preconceived notions and assumptions from former studies of the life of David. Allow God to give you a fresh approach to His ageless Word. Grant Him the delight of teaching a completely willing student. Begin your study by reading Today's Treasure. Pray that God will speak to you through His Word.

In the margin please write a brief prayer of commitment to the God who has drawn you personally to this study.

I am blessed beyond measure to take this journey with you. The member book you hold in your hands is the revised, updated version. I first studied this remarkable narrative 16 years ago; but, true to His faithful form, God engaged my attentions and stirred my spirit with the same force the second time around. Isn't that part of what we love about the study of Scripture? Because it's a living word, it falls just as fresh in every re-encounter if we're willing to approach it with a fresh heart. The words of commentator Robert Alter elated me as I took this second look. May God use them to stir your anticipation as well:

> The major sequence that runs … from 1 Samuel 1 to 1 Kings is one of the most astounding pieces of narrative that has come down to us from the ancient world. The story of David is probably the greatest single narrative representation in antiquity of a human

life evolving by slow stages through time, shaped and altered by the pressures of political life, public institutions, family, and the impulses of body and spirit, the eventual sad decay of the flesh… And nowhere is the Bible's astringent narrative economy, its ability to define characters and etch revelatory dialogue in a few telling strokes, more brilliantly deployed.[1]

Oh, how I pray that the Holy Spirit will invade our study with such internal force that the these ancient historical figures will come alive before our very eyes. We will encounter many colorful personalities over the next 10 weeks.

Our journey begins with Saul and Jonathan, a father and son who had a tremendous impact on David. Saul was the reigning king of Israel. Jonathan, his son, was heir apparent to the throne. Our study begins in the middle of the reign of King Saul, the people's choice.

Hopefully, you have seen video session 1, which sets our study in historical context. If not, first take time to read 1 Samuel 8–11. One of the most definitive points made in our introduction concerning Saul was that his position exceeded his passion.

Have you ever been in that kind of predicament? If so, when?

We are not victims of our passions or our lack of them.

At one time or another, most of us have been. Our present journey will illustrate a crucial concept that could practically save our lives and, undoubtedly, our integrity at times: We are not victims of our passions or our lack of them. God really can grant us a fiery heart toward Him and toward what He favors. This is the love David later described as "better than life" (Ps. 63:3).

Good news and bad erupted from Samuel's prophecy in 1 Samuel 13:14. The bad news was that the kingdom of Israel's first monarch would not endure. Saul had a bad habit of compromising the commands of God. The king refused to wait on the Lord, trust in His Word, and follow His directions. Saul proved that a person can have good characteristics without having good character. The good news was: "The LORD has sought out a man after his own heart."

Our first assignment introduces us to Jonathan, son of King Saul, a man quite different from his father. The one who became so dear to David is sure to become dear to us. Read 1 Samuel 14:1-23.

Describe the relationship between Jonathan and his armor bearer based on these verses. Try to be specific.

First Samuel 14:6 is probably the most powerful statement in the reading assignment. In the margin write your own paraphrase of the portion of Scripture that begins with "Perhaps the LORD."

Jonathan and his armor bearer were impressive men and worthy examples. Let's allow two points to draw our attention.

1. Jonathan's perception of the Lord's ways. His keen perception of the Lord certainly did not come from his father because Jonathan's understanding exceeded that of Saul. Jonathan had his own relationship with the Lord, completely separate from his father's. Jonathan made two profound statements in verse 6:

- "*Perhaps* the LORD will act in our behalf."
- "*Nothing* can hinder the LORD from saving, whether by many or by few."

Consider how these statements reveal Jonathan's distinct perception of God's ways: Jonathan *knew* the Lord could save, no matter *who* or *how many* were fighting the battle. In fact, he knew that if God chose to save, *nothing* could hinder Him. His faith in God's strength and determination was solid: God could do anything. His only question was whether or not God would choose to do it through them that day. Reread Jonathan's words: "*Perhaps* the LORD will act in *our* behalf." He *knew* God could do it; he didn't know if He *would*. Whether or not He did, Jonathan understood God's response to be based on sovereignty, not weakness. Jonathan's attitude reminds me of several other young men who also faced the strong possibility of death.

Read Daniel 3:16-18. How was the apparent attitude of Shadrach, Meshach, and Abednego similar to Jonathan's attitude?

Read the following and choose the answer that most often reflects your attitude when the odds seem stacked against you.

- ☐ God could help me, but He doesn't seem to want to very often.
- ☐ My beginning faith fades quickly when I don't see results.
- ☐ I often feel alone, as if God is not interested in my battles.
- ☐ God works mightily through the mighty and no one else.
- ☐ Other: _____

I want to have faith like that of Jonathan and the three men in the blazing furnace, don't you? As you pursue this study, you are strengthening your faith.

Read Romans 10:17 and fill in the diagram below, charting the two components that lead to faith.

hear the word → *believe the Message* → FAITH

You might have said that hearing through the Word of God results in faith. Two critical elements result in faith: the message of Christ and our experience of hearing the message. Jonathan was not the only impressive individual in our first reading assignment. Look at the significant example of his armor bearer.

2. The armor bearer's commitment to Jonathan's authority. You probably noted the armor bearer's constant obedience to Jonathan's commands. You can draw a wonderful parallel between the armor bearer and a Christian.

What is God's command to us in Ephesians 6:10-13?
- ☐ Stand and watch the salvation of the Lord.
- ☑ Put on the whole armor of God.
- ☐ Ignore the enemy and he will have to flee.

What is the stated purpose of the command to put on the armor?
- ☐ We will intimidate our enemy.
- ☐ We keep from getting slaughtered.
- ☑ We can take our stand against the Devil's schemes.

Whose armor are we supposed to put on? ___God's___

We are God's present armor bearers. We're not just to carry it. We are to put it on. I want you to see just how much we compare to Jonathan's armor bearer. Take a good look at the word "struggle" in Ephesians 6:12. The Greek word *pale* means, "A wrestling, struggle, or hand-to-hand combat." The word described the wrestling of athletes and the hand-to-hand combat of soldiers. It denoted the struggle between individual combatants in distinction from an entire military campaign.[2] Our "struggle" against our enemy is a very personal battle. *Pale* does not describe a corporate battle. It describes a struggle that involves only ourselves, the One whose armor we bear, and our enemy.

> We must listen carefully to the instructions of the One whose armor we bear.

Jonathan's armor bearer set a wonderful example. Take a look back at 1 Samuel 14 and let's draw a few applications that may help us in our battle:
- The armor bearer listened carefully to Jonathan's instructions. To be victorious, we must also listen carefully to the instructions of the One whose armor we bear. The Sword of the Spirit, the Word of God, will both prepare us and protect us.
- The New International Version describes Jonathan's armor bearer as being with his master "heart and soul" (v. 7).

What you think the armor bearer meant by pledging himself to Jonathan "heart and soul"?

At this point in your journey, how often would you describe yourself as being with God "heart and soul"?
- ☐ often   ☐ occasionally   ☐ rarely
- ☐ I don't believe I've ever really been with God "heart and soul."

In the margin write a brief prayer regarding any desire you have to be with God "heart and soul."

• The armor bearer followed behind Jonathan. His master led him into battle. He did not choose the battle. Jonathan made sure he went ahead of the armor bearer so that he could take the blows of the enemy. When we received Christ as Savior, we enlisted in an army we weren't acutely aware existed. We would avoid our spiritual battles if we could, but our Master is always careful to lead the way. We must always "climb up" after Him. Notice that 1 Samuel 14:13 says, "The Philistines fell before Jonathan, and his armor-bearer followed and killed behind him." Our enemy will fall before our God. We are only deadly to the enemy when we go behind Him.

Based on the impressions of Jonathan you received in day 1, how would you describe him?

Read 1 Samuel 14:24-52. How did Saul put his army in jeopardy?
☑ He forced his men to fast.
☐ He forced them to settle in enemy territory.
☐ He forced them to fight an enemy too powerful for them.

According to 14:31-33, what things happened as a result of their "fast"?

What tragedy almost resulted from Saul's selfish command?
☑ Jonathan was almost put to death.
☐ David nearly lost his life.
☐ Saul was nearly captured by the Philistines.
☐ The men almost died of starvation.

Note an important fact about fasting. God, not man, must call "fasts." Fasting called by God will result in strength, not weakness. Fasting for any other reason works against us rather than for us. It is a wonderful and highly effective discipline of God, but we must follow His instruction for fasting so we will be empowered rather than depleted in our battles.

Unfortunately, we're highly capable of fasting for all sorts of misguided reasons. In the last 25 years of women's ministry, I can't count the times I've seen women use fasting as an excuse for radical dieting and weight loss. Not only is it dangerous but it also can be deadly. On the other hand, our motive for fasting may be good. It's just not necessarily God.

Have you ever withheld food from yourself for a considerable length of time when it wasn't God's idea? ☐ yes ☐ no

If so, in the margin describe how you felt and what eventually happened.

Hasty, self-centered vows can cost us. Not only did Saul's army end up sinning against God but Saul easily could have lost his son. God tried to teach Saul a very serious lesson that day. Saul's pride could have caused him to keep a foolish vow. Better to repent than to add foolishness to foolishness.

In each battle we've studied today, we've seen evidence that God is for us in battle, not against us. He wants us fortified before our enemy with faith like Jonathan's, obedience like the armor bearer's, and proper fuel like Saul's army should have received. May He grant us the wisdom that leads to divine strength. I'm so glad you came along today. I'll meet you here tomorrow.

DAY 2

An Arrogant King

TODAY'S TREASURE

"But Samuel replied: 'Does the LORD delight in burnt offerings and sacrifices as much as in obeying the voice of the LORD? To obey is better than sacrifice and to heed is better than the fat of rams.'" 1 Samuel 15:22

Begin your study by praying that God will speak to you through His Word. Today we observe a confrontation between King Saul and Samuel the prophet. The confrontation speaks to us as we consider our approach to God's instructions. The Scriptures we will read will likely leave quite an impression on you.

Read 1 Samuel 15:1-35. In one sentence state what you believe is the theme of this chapter.

What is the most shocking or troublesome verse or statement in this chapter in your opinion and why?

Which of the following words best describes God's response to Saul's actions in verses 11 and 12?

☐ fury ☐ jealousy ☐ indifference
☐ bitterness ☑ grief ☐ guilt

According to verse 11, how did Samuel respond to Saul's disobedience?

troubled/unhappy. Prayed to God.

Saul had gone to Carmel to set up a monument in his own honor. What does that suggest to you about Saul's heart?

When Samuel confronted Saul, what reason did Saul give for sparing the livestock (v. 15)? Choose one.

☐ The livestock could provide food and clothing for the Israelites.
☑ The best livestock was spared to offer as sacrifices to God.
☐ The stock of the Amalekites was healthier than Israel's livestock.
☐ The livestock would be an impressive addition to Israel's assets.

In your opinion, which of the following statements most reflects Saul's apparent attitude according to verses 20 and 21?

☑ Partial obedience is still obedience.
☐ God doesn't make His instructions clear enough to be followed.
☐ God's ideas are good unless a better one comes along.

What does verse 22 mean to you? Respond in the margin.

To obey is better than sacrifice.

Our God seems so unlike the One who ordered an entire people destroyed, doesn't He? If God is love, light, and cannot tempt us to sin, we must need to know more to adequately evaluate this grave command of God. We need to know the history of the Amalekites. They were the first people to attack the Israelites after their exodus (Ex. 17:8-16). After initial defeat, they attacked Israel again, forcing them back into the Sinai wilderness (Num. 14:39-45).

Read Moses' words to the Israelites in Deuteronomy 25:17-19. Note everything you learn about the Amalekites by completing the following:

They met the Israelites on their way out of Egypt and … *cut off all who were lagging behind.*

They had no … *fear of God.*

The Israelites would eventually blot out … *the memory of Amalek*

The Israelites must not … *forget.*

Jonah 3:10 and 4:1-2

God is sovereign. He owes us no explanation as to why He ordered this entire population to be exterminated. However, we can assume they were a vile and godless people because God is merciful and compassionate.

You are a gracious & compassionate god, slow to anger &

Look up the Scriptures in the margin and note what they have to say *abounding* about God's mercy on wicked people.

Ezekiel 33:11

The passages from Jonah and Ezekiel clearly demonstrate God's desire to forgive and rescue all people from evil. From all the Bible says about the Amalekites, I assume they rejected every opportunity to repent of evil and turn to God.

Saul made some serious and inappropriate presumptions. He kept King Agag alive, not to spare his life out of mercy, but to present him as a trophy—a public exhibit. He did not slaughter the sheep and cattle for the very same reason: He saved the best to make himself look better. First Samuel 15:9 ends with a sad commentary on Saul's actions: "These they were unwilling to destroy completely, but everything that was despised and weak they totally destroyed." Saul had the audacity to improve on God's command.

Several breaches in character become evident in this dramatic chapter. Let's consider each of these traits.

1. Saul was arrogant. If we needed any further proof of Saul's pride and audacity, verse 12 certainly provides it. Saul went directly to Carmel and built a monument to himself. A short time later Samuel reminded Saul that God had anointed him king over Israel when he was small in his own eyes.

Check the following words that describe what you think Samuel meant by the term "little in your own eyes."
  ☐ self-conscious ☑ low self-esteem ☐ self-denying ☐ humble

Of the four answers to the last question, circle the ones that describe a positive, Christ-honoring form of being "little in your own eyes."

For Saul being little in his own eyes meant being self-conscious. We could certainly speculate that his self-esteem was inappropriately low. The Bible encourages self-denial and humility as positive forms of recognizing our "smallness" before God.

Briefly describe a time in your life when you knew God was humbling you so that He could more fully use you.

What are a few ways you could keep your heart humble before God?

2. Saul refused to take responsibility for his actions. He first excused himself for disobeying God by claiming he spared the best of the sheep and cattle for a sacrifice to the Lord. Amazing, isn't it? Comparable reasoning might be a person claiming the reason he robbed a bank was to give a greater tithe and offering to the Lord. (Frankly, I'm surprised we haven't seen that one come up in the news.) Believe it or not, we can sometimes use God as our excuse for disobedience too. One woman told me she was certain God's will was for her to leave her husband because she simply wasn't happy. Another woman explained to me that she had found the man God intended her to marry, though she was already married.

Can you think of an example of disobedience in God's name?

Saul not only tried to use God as his excuse for disobedience but he also claimed he was afraid of and gave in to the people (v. 24). The king of Israel with God on his side scared of his people? Somehow I doubt it, don't you?

When we've done something wrong or foolish, we find shouldering the responsibility difficult, don't we? At times we are all tempted to blame someone else when we've blown it. I wonder if the outcome might have been different if Saul simply had admitted he'd made a wrong choice.

Unlike Saul, we have lots of opportunities for good choices. Our first choice should be to obey God. Our second choice should be to take responsibility for poor decisions when we make them. Let's try an experiment this week: Ask God to make us keenly aware when we try to "pass the buck" instead of taking responsibility for something we should or shouldn't have done.

Be courageous enough to record in the margin any instances when you recently were tempted to blame someone else for your actions.

I'm amazed at the inclinations of our human nature. Thank God He can change that nature. Don't get discouraged. Awareness is the first step to change.

3. Saul minimized the seriousness of disobedience. In verse 23 Samuel compared rebellion to the sin of divination or witchcraft. The comparison seems puzzling until we consider that rebellion is a means by which we attempt to choose our own futures by our independent actions. Divination attempts to foretell or sway the future. In the same verse God likens arrogance to the evil of idolatry. When we are arrogant, who becomes God in our lives?

The chapter concludes with a harrowing scene. Samuel hacked King Agag to pieces. Samuel's actions were neither in haste nor based on displaced piety to say, "I told you so." He acted in grieved obedience.

As we conclude our lesson today, what did you learn about Samuel's heart in verses 11 and 35? Respond in the margin.

troubled/ mourned
angry   disappointed, grieved

> I wonder if the outcome might have been different if Saul simply had admitted he'd made a wrong choice.

Based on 1 Samuel 15:22, why do you think obedience is more important to God than sacrifice?

Obedience demonstrates that god is loved + accepted as Sovereign Lord.

Perhaps Samuel's heart was the reason God used him as He did. Samuel's heart never grew cold and condemning. God allowed Samuel to be emotionally involved but enabled him to maintain objectivity so that he could speak "the truth in love" (Eph. 4:15). Saul learned that obedience was better than sacrifice. Samuel learned that sometimes obedience is the sacrifice.

DAY 3
Straight to the Heart

TODAY'S TREASURE

"The LORD said to Samuel, 'Do not consider his appearance or his height, for I have rejected him. The LORD does not look at the things man looks at. Man looks at the outward appearance, but the LORD looks at the heart.'" 1 Samuel 16:7

I love wrapping familiar passages around me like a security blanket and feeling their warmth.

Begin by praying that God will speak to you through His Word. Can you tell from our "Treasure" that we have a special chapter to study today? I love to discover new truths through Scriptures, but I also love wrapping the familiar passages around me like a security blanket and feeling their warmth. Perhaps we'll have the joy of experiencing the best of both worlds today. We'll study the old and familiar with a fresh new look. I can't wait to get started!

Read 1 Samuel 16:1-13. What profound assignment did God give the prophet Samuel in verse 1?

I am sending you

Why was Samuel initially reluctant to go to Bethlehem? Choose one.
- ☐ His health was failing.
- ☑ He was afraid Saul would kill him.
- ☐ He felt unworthy.
- ☐ His sons were unruly.

Samuel first assumed God's choice was Eliab, Jesse's oldest son. Based on God's response to Samuel, why do you think Samuel chose Eliab?

His appearance, his height, the oldest.

When Samuel asked Jesse if he had any other sons, Jesse answered, "There is still the youngest ... but he is tending the sheep." What other words come to your mind when you think of the word "tending"?

caring for, providing for, protecting.

Which of the following words describe Jesse's youngest son?
- ☐ rugged
- ☑ ruddy
- ☑ handsome
- ☐ tall
- ☐ strong
- ☐ shy

In the margin write the Lord's commandment to Samuel in verse 12.   *Rise & anoint him.*

How did the Spirit of God manifest Himself in the life of David from the time He came upon him?
- ☑ in power
- ☐ in glory
- ☐ in countenance
- ☐ in zeal
- ☐ in authority

Samuel's stubbornness amuses me. Notice his response to Jesse once he learned that Jesse had one more son. "Send for him; we will not sit down until he arrives." He certainly knew how to get them moving. Don't forget how everyone trembled when he arrived in Bethlehem. No one wanted to have the prophet of God drop by unannounced.

David, a young teenager, arrived on the scene with no idea what awaited him. He was handsome with a reddish complexion and no doubt smelled like sheep. He obviously was not his own father's first choice nor would he have been Samuel's. The prophet initially assumed God's choice was Eliab. This choice made the most sense. He was the eldest son, and he looked like a king.

God taught Samuel a very important lesson. "Man looks at the outward appearance, but the LORD looks at the heart." He reminded Samuel that the human mind has an overwhelming tendency to make assumptions based on appearances. God's choices don't always make sense to us.

When my oldest brother was born, my mother wholeheartedly gave him to the Lord. By age five he was showing remarkable signs of musical talent. He earned many honors by high school and developed impressive leadership skills. He earns a very good living as a conductor and composer in the secular entertainment world. My big brother has always been a hero to me. He not only is the most talented person I've ever known but he is one of the dearest.

I came along in the family order as the fourth of five children and never could find my niche. I could not sing or play an instrument. I was not outstanding at anything. Strangely, God heard my mother's devotion, and He honored her desire to give a child back to the Lord to serve Him. For reasons

I will never know, He did not choose the one who made the most sense. In fact, my beloved older brother has chosen an entirely different religion that does not include Christ as Savior. God appears to have pulled out the one who made the least sense—me. I can't even tell you what He saw in my heart worth using. He is simply a God of grace, looking for those who will not take an ounce of credit for what He alone can do.

Can you think of a time when God's obvious choice for you did not make sense based on outward appearances? If so, in the margin describe the experience.

God's choices don't always make sense to us, but they are never haphazard or random. A few considerations about David shed light on why God may have chosen him. The first consideration is his genealogy. Let's do a little research.

The Old Testament Book of Ruth tells of a woman and her mother-in-law after the deaths of their husbands. Ruth is not only one of the most important women in Hebrew history but she also had a special relationship to David.

Read Ruth 4:13-17. Who was Ruth in relation to David?
- ☑ David's great-grandmother
- ☐ David's grandmother
- ☐ David's aunt
- ☐ none of the above

Look at Matthew 1:1-17. Whose genealogy is listed? *Jesus*

What two titles is Christ given in verse 1?
- ☑ the son of David
- ☐ the son of God
- ☐ the son of man
- ☑ the son of Abraham

The genealogy David and Christ shared was of obvious importance. In verse 3, you can see that both were descendants of Judah, one of the sons of Jacob. In the prophecy Jacob spoke over Judah, he told him that "The scepter will not depart from Judah, nor the ruler's staff from between his feet" (Gen. 49:10). You see, David was not a random choice. He was one of the most important figures in the genealogy of Christ, the Lion of the tribe of Judah (Rev. 5:5).

I never fail to be encouraged by Christ's heritage. On the list you will find names of many offenders but few blameless characters.

How do you respond to the fact that the only perfect person on Christ's genealogy is Christ Himself? Respond in the margin.

In many ways David's life foreshadowed or pictured details of Christ's life. God illustrated the unknown about the Messiah through the known about David. David was not divine nor perfect, as we will quickly see, but God will use him to teach us truths about the One who is. I think you'll enjoy knowing that the name Jesse is a "personal name meaning, 'man.'"[3] Christ referred to Himself as the "Son of Man" more than any other title. He asked His disciples, "Who do people say the Son of Man is?" (Matt. 16:13). Isn't it interesting that the King of Israel who often prefigured Jesus was also technically the "Son of Man"?

David's occupation also made him a candidate for kingship. At first glance, few similarities appear between a shepherd and a king, but we will discover that David received invaluable experience keeping sheep. Psalm 78:70-72 states: "He chose David his servant and took him from the sheep pens; from tending the sheep he brought him to be the shepherd of his people Jacob, of Israel his inheritance. And David shepherded them with integrity of heart; with skillful hands he led them."

What evidences do you see in these verses to refute the idea that God called David in spite of the fact that he was a common shepherd?

What are a few of your occupational skills?

Have you ever felt that your occupational skills were useless in areas of service to God? ☐ yes ☐ no

Can you think of any ways God can use or has used you because of your skills and not just in spite of them? If so, list them in the margin.

Few things seem less spiritual than keeping smelly sheep, yet God used David's skills for eternal purposes. Those who went to "fetch him" (KJV) could not have easily torn David from his sheep. You can be certain he did not leave his sheep shepherdless. Someone had to stay in David's place while he ran home. He even returned to his sheep after the anointing (v. 19).

When David arrived at home, Samuel saw that he was "ruddy, with a fine appearance and handsome features." Still, Samuel did not move. He had already made a mistake based on appearances. Then God said, "Rise and anoint him; he is the one."

These words send chills up my spine.

Complete the following from 1 Samuel 16:13. "So Samuel took the horn of oil and anointed him in the presence of his brothers, and from that day … "
the Spirit of the Lord came upon David in power

"But you will receive power when the Holy Spirit comes on you; and you will be my witnesses in Jerusalem, and in all Judea and Samaria, and to the ends of the earth."
ACTS 1:8

The Holy Spirit just can't seem to arrive without power, can He? (See Acts 1:8 in margin.) As we study the life of a certain shepherd boy, we will no doubt see testimony of that power again and again. Samuel stood before a young lad and with awe and reverence poured the oil on his head. Although the oil surely blurred the vision of the one whose eyes it bathed, God's vision was crystal clear. He had said, "I will send thee to Jesse the Bethlehemite: for I have provided me a king among his sons" (1 Sam. 16:1, KJV). The Hebrew word for *provided* is *ra'ah*. It means "to see, to look at, view, inspect, regard, to perceive; ... to feel; to experience."[4] Second Chronicles 16:9 says, "For the eyes of the LORD run to and fro throughout the whole earth, to show Himself strong on behalf of those whose heart is loyal to Him" (NKJV).

That day so many years ago, the eyes of the Lord looked throughout the whole earth and fell on an obscure village called Bethlehem. There He found a heart—one like unto His own. He found a heart tendered to little lost sheep, and He showed Himself strong on behalf of that heart, just like He promised.

N.B!

DAY 4
Chords of Comfort

TODAY'S TREASURE

"Whenever the spirit from God came upon Saul, David would take his harp and play. Then relief would come to Saul; he would feel better, and the evil spirit would leave him." 1 Samuel 16:23

Begin by praying that God will speak to you through His Word. In the previous lesson we witnessed the anointing of a man after God's own heart. Today we focus our attention on the remaining verses that provide the bridge connecting the lives of King Saul and young David. Read 1 Samuel 16:13-23.

Verses 13 and 14 tell of two contrasting activities of the Holy Spirit. In the margin describe the two activities and the results that came from them.

How did David come into Saul's service?

What was David's first position under Saul's authority?
☐ servant ☑ armor bearer ☐ guard
☐ cup bearer ☐ door keeper

List every description you discover about David in verse 18.

Son of Jesse
knows how to play the harp
brave man
warrior
speaks well
fine looking   *the Lord is with him*

What effect did David's music have on the tormented king?
- ☐ help him sleep
- ☐ felt better
- ☑ evil spirit left
- ☐ all of the above

The Holy Spirit had a different relationship with people before Christ died on the cross. Now His Spirit lives in all believers (Rom. 8:9). Before Calvary, the Holy Spirit worked to empower specific types of service rather than to bring a new relationship with God through salvation. Fewer than 100 people in the Old Testament were ever characterized by the Holy Spirit being on or in them. The Holy Spirit came on only those who were being empowered for specific tasks or positions.

We can draw another important contrast between the Holy Spirit in the Old Testament and in the New. Saul's experience demonstrates that the Holy Spirit could depart from a person. After the atoning death of Christ, the Spirit comes to establish a new and permanent relationship with the believer. The Gospel of John offers believers assurance concerning the gift of the Holy Spirit.

Read John 14:16-17 and explain the assurance we now have.

Have you ever feared that you might have done something to make the Holy Spirit depart from you? ☑ yes ☐ no

Read Romans 8:38-39. How do these verses encourage you toward security in your relationship to God through Jesus Christ?

Nothing can separate us from the love of God that is in Christ.

Saul did not have the same assurance we have of the continuing presence of God's Spirit. We have nothing comparable to Saul's experience. I can imagine nothing more horrifying than the Holy Spirit departing from me.

Unfortunately, the departure of the Holy Spirit did not just leave Saul empty. It left a door open to evil. As the Holy Spirit poured on the one God had chosen as king, the Holy Spirit drained from the one who was the answer to the people's selfish demands.

Although David's anointing did not end Saul's reign as king, it marked the end of the power and favor of God on him. Just as God prepared Abraham for many years before he was ready to assume his position, God prepared David for his role as king long before he was crowned.

The exit of the Holy Spirit left Saul open to the torment of an evil spirit. If he had been a man of character, Saul might have cooperated with God to add David to his royal ranks through less painful means. But Saul had already proved himself to be self-centered and rebellious. God used Saul's selfishness to bring David to the royal courts.

> "You, however, are not in the flesh, but in the Spirit, since the Spirit of God lives in you. But if anyone does not have the Spirit of Christ, he does not belong to Him."
> **ROMANS 8:9, HCSB**

God is sovereign. He <u>allowed</u> the evil spirit to torment Saul. He knows what methods will work to bring about His will. David had to be summoned to the kingdom. I believe God <u>allowed</u> an evil spirit to torment Saul because He knew Saul would seek David's services.

The Hebrew word for torment is *ba'ath,* which means "to be frightened, to overtake, to strike with fear, to be afraid, to dread, to be terrified, to be overtaken by a sudden terror. It is the strongest form of intimidation."[5] Mentally apply this definition to Saul. In essence, God allowed the spirit of fear to come on him. Few things torment me like fear. You name it, and I've feared it. For instance, I feared that my children would never grow up. Then I feared they'd grown up too fast. I feared them living on their own and also feared they'd move back in. I've even feared good things if they called for change. It can be disabling, can't it?

Think back on the most memorable time in your life when you were tormented by fear. Describe the situation.

Saul's attendants searched for a remedy for his torment. His servants found a young man who could play the harp, and they assured the terrorized king that David's songs could comfort Saul's soul. David used the harp to bring joyful praises to God and relief to the torments of Saul. You may rightly imagine that many of your favorite psalms were first sung by the young voice of David, wavering and cracking somewhere between boyhood and manhood to the accompaniment of a well-worn, deeply loved harp. Surely the very sound of its strings summoned the attentions of many a straying sheep. The words that accompanied it still do.

Look carefully at 1 Samuel 16:18. What is the next piece of information we learn about David after we are told that he played the harp?

From 1 Samuel 16:18, how would you describe David? Respond in margin.

In two simple descriptions, God told us volumes about a man after His own heart. We are shown that David had the tenderness and the sensitivity of an artist. He was a musician and a song writer. David did not simply have talent. Talent alone could not have soothed the torment of Saul. David plucked the strings of his harp with tenderness and sensitivity. He chose melodies that ministered to the aching soul. Yet we are also told he was a warrior, brave and strong. The fingers that gently plucked the strings of a harp could wind fiercely around a sling or a sword. We will see his gentle song turn into a corporate rebuke as he faced the Philistines.

"One of the servants answered, 'I have seen a son of Jesse of Bethlehem who knows how to play the harp. He is a brave man and a warrior. He speaks well and is a fine-looking man. And the LORD is with him.' "
1 SAMUEL 16:18

These complementary parts of David's character will appear throughout our study. David was a complex man. He could be both passionate and withdrawn, dependable and shocking, righteous and wicked—just like us.

What a mistake we make in our society when we consider gentleness and masculinity exclusive terms. My brother who has such a gift to play the piano could also put a basketball through a hoop, but he was told in junior high he had to make a choice between the two. He was forced to choose either band or sports. He went with his greater gift at the cost of being labeled effeminate. He and his wife have recently celebrated 33 years of marriage. Those who ridiculed were wrong. He still makes his living on a keyboard. I wonder if our society pushes some individuals into the world of homosexuality by failing to value tenderness and sensitivity in men.

Do you think you possess both qualities of tenderness and strength? ☐ yes ☐ no Are you more comfortable with one than the other? If so, share your thoughts regarding the possible reasons.

Two qualities I've come to admire most in both men and women are tenderness and strength. I no longer see them as exclusive terms. Quite the contrary; I've come to realize that one without the other leaves an individual lacking wholeness. I deeply desire to be a woman of tenderness and strength because my dearest role model possessed both.

Christ Jesus is the artist. He created the world with colors and textures human artists have tried for thousands of years to imitate. Christ Jesus is the musician. He gave the angels their voices. Christ Jesus is the tenderhearted, ministering to our every need.

Christ Jesus is also the warrior, forever leading us in triumphant procession, if only we will follow (2 Cor. 2:14). In our greatest weakness, He is strong. Christ Jesus is the blessed embodiment of both characteristics. He has set an example before us of true manhood and true womanhood. No greater man or woman exists than one in whom tenderness and strength can be found. David was such a man.

As we close today, perhaps God brought someone to mind who has been an example to you in both tenderness and strength.

In the margin briefly describe a man or woman you know who possesses both these characteristics.

Conclude with a time of prayer. Invite God to fill whatever may be lacking in you today in the areas of tenderness and strength.

DAY 5
One Smooth Stone

TODAY'S TREASURE

"David said to the Philistine, 'You come against me with sword and spear and javelin, but I come against you in the name of the LORD Almighty, the God of the armies of Israel, whom you have defied.' " 1 Samuel 17:45

I had the joyous privilege of growing up in Sunday School. I sat in a miniature wooden chair in a Sunday School room by the time I could stand. I held my mother's skirt as she walked me to my class as ever-smiling, ever-patient teachers greeted me. I remember the lessons they taught and the water color prints they held to illustrate the stories. It never occurred to me how much easier it would have been for them simply to attend church rather than teach. I'm sure I never said thank you. I should have. Through the stories they told to a bunch of squirming preschoolers, a scary ghost became the living God to me.

We arrive today at an account in Scripture that has captured the imaginations of every little boy and girl who ever sat in a circle of small wooden chairs in a Sunday School room. Yes, dear teacher, some of us were listening. This is the story of David and Goliath. May we have the joy of reading it again as if for the very first time. Read 1 Samuel 17:1-58.

Dress Goliath for battle by drawing on the diagram the pieces of armor described in verses 5-7. This exercise is not to test your artistic abilities, so please don't stress over it.

bronze helmet

scale armor of bro[nze]

javelin

spear shaft

bronze greaves

Why did Jesse send David to the camp of his three older brothers?
- ☑ to take food to his brothers
- ☐ to fight against the Philistines with his brothers
- ☑ to take food to the commander of their unit
- ☑ to bring back assurance of his sons' well-being

What all was promised to the man who killed Goliath?
- ☐ He would be heir to Saul's throne.
- ☑ He would receive great wealth.
- ☑ He would receive Saul's daughter in marriage.
- ☑ His father's family would be exempt from taxes.

What were Eliab's feelings toward his youngest brother?

anger, intolerance

What was David's claim to Saul in verse 37?

The Lord ... will deliver me.

Why didn't David wear Saul's armor?

not used to them

David's greatest weapon actually was not his sling.

Read verse 45 carefully. What do you believe was David's most powerful weapon against Goliath?

This day the Lord will hand you over to me.

David possessed both tenderness and strength. We saw his tenderness in the soothing way he played the harp. Today we see his strength as a warrior. David had an outlook on the battle that caused God to bring him victory against all odds. His example teaches us the following guidelines to victory.

1. *Take God's Word over the opinions of others.* Eliab said everything he possibly could to discourage David. He said David didn't belong, made fun of David's trade, and accused him of conceit and deceit.

David's response, "Now what have I done?" evidenced the fact that Eliab and David were not at odds for the first time. We see David not only as the warrior but as the annoying little brother. I can almost picture him running up behind his brothers, throwing his hands over their eyes, and saying, "Guess who?" They apparently weren't pleased to see him. He could have kept his bread and stayed home for all they cared.

I have to wonder if Eliab's response resulted from almost being anointed king. The first drop of oil had almost fallen on his head when God stopped the prophet Samuel and chided him for looking on the outward appearance. For whatever reason, Eliab was very critical of David.

Take God's Word over the opinions of others.

29

I'm not sure anyone can encourage or discourage us like family. The views of our family members toward us are very convincing, aren't they? If people who know us the best encourage us the least, we have few chances to develop confidence.

David remained undaunted by Eliab's criticisms for one reason: David took God's Word over the opinions of others. As Hebrew lads, David and his brothers heard the promises of victory God made to the nation that would call upon His name. David believed those promises. A verse that I've taught my children to memorize from David's own pen is Psalm 71:5.

Write Psalm 71:5 in the margin.

Do you remember a time when a family member discouraged you deeply? ☑ yes ☐ no   If so, describe what happened.

For you have been my hope, O Sovereign Lord, my confidence since my youth.

God's Word tells us we are loved, gifted, and blessed. We can do anything God calls us to do through Christ who strengthens us (Phil. 4:13). We must develop more confidence in God's Word than in the opinions of others.

If the opinions of others are stumbling blocks to you, use the margin to write a brief prayer asking God to be your confidence.

David took God's Word over the opinions of others, but that's not all. Let's look at a second guideline to victory his example extends to us.

2. *Measure the size of your obstacle against the size of your God.* David wanted God to use him to bring Israel victory in the name of the Lord. He had just one obstacle: Goliath. Goliath was over 9 feet tall with over 140 pounds of armor shielding him.

We tend to measure our obstacles against our own strength. Thus we often feel overwhelmed and defeated before the battle begins. Smoking can be such an obstacle. The doctor says, "You must quit smoking because of your health." The woman may be convinced God's will is for her to be healthy. The victory would be good health. But the obstacle is a giant—a 20-year addiction that seems much stronger than she is. She feels discouraged because she is measuring her obstacle against the size of her strength rather than the size of her God. I'm not suggesting that if we measure our obstacles against God, our battles will be effortless. David still had to face his giant obstacle and use the strength he possessed, but his confidence in God caused a simple pebble to hit like a boulder.

Is there an area in your life in which God wants to give you a victory but an obstacle seems too big to overcome? ☐ yes ☐ no

If so, what is the victory God wants to give you?

What obstacle must you overcome?

Can you make a commitment today to begin measuring your giant obstacle against your God and not your strength? ☐ yes ☐ no

3. Acknowledge an active and living God in your life. The description David often used of his Commander-in-Chief shows another basis for his courage.

How did David refer to God in 1 Samuel 17:26?

the living god

Do you approach every circumstance and conflict as a member of the army of the living God? Do you continually regard God as able? Is He not only the Lord Almighty on the page but the Lord Almighty on the pavement? Do you stand in His name? Our victory rests not on faith in our spirituality. Our victory rests on faith in our God. We're often intimidated in battle because we are uncertain of our faith. We must remember we don't stand in victory because of our faith. We stand in victory because of our God.

> We don't stand in victory because of our faith. We stand in victory because of our God.

Faith in faith is pointless. Faith in a living, active God moves mountains. Moses acknowledged Yahweh as the living God and led multitudes to freedom from slavery. Joshua acknowledged Yahweh as the living God and led multitudes into the promised land. Daniel acknowledged Yahweh as the living God, and the angel shut the mouths of lions.

You serve the same God. Are you allowing Him to live smack in the middle of your life? If so, I bet you've crossed a few Red Seas, tumbled down a few walls, and escaped a few lions yourself. He is alive. He is active. He wants to make you living proof. Remember, the cross would have been God's worst defeat had the people not had cause to exclaim, "He's alive!"

Conclude your lesson today by testifying about a time in which God showed His might on your behalf in a specific battle you've fought.

Stories don't get any better than David and Goliath, do they? Stories like the one we've studied today can cause preschoolers, who once listened from baby bear chairs, to stand in front of mama bear chairs and teach Sunday School. Some stories are worth retelling. A living God is worth believing. Thank you for making it all the way through week 1. I'll see you in class.

[handwritten margin notes top-right:] God chooses the less h... to be the most likely. 1 Cor 1:26-29

Acts 1:24 God looks @ heart.

[handwritten margin notes left:]
I have provided me a king (V1)
Conflict between S+S - do you come in peace?
David - beloved one
Jesse - man
Why does God tell you just so much?

PART 1

A Deeper Look at David's Anointing

Read 1 Samuel 16:1-11.

1. God often ___places___ His servants in positions to ___test___ their reasoning (vv. 1,3).

- Robert Alter says of David, "By his sheer youth, he has been excluded from consideration as a kind of male ___Cinderella___ left to his domestic chores instead of being ___invited___ to the party."[1]
- "The LORD looks at the heart." Compare 1 Samuel 16:7 to Acts 1:24.
   Kardiognostes: ___Knower___ of the heart

[handwritten left margin:]
Acts 1:24
Ps. 139:12
Ps 24

[handwritten:] Secret shame + talkative personality = a lie

Read 1 Samuel 16:11-13.

- "Fine appearance" is literally "___beautiful___ of ___eyes___."[2]
- "Handsome features" is literally "___good___ of ___looking___."[3]

2. God's ___anointing___ on David offers glimpses into His anointing upon ___us___.

[handwritten:] Messiah } the anointed.
Christos }

- THE ___POWER___—The word *Spirit* (*ruah* in Hebrew, *pneuma* in Greek)—carries the basic meaning of ___breath___ or ___wind___. Both represent the power of the ___invisible___ to ___move___ the ___visible___.

  [handwritten: Acts 1:8 1 Cor]

  [handwritten: John 20:21-22]

- THE ___SPEED___—*Came upon*—literally means "___rushed___" (1 Sam. 16:13). *[handwritten: immediatly]*

- THE ___SECRECY___ *[handwritten: anointing in home, family; Spirit comes in private way; but end result is public.]*

- THE ___PERMANENCE___ *[handwritten: from that day on.]*

PART 2
A Deeper Look at David's Entrance into Saul's Service

[handwritten: V18 - servant is still a boy/lad.]

Read 1 Samuel 16:14-23.

[handwritten: V18.]

1. When God finds a heart given over to Him, He forms from it a life with ___facets___ and ___features___ that normally wouldn't fit.

   [handwritten: He makes us unusual]

2. Though every life is ___worthy___ of love, the activated Spirit of God within a person can make him or her irresistibly ___lovable___.

   [handwritten: 21]

   [handwritten: Saul loved David.]

1. Robert Alter, *The David Story* (New York: W. W. Norton & Company, 2000), 97.
2. Robert L. Hubbard Jr., gen. ed., "The First Book of Samuel" in *New International Commentary on the Old Testament* (Grand Rapids, MI: Eerdmans Publishing Company), 423.
3. Ibid.

[handwritten: You cannot build a relationship w. somebody because they make you feel better about yourself.]

Sowing the Seeds of Jealousy

Day 1
An Amazing Covenant

Day 2
A Jealous Eye

Day 3
The Great Escape

Day 4
Common Bonds, Uncommon Friends

Day 5
The Blessed Reminder

DAY 1
An Amazing Covenant

TODAY'S TREASURE

"Jonathan made a covenant with David because he loved him as himself."
1 Samuel 18:3

David's life was rarely boring! This week we begin with the unusual relationship between David and Jonathan. Then we will turn to Saul's volatile reaction to the victory young David reaped for Israel. We will identify the flaws God had seen all along in Saul's character. We'll confront the destructive nature of jealousy and discover the only circumstances under which jealousy can be righteous. We'll also share a deeper look at two uncommon friends. Begin by praying that God will speak to you through His Word.

In week 1 we saw how King Saul's rebellion led to the departure of the Holy Spirit. We also observed David's anointing as God's chosen king. Fifteen years passed before God's anointed was crowned king. Not one of those years was wasted. God taught His servant that submission to Him is the best preparation for an assignment from Him. God allowed David to face many difficult trials, but in turn He taught David volumes about Himself. Each trial prepared a man after God's own heart to do a work after God's own heart.

This week we will witness a tragic turning point in the relationship between Saul and David, but today we behold a tender scene between two young men. Our reading assignment is brief in words but full in content.

Read 1 Samuel 18:1-4 and describe Jonathan's feelings for David.

Which of the following statements best describes David's feelings for Jonathan according to 1 Samuel 18:1-4?
- ☐ David loved Jonathan as himself.
- ☐ David was overwhelmed by the covenant with Jonathan.
- ☐ David regarded Jonathan as his best friend.
- ☑ David's feelings toward Jonathan are not mentioned.

What belongings did Jonathan give to David in the covenant?
- ☑ bow
- ☐ turban
- ☑ tunic
- ☑ robe
- ☑ sword
- ☑ belt
- ☐ shield

Who but God can explain the ways of the heart? Sometimes friendships bloom over months or years. Other times someone touches your heart almost instantly, and you seem to have known him or her forever.

Have you ever felt an almost instant bond to a new friend? If so, what can you identify as reasons you believe you felt such a kinship?

A covenant was a contract accompanied by signs, sacrifices, and a solemn oath.

Jonathan's expressions of love and friendship toward David paint one of the most beautiful portraits of covenant in the Word of God. The word "covenant" in 1 Samuel 18:3 is derived from the Hebrew term *berith*, which means, "determination, stipulation, covenant. It was a treaty, alliance of friendship, a pledge, an obligation between a monarch and his subjects, a constitution. It was a contract that was accompanied by signs, sacrifices, and a solemn oath that sealed the relationship with promises of blessing for obedience and curses for disobedience."[1]

According to the preceding definition, what three elements accompanied the making of a covenant?

1. _Signs_ 2. _Sacrifices_ 3. _solemn oath_

Although they are less obvious than in other covenants in Scripture, each of the three elements of covenant can be found in the covenant relationship between Jonathan and David recorded in 1 Samuel 18:1-4. We will look at a covenant in which the elements are more obvious. Through it we can understand what we're looking for in Jonathan and David's covenant.

Read Genesis 15. Look for the sign of the covenant, the sacrifice of the covenant, and the solemn oath of the covenant.

Briefly describe each element in God's covenant with Abram.

1. Sign (how the covenant was demonstrated):

V4 a son coming from your own body. V17?

2. Sacrifice:

V9 heifer, goat, ram, dove, pigeon

3. Solemn oath:

V18 to your descendants I give this land

You may have noted that the sign of the covenant was the smoking firepot with a blazing torch passing between the pieces of flesh. The sacrifice was the heifer, goat, ram, dove, and young pigeon. The solemn oath was the promise to give Abram and his descendants the land.

Compare Jonathan's covenant with David by noting the same three elements. Reread 1 Samuel 18:1-4, looking for hints of the three elements of covenant. Don't be discouraged that they are less obvious than the elements in God's covenant with Abram. The sign will likely be the only obvious element. We will discover the other two together.

The sign: Which of the following was the demonstration of the covenant Jonathan made with David?

☐ Jonathan loved David as himself.
☐ David never returned to his father's house.
☑ Jonathan gave David his robe, tunic, and weapons.

God demonstrated His covenant with Abram by the blazing fire pot passing between the pieces of flesh. Jonathan showed his covenant with David by giving him his robe, tunic, and weapons. We will see the greater significance of Jonathan's demonstration as we consider the sacrifice and the solemn oath.

The sacrifice: In Jonathan's covenant with David the sacrifice is less obvious than the birds and animals in God's covenant with Abram, but it is profound. Look ahead for just a moment and read 1 Samuel 20:30-31.

What were King Saul's obvious intentions for his son Jonathan?

the next king

Jonathan was a prince and heir apparent to the throne. His father obviously planned for Jonathan to be the next king of Israel, but this son had other plans. In David, Jonathan saw character fit for a king. He was so determined that the throne be occupied by God's chosen instrument that he offered everything he had. In this unique covenant, Jonathan sacrificed himself. Jonathan removed his royal regalia—his robe and tunic—and placed it on David, symbolizing that David would be king instead of him.

Can you picture the face of the recipient whose clothing probably still carried the faint scent of sheep? Jonathan acknowledged David as prince of the Hebrew nation, a position that he could have jealously and vehemently claimed as his own. Men like Jonathan are a rarity. Few people have "in mind the things of God" at risk of their own favor and position (Matt. 16:23).

Do you have the privilege of knowing someone like Jonathan, someone who has given up power or position for God's will? ☐ yes ☐ no   If so, briefly describe that person and his or her faithfulness.

"After David had finished talking with Saul, Jonathan became one in spirit with David, and he loved him as himself. From that day Saul kept David with him and did not let him return to his father's house. And Jonathan made a covenant with David because he loved him as himself. Jonathan took off the robe he was wearing and gave it to David, along with his tunic, and even his sword, his bow and his belt."
1 SAMUEL 18:1-4

"Jesus turned and said to Peter, 'Get behind me, Satan! You are a stumbling block to me; you do not have in mind the things of God, but the things of men.'"
MATTHEW 16:23

"But if my father is inclined to harm you, may the Lord deal with me, be it ever so severely, if I do not let you know and send you away safely. May the Lord be with you as he has been with my father."

1 SAMUEL 20:13

The solemn oath: Compare 1 Samuel 18:4 and 20:13. How did Jonathan's actions in the first Scripture illustrate what he then clearly verbalized in the second passage?

The oath of Jonathan's covenant with David does not take place in words in chapter 18. However, it is symbolized in 1 Samuel 18:4; then it is verbalized in 1 Samuel 20:13.

Jonathan symbolized the solemn oath by giving David his weapons of protection: his sword, bow, and belt. He symbolically gave all he had to protect David from harm and ensure his position as future king. Jonathan verbalized his solemn oath by pledging in 1 Samuel 20:13 to protect David from harm at great personal risk.

We've compared two examples of covenant today, but we've not yet noted the most meaningful aspect they share: the basis of the covenant.

According to Deuteronomy 7:6-9, why did God choose Israel?
- ☐ They loved God.
- ☐ They were the fewest of all peoples.
- ☑ He loved them.
- ☐ They had honored God with their sacrifices.

V 8

Reconsider Jonathan's covenant with David. What was the basis of their covenant (1 Sam. 18:1)?

J loved D

Does 1 Samuel 18:1-4 mention David returning the love? ☐ yes ☑ no

God's covenant with the nation of Israel was based on His love for them. In this same way, Jonathan's covenant with David was based on Jonathan's love, not David's response. We who have accepted Christ as Savior are part of the most wonderful covenant God ever made with man. God loves us for a singular reason—He chooses to love us.

According to 1 John 4:10,15 how does our covenant compare to the two we've studied today?

I trust that you observed: The sign—God sent His only Son. The sacrifice—He "sent his Son as an atoning sacrifice for our sins" (v. 10). The solemn oath—"If anyone acknowledges that Jesus is the Son of God, God lives in him and he in God" (v. 15).

The basis of this covenant is the same as the basis of Jonathan's covenant with David—"Not that we loved God but that he loved us" (v. 10). What greater covenant could possibly exist?

Covenant is an important theme in the Word of God. God's covenant with Abram made Jonathan's covenant with David a little clearer. I pray that our look at both covenants makes God's covenant with us a little dearer.

Conclude your lesson by briefly recording how you entered into the covenant with God through Christ (when and how you accepted Christ as Savior).

If you could not answer the question and are unsure that you have entered into the covenant of eternal life through the death of Christ, would you consider accepting Christ as Savior right now? The steps to eternal life are very simple, but the results are profound and everlasting:

- Tell God that you are a sinner and that you cannot earn eternal life.
- Tell God that you believe Jesus Christ is the Son of God and that He died on the cross for you.
- Ask Jesus to forgive you of your sins and to live in your heart through His Holy Spirit.
- Commit your life to love and to serve Him.
- Thank Him for your new salvation.

If you have accepted Christ as Savior, would you please write your commitment below and share your decision with your group leader or a pastor? If you are already a Christian, take time to pray. Thank God for His salvation, and pray for someone you know who has never accepted Christ as Savior.

DAY 2
A Jealous Eye

TODAY'S TREASURE

"'They have credited David with tens of thousands,' he [Saul] thought, 'but me with only thousands. What more can he get but the kingdom?' And from that time on Saul kept a jealous eye on David." 1 Samuel 18:8-9

Begin by praying that God will speak to you through His Word. John Dryden, a sixteenth century philosopher, once called it "the jaundice of the soul."[2] The Song of Solomon says it is as "cruel as the grave" (Song of Sol. 8:6, KJV). Others call it the green-eyed monster. It sends some to jail; others to insanity. It is *jealousy*.

In stark contrast to Jonathan's self-sacrifice and solemn allegiance, Saul regarded David as the ultimate threat. In our first reading assignment today, we will see a seed of jealousy planted deep within the soul of Saul. That seed will express itself with a vengeance over many chapters to come. Both reading assignments today expose the evil in the heart of Saul. Read 1 Samuel 18:5-16.

How did David perform the duties Saul assigned to him?
- ☑ He performed all his duties successfully.
- ☐ He did what was right in his own eyes.
- ☐ He was reluctant to obey the commands of Saul.

What did Saul do as a result of David's performance?
- ☐ He made David his armor bearer.
- ☐ He made David second in command.
- ☑ He gave David a high rank in the army.

What first incited the jealousy of King Saul (v. 7)?

praise for David's accomplishment over Saul's

How did Saul's inward jealousy become an outward violent expression?

evil spirit

Why was David a great success in everything he did (v. 14)?

the Lord was with him

In our first reading assignment, we identified several powerful feelings Saul had toward David. Read the list of feelings below and cross out any that do not describe Saul's feelings as mentioned in 1 Samuel 18:5-16.

~~admiration~~	jealousy	~~hatred~~	fear	~~joy~~
gall	anger	~~anticipation~~	anxiety	

I believe that fear is the root of virtually all jealousy. Consider the possible relationship between fear and jealousy by responding to the following scenarios:

Why might a wife be jealous of an attractive single woman working with her husband?

Why might a man be jealous of a new, talented employee hired in a similar position in his company?

Do you see how fear might contribute to both cases of jealousy? We could cite countless examples of jealousy fueled by fear, but we need look no further than 1 Samuel 18. Saul was terribly jealous of David.

In your opinion what fear might have fueled Saul's jealousy?

losing his kingship to D.

Just as fear often leads to jealousy, most negative emotions lead to others. I see at least four emotions attributed to Saul in his reactions to David. In verse 8 we see anger and gall, which ordinarily means bitterness. In verse 9 we see jealousy, and in verses 12 and 15 we see evidences of fear. When emotions are unchecked by the Holy Spirit, one negative emotion can easily feed another, joining together as links in a chain of bondage.

The Hebrew word for the kind of anger Saul experienced is informative, "Anger: *Charah*—to burn, be kindled, glow with anger, be incensed, grow indignant; to be zealous, act zealously. Unlike some of its synonyms, *charah* points to the fire or heat of the anger just after it has been ignited."[3] *Charah* captures the moment a person explodes with anger—before any sense of control takes over, before a rational thought can be processed.

When was the last time you exploded over something? Go ahead, you can record it. Questions like this keep us humble.

Did you have regrets later? ☐ yes ☐ no   If so, in the margin describe how you felt.

> Just as fear often leads to jealousy, most negative emotions lead to others.

It's dangerous to approach a day without praying to be filled with the Holy Spirit.

Rarely do we accomplish anything profitable at the moment we become angry. Actions or words immediately following the ignition of anger are almost always regrettable. Moments like the one *charah* describes are exactly the reason it's so dangerous to approach a day without praying to be filled with the Holy Spirit. Through the life of Saul, we see a portrait of what our lives might be like if the Holy Spirit departed from us. We get a frightening enough glimpse of peril when He's quenched in us.

Saul felt many things toward David, but the most consistent emotion was jealousy. Two men will pay a tremendous price for the jealousy of Saul. We will behold some of the suffering jealousy showered on the lives of both Saul and David. Few experiences are more miserable than being the subject of someone's unleashed jealousy. Perhaps the only thing worse is being the one in whom the jealousy rages. Before we go on to our second reading assignment, let's count the cost of being subject to someone's jealousy; then we will determine whether jealousy is ever a healthy emotion.

In Acts 5:17-18 what happened as a result of jealousy?

Arrested apostles + put them in the public jail.

According to Acts 5:19, who rescued them?

An angel of the Lord.

In the margin describe the results of jealousy in Acts 13:44-50.

Jews jealous of Paul & Barnabas, they turn away from the Jews towards the gen

In Acts 13:49 what did God do through them in spite of the jealousy?

The word of the Lord spread through the whole region.

If you are the innocent subject of someone's unchecked jealousy—in the workplace, at church, in a relationship—tell God on him or her. Let God work. Pray for Him to deliver you, to sow peace in your persecutor's heart, and to move mightily in spite of the wrongful response of another. If you are a sower of jealousy in your own heart, I tenderly urge you to ask God right now to release you from its bondage and fill you with His Spirit.

What does 1 Corinthians 3:3 tell you about jealousy?
- ☑ Jealousy is characteristic of worldly behavior.
- ☐ Jealousy is evidence that the enemy is at work.
- ☐ Jealousy is overcome by forgiveness.

Is jealousy ever a proper response? Does it ever sow good rather than evil? Believe it or not, the answer is yes!

What is a righteous kind of jealousy according to 2 Corinthians 11:2?

a godly jealousy.

What does Exodus 20:5 tell us about jealousy? *God is jealous: You shall have no other gods before me.*

What kind of jealousy does God possess? Fill in the missing words.

Joel 2:18: "The LORD will be jealous _____*for*_____ his land and take pity on his people."

Zechariah 1:14: "This is what the Lord Almighty says, 'I am very jealous _____*for*_____ Jerusalem and Zion.' "

Zechariah 8:2: "This is what the Lord Almighty says, 'I am very jealous _____*for*_____ Zion; I am burning with jealousy for her.' "

Now reread 2 Corinthians 11:2 and fill in the missing word.

"I am jealous _____*for*_____ you with a godly jealousy."

Do you see a common characteristic in all righteous jealousies? A big difference exists between being jealous *of* someone and being jealous *for* someone. God is jealous on our behalf. He is jealous for us to know the one true God. He is jealous for us to be in a posture of blessing. He is jealous for us to be kept from the evil one. He is jealous for us to be ready for our Bridegroom. Jealousy *for* someone's best is of God. Jealousy *of* someone's best is of the enemy.

Is there anyone you can honestly say you are jealous "for"? Who is it and what is the nature of your righteous jealousy on his or her behalf?

Read 1 Samuel 18:17-30. Why was Saul pleased that his daughter was in love with David, and what does his attitude tell you about his heart?
S. saw an opportunity to have David killed.

Why do you think Saul became more afraid once he realized his daughter loved David? Respond in the margin. *V 28: Saul realized that the hand was with David.*

So our David is married. We know little about Michal, but Saul considered the marriage a way to destroy David (v. 21). Can you imagine the evil in the heart of a man who would use his own daughter as a pawn in a personal vendetta?

Perhaps Saul was raised on a well-known story of another man gifted with strength, one who struck down a thousand men with the jawbone of a donkey but who could not tame one woman. Samson went from the hands of Delilah into the hands of the Philistines and ultimately to his death (Judg. 15–16). Saul obviously had high hopes that Michal would be the death of David, but David had something much greater than high hopes. He had a Most High God.

DAY 3

The Great Escape

TODAY'S TREASURE

"Jonathan spoke well of David to Saul his father and said to him, 'Let not the king do wrong to his servant David; he has not wronged you, and what he has done has benefited you greatly.' " 1 Samuel 19:4

In our previous lesson we saw the seed of jealousy sown in the heart of Saul. Fear, anger, and bitterness fueled a jealousy that quickly grew out of control. Today we see the power of jealousy contrasted with the power of love and the Spirit. Today's reading is fascinating. As I first read 1 Samuel 19, I could almost see the scene unfold on stage. Picture the scene with me. Read 1 Samuel 19:1-18.

In what ways did Jonathan respond to his father's orders to kill David?
- ☑ He warned David of his father's intentions.
- ☐ He pretended to follow his father's instructions.
- ☑ He reminded his father how David had benefited him.
- ☐ He broke his covenant with David to honor his father.

What was the result of Jonathan's efforts in David's behalf?
- ☐ Saul regarded Jonathan as a traitor.
- ☐ Saul's anger toward David deepened.
- ☑ Saul and David were briefly reconciled.
- ☐ An evil spirit struck Saul.

How did Michal demonstrate her love for David in 1 Samuel 19?

Warned D + helped him to escape.

In verse 17 what excuse did Michal give her father for deceiving him?

David threatened to kill her.

Now that's drama, isn't it? We continue our look at the power of jealousy. First consider how Saul's jealousy continued to grow. Jonathan was momentarily able to bring his father back to reality. He tried to convince Saul that David had been good for him and for the kingdom. Jonathan reminded Saul that he had initially been glad over David's victory.

Keep in mind that Jonathan risked his own life in keeping the covenant with David. Saul did not hesitate to order Jonathan's death once before. If Saul's men had not talked him into being rational, he would have killed his own son. (See 1 Sam. 14:43-45.) Well-chosen words calmed Saul's jealous rage, but it returned with a vengeance. Without God's intervention, we can offer only a small bandage to someone hemorrhaging from uncontrolled emotions. We may bring calm for a moment, but our efforts will have little lasting effect.

Do you remember a time when you momentarily talked someone out of a negative spiral of emotions only to see the person become captivated again? ☐ yes ☐ no   If so, in the margin briefly describe the events.

Have you ever been talked out of a negative spiral of emotions only to be captivated by those feelings again? If so, describe the situation.

Our words can only treat the symptoms. Only God can heal the disease of uncontrolled emotions. We've probably all been in Saul's place at one time or another. Something makes us furious; then someone tries to "talk some sense into us." We feel a little better and pledge to put our anger away forever. Then, here it comes again with the power of gale-force winds.

Our emotions negatively ignited can be more powerful than we are. Our best recourse when negative emotions begin controlling us is to fall before the throne of grace and seek God. Take solace in the fact that Christ knows how it feels to be tempted by feelings (Heb. 2:18; 4:15).

Saul failed to acknowledge his rage and jealousy as evil. His imaginations did nothing but further sow the seed within him, and his jealousy became relentless. Our imaginations will also fuel the fires of jealousy if we are not careful. Jealousy is a powerful emotion, but so is love.

> Our imaginations will fuel the fires of jealousy if we are not careful.

Why did Saul have cause to be frightened when he realized that Michal loved David (1 Sam. 18:28-29)?

She would protect him.

Saul was right about love threatening his plans for Michal to bring harm to David. The power of love often exceeds the power of loyalty. He thought he could trust Michal to make David miserable. He thought she would be a puppet in his hands against the young warrior until he realized she loved him.

Michal's masterful deception could easily have led to her death. Surely she was only spared because she convinced her father that David would have killed her if she hadn't let him get away.

Our first reading assignment ended in verse 18 with a vital piece of information. To whom did David run?

☐ Jonathan ☐ Jesse ☑ Samuel ☐ Eliab

Why do you think he ran to this particular person?

Have you ever had a time when someone encouraged you toward a position and once you got in the middle of it, you went back and said, "What have you gotten me into?" Did you ever feel that way about marriage? parenthood? career? church work? David probably shared your doubts and questions.

David went straight to Samuel because he was the one God used to anoint David as leader of Israel. He likely had questions for Samuel, such as "Are you sure God told you to anoint me?" Regardless of his questions, David went to tell on Saul, and no doubt Samuel confirmed David's calling.

We've seen proof in our first reading assignment today that love can be more powerful than jealousy. Our second reading assignment and commentary will be brief, but we will see that the Spirit of God is also more powerful than jealousy. Read 1 Samuel 19:19-24.

These events are almost humorous, aren't they? Saul sent one man after another to capture David, but every time they entered the presence of Samuel's prophets, the Spirit of God fell on them and they prophesied too. Finally Saul apparently thought, *Fine. I'll do it myself.* The same thing happened to him.

What do you think these words in the NIV mean: "But the Spirit of God came even upon him"?

The Spirit has left him. He was the enemy of God's chosen one.

When God gets involved, we see real results. Don't miss celebrating that when a group of evil men met a group of godly men, godliness won. How encouraging to remember that the Spirit of God is more powerful than the spirit of wickedness. As 1 John 4:4 reminds us, "You, dear children, are from God and have overcome them, because the one who is in you is greater than the one who is in the world."

Today we've seen that love is more powerful than jealousy, godliness is more powerful than wickedness, and the Spirit of God is more powerful than anything. The best laid plans of kings and queens crumble under the mighty Spirit of God. Acts 1:8 tells us that when the Holy Spirit comes on us we will receive power. The Greek word is *dunamis*. We call it *dynamite*. That's what it takes to burst the walls of rage and jealousy within us. First John 3:20 says, "God is greater than our hearts."

As children of God, we do not have to be derailed by the way we feel. Our God is greater. Give Him your heart.

How encouraging to remember that the Spirit of God is more powerful than the spirit of wickedness.

DAY 4

Common Bonds, Uncommon Friends

TODAY'S TREASURE

"Show me unfailing kindness like that of the LORD as long as I live, so that I may not be killed, and do not ever cut off your kindness from my family—not even when the LORD has cut off every one of David's enemies from the face of the earth." 1 Samuel 20:14-15

Begin by praying that God will speak to you through His Word. Today we have a rather long chapter, but it describes a comparatively simple scene. We find David caught in the whirlwind of Saul's jealousy, and this threat of death gave way to the reaffirmation of Jonathan's covenant. We're going to talk about friendships, the once-in-a-lifetime kind. In the reading assignment, observe the relationship between Jonathan and David and the events that caused their separation. Read 1 Samuel 20:1-42.

Why did David flee to Jonathan?

To find out why Saul is determined to kill him & if he had done anything to deserve it.

Mark each of the following statements as true or false based on 1 Samuel 20:1-24. If the statement is false, draw a line through the error and correct the statement in the margin.

_____X_____ Jonathan believed that his father was going to kill David. *V 2*

_____✓_____ Jonathan was to tell Saul that David went to his hometown. *V 6*

_____✓_____ Jonathan pledged to tell David if his father planned to harm him. *V 13* *send your word*

_____X_____ Jonathan would cast his spear to let David know Saul's response. *V 20* *arrow*

Jonathan signaled his father's unfavorable response to David just as he promised. Describe the scene between Jonathan and David after the boy had gathered the arrows and departed.

Offer a few reasons why you believe David "wept the most."

We've read about tragic events today, but we've seen priceless expressions of deep friendship. In 1 Samuel 18:1-4 we studied the making of the covenant between Jonathan and David. Today we saw the keeping of that covenant. Anyone can make a covenant, but only the faithful keep their covenants.

I've waited to emphasize a special portion of Scripture from our reading assignment on day 1. First Samuel 20 poignantly pictures words so beautifully expressed in 1 Samuel 18:1. The Word of God tells us, "Jonathan became one in spirit with David, and he loved him as himself" (1 Sam. 18:1). The King James Version helps us draw a more vivid mental image: "The soul of Jonathan was knit with the soul of David." The Hebrew word translated "knit" in the King James Version and "became one" in the New International Version is *qashar,* which means "to tie … join together, knit."[4] Jonathan and David are examples of two people knit together by something more powerful than circumstances or preferences.

The Spirit of God sometimes cements two people together as part of His plan. God would never have chosen David to be His future king if He had not planned to sustain him and ultimately deliver him safely to his throne. Jonathan was an important part of God's plan. They were uncommon friends joined by a common bond: the Spirit of God. First Samuel 18:1 tells us that Jonathan and David were united, but 1 Samuel 20 shows us. Consider these tender expressions of uncommon friendship.

Uncommon friends can speak their minds without fear. Imagine the tone David probably used with Jonathan in 1 Samuel 20:1-4. His words suggest nothing less than panic. Jonathan could easily have received David's words as an insult. After all, David practically took his frustration out on Jonathan and asked him to explain his father's actions. As you carefully consider the words they traded, you can almost hear their elevated and emotional tones.

Jonathan responded to David's panic with the words, "Look, my father doesn't do anything, great or small, without confiding in me. Why would he hide this from me? It's not so!" (v. 2). I believe they exchanged heated words. David came very close to holding Jonathan responsible for Saul's actions, and Jonathan came very close to getting defensive.

Their initial words to one another would be only natural under their circumstances. What is not natural, however, was their freedom to speak their minds to one another and move on to resolution without great incident. Notice that at this point Jonathan didn't believe Saul was really trying to take David's life; yet he acknowledged that David's feelings were authentic by saying, "Whatever you want me to do, I'll do for you" (v. 4). He didn't necessarily agree with David, but he agreed that David was upset and needed his help instead of his doubt.

Jonathan and David are examples of two people knit together by something more powerful than circumstances or preferences.

Each of us can probably remember times when people have focused their frustrations on us and held us responsible for something beyond our control. How do you usually respond to this kind of scenario?

☐ I ordinarily become a little defensive.
☑ I ordinarily become very defensive.
☐ I ordinarily allow the person to safely blow some steam.
☐ I ordinarily refuse to talk to her until she settles down.

Allowing others to speak their fears even when we can't understand is characteristic of uncommon friendship. Willingness to listen and then let the potential insults pass is not a sign of weakness. It is a sign of strength. The bonds of uncommon friends are deeper than the width of their differences.

Can you think of a time when a friend let you off the hook when you centered your frustration on her or him? ☐ yes ☐ no If so, briefly explain.

Uncommon friends can share their hearts without shame. The scene between Jonathan and David in 1 Samuel 20:41 touches my heart every time I read it. Something about two men unafraid to share their hearts with one another never fails to move me. Uncommon friends can be vulnerable with one another and still retain their dignity. The friendship between Jonathan and David was far more than emotion, and it was a safe place to trust and show feelings. They shared a common goal: the will of God. Each life complemented the other. They had separate lives but inseparable bonds.

My husband Keith is a plumber by trade. His best friend Roger is a lawyer and judge. They are uncommon friends. They don't talk every day. They don't necessarily talk every week, but their bond remains firm. They play jokes on one another. They take up for one another. Roger often sends Keith cards or cartoons. Keith drops by Roger's office unexpectedly with lunch from time to time. When they see one another, they hug. When they hurt, they sometimes cry. They are "real men" with a rare friendship.

Do you sometimes struggle with the appropriate response when someone is very emotional with you? ☐ yes ☐ no

Read Romans 12:15. Based on this verse, what do you believe people really need from us when they are extremely emotional?

Rejoice with those who rejoice; mourn " " " " mourn.

Do you have a friend with whom you feel safe sharing your heart?
☑ yes ☐ no If not, and you wish you had an uncommon friend, in the margin express a prayer for one.

Uncommon friends can stay close even at a distance. Most friendships require time and attention. We established on day 1 that Jonathan and David's friendship did not grow out of a lengthy period of time as most friendships do. They were brought together by spiritual ties, not sequences of time. They had "sworn friendship with each other in the name of the LORD" (v. 42). God brought them together. Their friendship was a bond of three.

Read Ecclesiastes 4:9-12. The entire segment of Scripture applies perfectly to Jonathan and David, but give special attention to the last statement in verse 12.

How could you apply this statement to God's part in Jonathan and David's friendship?

A cord of 3 strands is not quickly broken.

Do you have a "three strand" friendship? In other words, is God an active part of one of your friendships? ☐ yes ☐ no   If so, in what ways do you and your friend keep God an active part of your friendship? If not, how can you involve God more fully in your friendships?

My kindred soul,
    it seems

Parts of a whole

Higher things foreknown

Than friends

Uncommon works

Eternal ends.

Unworthy guests

Worthy goals

May we walk worthy,

Kindred soul.

Partners in

The higher things

'Til captives hear

And freedom rings!

I have known the joy of several uncommon friends in my life. God has undeniably tied my spirit to the spirits of several wonderful people who have influenced my life and allowed me to share my heart with them. My husband is one such friend. After troubled times in our marriage, we have always found our way back together because our hearts are undeniably yoked. We just can't seem to keep from falling back in love with one another after difficult times.

God has also tied my heartstrings to a small band of women I see many times a week. They are more than friends. They are partners in the gospel, brought together by God for this ministry. We have an unexplainable yoke in our spirits that God ordained for His purposes. We are equally dedicated to one specific goal: to share the Word of God. They do their part. I do mine. God braids the strands with His purpose and forms a cord not easily broken.

I wrote the words in the margin for those of us who have found our spirits tied to another by God Himself and for His great glory. May these words help us recognize how God can bind common lives like yours and mine in uncommon ways.

DAY 5

The Blessed Reminder

TODAY'S TREASURE

"The priest gave him the consecrated bread, since there was no bread there except the bread of the Presence that had been removed from before the LORD and replaced by hot bread on the day it was taken away." 1 Samuel 21:6

Begin by praying that God will speak to you through His Word. A very significant season of David's life begins in our chapter today. David was scarcely 20 years old when he was forced to leave his home, his livelihood, and his beloved friend as he fled from the madman who happened to be king of Israel.

I've had the opportunity to work with college students a few times. I always come away thinking how young they seem and how old and savvy I felt at that same age. I suffered enough trauma just leaving home to go to college where I had a secure room in the dorm, a guaranteed meal in the cafeteria, and more company than I could stand. I certainly have nothing with which to compare this season of David's young life. He was on the run with a madman on his heels. Saul had alerted half the country to kill him. David faced a terrifying prospect for a person twice his age. Today we will take a look at David's initiation to life on the run. Read 1 Samuel 21:1-9.

When David fled, he first went to Nob, to Ahimelech the priest, who reacted to David's arrival with trembling.

Why do you think Ahimelech was frightened by David's coming?

He knew D was a great warrior + possibly sent by Saul.

What lie did David tell Ahimelech?

V2 The king sent me on a mission.

What two things did David request from the priest in these nine verses?
☑ five loaves of bread   ☐ protection   ☐ prayer   ☑ a weapon

The priest had no bread to offer except the bread of the _____*Presence*_____.

Doeg the Edomite will become a memorable figure in our study next week. Who was he according to verse 7?
- ☐ one of the priests of Nob
- ☐ Ahimelech's head shepherd
- ☐ one of David's men
- ☑ Saul's head shepherd

The only sword in Nob was the one that had belonged to _Goliath_.

David did not haphazardly end up in Nob. He no doubt sought relief in the city of priests. Nob, a village between Jerusalem and Gibeah, was the venue where the tabernacle was relocated after the destruction of Shiloh. Like many of us in times of crisis, he may have desired to draw closest to those who seem closest to God—not a bad idea.

When was the last time you reached out to your pastor, Sunday School teacher, or someone you regard as being "close to God"? Why did you reach out to that particular person in your time of need?

In the first verse of chapter 21, we see that Ahimelech "trembled" when he met David. Ahimelech was probably not aware of the warrant out for David's life. If he'd known Saul was seeking to kill David, he would not have asked why David was alone. Perhaps verse 9 provides a little insight. Ahimelech knew of Goliath's demise at the hands of this young man. He also may have remembered David sporting through Jerusalem swinging Goliath's head in his hand. No doubt, David was rather intimidating. The priests certainly would have wanted no trouble from the Philistine army seeking revenge. Whatever the reasons, we are told that the sight of David struck fear in the priests' hearts.

> We will be witness to more than a few compromises in David's character.

Surely you noted that David responded to the priest with a lie. Through our study we will be witness to more than a few compromises in David's character. In this case the compromise was David's willingness to lie. He was probably attempting to spare the priest's life, hoping that Saul would not hold Ahimelech responsible for helping David. Famished from his flight, David asked the priest for five loaves of bread.

Christ fed the multitudes with ___5___ loaves of bread in Matthew 14:19.

Interestingly, David requested in verse 3, "Give me five loaves of bread, or whatever you can find." In all four of the Gospels, as Christ sent the disciples to search for food, five loaves were all they could find. For David, however, no bread could be found except the bread of the Presence. Perhaps God had a point to make with the five loaves. Let's do a little research about the bread of the Presence.

Read Leviticus 24:5-9, and fill in the following blanks. Verse 8 says: "This bread is to be set out before the LORD regularly, Sabbath after Sabbath, on behalf of the Israelites, as a _lasting_ _covenant_."

What was God's "everlasting covenant" in Isaiah 55:3?
- ☐ never cut off His people from their inheritance
- ☐ restore the promised land to the people of Israel
- ☑ promised His faithful love to David
- ☐ promised His faithful love to Abraham

Consider two possible reasons why the bread of the Presence might have purposely been used of God to feed David:

1. The bread of the Presence might have symbolized God's everlasting covenant with David. Somewhat like the stars of the sky symbolized the offspring of Abram (Gen. 15:5), the bread of the Presence was placed before God as a reminder or symbol of the everlasting covenant. Through the bread of the Presence God may have been "reminding" David that He had not broken the everlasting covenant He had made with David's kingdom.

2. The bread of the Presence might have symbolized the provision of God's presence in David's life. Just as the first possible reason was a corporate symbol for a kingdom covenant, I believe the second reason might have been a private symbol for a personal covenant. The Hebrew term for *presence* is *paneh*, which means "countenance, presence, or face."[5] The everlasting covenant symbolized by the bread of the Presence was a reminder of the pledge of God's presence to His people. As He offered bread to David through Ahimelech the priest, I believe God pledged His presence to David throughout his exile. God inspired David to write the following two verses.

Look up each verse and fill in the missing words.

Psalm 22:24, "For he has not despised or disdained the suffering of the afflicted one; he has not _hidden his face_ from him but has listened to his cry for help."

Psalm 31:16, "Let your _face shine on your servant_ save me in your unfailing love."

The original word for *face* in both the above verses is *paneh*, the Hebrew word for *presence* in the phrase "the bread of the Presence." God was doing more in this moment in Nob than feeding David's hungry stomach. I believe God was pledging His presence to David and promising to be his complete sustainer. God also extends His presence to you as your sustaining provision.

Read John 6:47-48. By what name did Christ call Himself?

I am the bread of life.

What hint do you see of covenant or something binding or perpetual in John 6:47?

the one who believes has eternal life.
h Very truly I tell you

Christ is the bread of God's presence to us. His scars are placed before God as a perpetual memorial that the wages of our sins have been paid. Christ said, "This bread is my flesh, which I will give for the life of the world" (John 6:51). Those who have eaten the bread of His Presence enjoy the same everlasting covenant He made with David thousands of years ago. He renews His promise to us in Hebrews 13:5: "Never will I leave you; never will I forsake you."

You have probably gone through difficulties in which you felt lost and afraid. In what ways has God reminded you that He was with you, that His "presence" was there?

Did the reminder of His presence calm your heart, or did you continue to fret and search for a refuge elsewhere? Why do you think you responded in this way?

God reminded David of His presence, but David continued to run frantically from village to village. Surely Samuel reminded David of God's plan when David fled to Ramah. God reminded David of His presence and provision through the priest of Nob.

God reminded David in another way. Is it coincidental that the only weapon in the city of Nob was Goliath's sword? Is it possible God was trying to remind David that he had overcome a greater enemy than Saul with God's help? None of these reminders seemed to help because David had forgotten to measure his obstacle against his God rather than against his own strength, as he had Goliath.

> Christ's scars are placed before God as a perpetual memorial that the wages of our sins have been paid.

At least David's search for refuge led to a rather humorous scene which we will view briefly as we conclude today's lesson. Read 1 Samuel 21:10-15. Had David been auditioning for a theatrical production, he would no doubt have gotten the part.

Describe David's "act."

pretended to be insane, making marks on the doors of the gate & letting saliva run down his beard.

Why do you think David put on this "act"?

he was afraid of Achish.

We've seen a new, creative, and shrewd side of our protagonist today, haven't we? Not only was he a harpist and a warrior, he could have won an Oscar for best actor! Some people act for pleasure. Others act for money. David was acting for his life. He pulled it off, too.

You may be wondering why the men of Gath didn't kill him on the spot. David knew something we might just be learning about the pagan people of his ancient era. They were terrified of a madman and far too superstitious to harm one. They feared he was a dangerous demon who had the power to cause them havoc from the next life.

Apparently, David wasn't just sheep smart; he was street smart. To David's good fortune, Achish had enough madmen to deal with and had no desire to have one "carrying on" in front of him.

David may have been short on patience and short on perceiving God's constant reminders, but David certainly wasn't short on personality, was he? Patience and perception might have helped him a little more than personality.

Ask God to make you aware of the constant reminders of His presence in your life so that you can have His assurance no matter your circumstances. In next week's study we will join David as he negotiates some pretty tough times. We'll begin to peek a little deeper into the heart God saw and loved.

Studying God's Word is habit forming. Keep praying for a hunger and thirst for His Word. Like David, God doesn't want you feeding from common loaves. He desires to feed you with the bread of His Presence. His table is always set.

viewer guide | session three

Jealousy is spurred on by fear.

Luke 6:45.
overflow of the mouth.

1 Cor 16:18

Gal 6:1

mental fragility –
1 crisis away.

2 Tim 1:7

1. No one has ever fully embraced the concept of " ___God___ ___alone___ "
apart from grave ___disappointment___ (Ps. 62:5). *Let down by man.*

2. We are never in greater need of ___humility___ than when we are
confident someone else is ___wrong___.

3. We will either ___wrestle___ all our lives with unmet ___expectation___
or intentionally ___rest___ our souls in God. *Turning any soul to face*
dedicated to ___God alone___

• *Selah* is a musical term that means to ___pause___ or bring
a suspension.[1]

wrestle

rest

• "Find rest" in verse 5 comes from a term that means "to ___stop___ ...
___cease___ ... hold peace, quiet self, rest ... tarry, wait."[2]

V8

• The balance is this: We can't ___put___ it ___up___ until we have
___poured___ it ___out___. *Sapak* means "to spill forth, to pour out
(a drink offering), to bare one's soul in ___sorrow___ or ___anger___.
Used literally to denote pouring out the ___contents___ of a
vessel."[3] Strong's dictionary adds: "to mound up ... to ___sprawl___
out ... to ___gush___ out."[4]

Eph 5:18

You cannot expect from
people what only God can deliver.

4. Significant rest comes to the soul when we accept that God alone is
   in charge of our _honor_. God does not just _defend_
   our honor. He _defines_ it.

5. To _cease_ trusting altogether is more harmful for the soul than
   trusting in man. The message of the psalm: Trust in God
   at all times. *Ps 116:11 all man are liars - epitomy of cynicism.*

   "Trust in God is not a place of refuge to which the believer can retreat
   from the turmoil and the disappointments of the world in order to find
   there his satisfaction and rest. Trust in God is a _cell_ of
   organic _life_, a power-centre which does
   not remain in _in isolation_, but cannot help bearing fruit
   because it feels inwardly constrained to prove its living reality through
   acts of faith."[5]

fine people does not make fine gods.

Trust God w. that person you can't trust / won't

1. James Strong, *Strong's Exhaustive Concordance of the Bible* (Peabody, MA: Hendrickson Publishers, n.d.), #5542.
2. Strong, #1826.
3. Spiros Zodhiates, gen. ed., *The Complete Word Study Dictionary NT* (Chattanooga, TN: AMG Publishers, 1992), #9161.
4. Strong, #8210.
5. Artur Weiser, *The Psalms* (Philadelphia: Westminster Press, 1962), 450.

Survival Skills and He Who Wills

Day 1
For Crying Out Loud

Day 2
The Inhumanity of Humanity

Day 3
Count Your Many Blessings

Day 4
A Chance for Revenge

Day 5
A Surly Man and a Smart Woman

DAY 1
For Crying Out Loud

TODAY'S TREASURE

"I pour out my complaint before him; before him I tell my trouble. When my spirit grows faint within me, it is you who know my way." Psalm 142:2-3

Pray that God will speak to you through His Word. This week will help us hold on to our faith when we face evil. We glimpse David's naïveté and share his horror over the boundless evil in the heart of King Saul. David's responses to his circumstances will challenge us to evaluate our own. His relationships will capture our attention and cause us to feel as if we know him. David rarely responded halfheartedly. He met his circumstances with the deeply felt emotions of a whole heart. Sometimes the unimaginable happens, and we respond with shock and horror.

This vital season of David's experience provided painful preparation for the throne God had promised. We'll study David's responses to life on the run as he fled a wildly jealous king. Can you imagine the devastation David must have experienced having all his hopes dashed to pieces?

David probably had never been away from home before Saul summoned him to service. Surely, like a high school graduate about to go to college, he had been too excited to sleep the night before he left his father's house. Filled with dreams and wonderful expectations, young David was met by a nightmare. He had not only left his home, but now he ran from his "home away from home." He was separated from his new wife and his best friend and forced to beg bread from the priest of Nob. Our first reading assignment takes place exactly where our last concluded. Glance back over the events recorded in 1 Samuel 21; then proceed by reading 1 Samuel 22:1-5.

> What did David's family do when they heard he was hiding out at the cave of Adullam?
> - ☐ They summoned for help.
> - ☑ They went to him.
> - ☐ They brought their weapons.
> - ☐ They wept for him.

David had quite an initiation into leadership. Dealing with sheep must have been much less complicated than dealing with people.

Based on verse 2, how would you describe David's "flock" of people?

outcasts

David asked the king of Moab if his parents could stay with him for a while (v. 3). Why do you think he might have made this request rather than sending them back home to Bethlehem?

For safety from Saul

First Samuel 22:1 tells us "David left Gath and escaped to the cave of Adullam." The cave of Adullam, a word meaning "sealed off place," was about 20 miles southwest of Jerusalem.[1] David had traveled approximately 10 miles by foot from Gath to the place of strange refuge he found in the crevice of a mountain.

Cave-pierced mountains are quite prevalent in the area of Palestine where David's exile took place. People found refuge in these caves up until the time of Roman rule, when Jews fled Roman persecution. I wonder how many of those Jews found solace in knowing their beloved King David had also escaped persecution in a similar refuge centuries earlier?

Today we begin to develop a deeper sense of appreciation that the shepherd boy, able young warrior, and the anointed one of God was also a writer of psalms. Had 1 Samuel 22 been our only text, we would never have known some of what David experienced in that dark, damp refuge. Thankfully, God inspired David to write his feelings, then engraved them forever in holy writ.

Your second reading assignment will take you to the psalm David wrote after entering this dismal cave, checking all earthly securities at the door. The New International Version identifies Psalm 142 as: "A maskil of David. When he was in the cave. A prayer." Please read the psalm prayerfully.

_X_ I should not pray for myself but only pray for the needs of others.

_X_ Bringing my complaint to God is inappropriate.

_✓_ God cares how I feel.

_X_ Asking to be rescued from my peril is unspiritual.

Based on David's example in Psalm 142, in the margin read the four statements about prayer and mark each one true or false.

Fill in the blank: "I cry ___*aloud*___ to the LORD" (v. 1).

What was David's comfort when his spirit grew "faint within" him?

it is you who watch over my way.

In one sentence state what you believe to be the theme of Psalm 142.

a prayer in distress.

What two results did David believe his deliverance would bring?

v7. that I may praise your name
the righteous will gather about me.

Few of us have been forced to find refuge in a cave, but we've all felt some of the same emotions David experienced. Psalm 142 offers a number of insights into David's heart. His responses provide a worthy example for us. What did David do when overwhelmed with unfair treatment and difficult circumstances?

1. David prayed. Be careful not to overlook David's most obvious response. The words of Psalm 142 provide an unquestionable testament that David responded to his difficulty with prayer. Few of us would argue about prayer being the proper response in our crises, but we often don't perceive prayer as being the most practical response. Sometimes we regard prayer as less practical when our need is more concrete. We think, *God can save me from my sins but not from my situation.*

In the margin note things we tend to do before we pray about a crisis.

2. David cried aloud. The scene touches my heart as I imagine this young man sobbing in the cave. A few weeks ago I was nearby when a teen-aged boy slammed his hand in a car door and could not remove it for at least a minute. He was in immense pain. I watched him try to control his quivering lip as he struggled between his internal need to be reduced to a bawling baby and his external need to keep his dignity.

David was probably no different than the young man I saw. He wanted to act like a man, but he was virtually a boy in a situation any adult would regard as frightening. I wonder how much he wished for the old days when he was unimportant, unimpressive, and contentedly keeping sheep. He had not asked for God's anointing, yet he had met nothing but trouble since that day. We can only begin to imagine the thoughts, fears, and losses that brought this young man to tears.

What unforeseen events have made you question God's calling on your life?

How he handled his emotions is noteworthy. I believe that one of the ways he maintained sound emotional, mental, and spiritual health was crying aloud. Volumes could be written in favor of going ahead and crying when the lump wells up within you. Sometimes there's just nothing like a good cry. It clears the air, doesn't it? David was a real man by anyone's standards, yet he knew no better outlet than crying aloud to his God. "Cry aloud to the LORD" when you feel overwhelmed. He can take it!

3. David poured out his complaint to God. He told God his troubles. If we pour out our complaint to everyone else, we're going to be labeled a complainer. But if we pour out our complaint to God, we'll find help. Tell Him your trouble. Tell Him what's hurting you. You can even tell Him what's bugging you! I am convinced this is one of the major contributors to David's Godlike heart: He viewed his heart as a pitcher, and he poured everything in it on his God, whether it was joy or sadness, bitterness or fear. David not only poured out his heart as a personal practice; he urged others to do the same.

Pour out your hearts to him, because God is our refuge.

In the margin write David's words from Psalm 62:8.

4. David rehearsed his trust in God. In Psalm 142:3 he said, "When my spirit grows faint within me, it is you who know my way." David was so exhausted that he feared he would become negligent in his alertness to the snares his enemies set for him. His prayer to God also became a reminder to himself: "God knows my way." Prayer is for our sake as much as it is for God's pleasure.

When I see the words I've written in my journal extolling the mighty virtues of God, I am reminded of His constant activity in my behalf, and my faith is strengthened.

5. David longed for God's presence. Our feelings are worth sharing with God whether or not they accurately describe the truth. In verse 4, David said, "Look to my right and see; no one is concerned for me." Guards often stood to the right of their appointees, ready to take an arrow in their defense. David was reminding God he had no guard. He surmised from his aloneness that no one was concerned for him. His next words were, "I have no refuge; no one cares for my life." We often equate safety with people, not places. Take a good look at the words of the psalmist again. Although he had found a cave in which to hide, he felt he had no refuge because no one was there who cared personally for him.

Have you ever felt like David? When was the last time you felt like no one was there to be a refuge in your need?

Certainly many people cared for David, but because they were not in his presence, he felt forsaken. His feelings were not an accurate assessment of the truth, but they were worthy to share with God. Feelings can be a little like our laundry. Sometimes we can't sort them until we dump them on the table. God honored David's telling Him exactly how he felt.

How can we know? Look back at 1 Samuel 22:1 and read it again. Whom did God bring to David?

parents & brothers, father's household.

In my freshman year of college, I fell head over heels in love with a young man. Every time he broke my heart, I wanted to go home. Home was three-and-one-half hours away, and I had no car. I must have called my daddy a dozen times during that fretful courtship. Every time, no matter what time of the day or night, he got in the car and drove seven hours round-trip to pick me up. I'd feel better after a few days of my mom and dad's tender loving care, black-eyed peas, and corn bread.

In the same way, God knew David needed his daddy. Later God would mature David and teach him to stand alone. He wouldn't always send David's father to him. He doesn't send my father to rescue me anymore. But God always responded to David's cry for help.

6. David confessed his desperate need. In Psalm 142:6 he said, "Listen to my cry, for I am in desperate need; rescue me from those who pursue me, for they are too strong for me." A wise man knows when those who stand

Our feelings are worth sharing with God whether or not they accurately describe the truth.

against him are mightier than he. David had killed both a lion and a bear; then Goliath became "like one of them" (1 Sam. 17:36). David knew God had given him power to subdue all three enemies, so why did he feel overwhelmed? It may have been because he had never battled a secret enemy. This time he had members of Saul's entourage pursuing him with secret schemes.

Does David's plight sound familiar? According to Ephesians 6, we also fight an entire assembly of unseen powers and principalities. Without the intervention of God and His holy armor, we are mud on the bottom of the enemy's boots. How wise to humbly seek God's aid by admitting, "rescue me … for they are too strong for me." David must have embraced a similar belief or he wouldn't have responded to his crisis as he did.

In the margin list the six responses David had to his peril.

prayer
cry aloud
poured out his heart.
trust God.
longed for God's presence
confessed own
inability.

Reconsider each of David's responses from a personal point of view and answer the following questions.

1. Which of the responses do you most often practice when you are in difficult circumstances?

2. Which of the responses do you practice the least and why?

3. On the following scale mark with an *X* where your most typical approach to prayer would fall.

VERY GENERAL ←——————————————D—→ VERY SPECIFIC

4. Where do you think David's approach to prayer would fall? On the same scale, mark his approach with a *D*.

I need constant encouragement to remain specific in my prayer life. You probably do, too. We often get far more specific sharing our hearts with a friend than we do with our God who can truly intervene and help us! "Pour out your hearts to him, for God is our refuge" (Ps. 62:8).

Look at our original text in 1 Samuel 22. Don't miss David's first taste of independent leadership! Read the description again in verse 2. What could be less appealing than leading a group made up of the three Ds: the distressed, the debtors, and the discontented? Ultimately, David would rise to the throne as the forerunner of Jesus Christ, the King of kings. His kingdom would be known throughout the world. He would be favored by the living Lord as His chosen, His anointed. God had to bring David down to a lowly position before He could raise him up to stand on solid ground.

DAY 2

The Inhumanity of Humanity

TODAY'S TREASURE

"I will praise you forever for what you have done; in your name I will hope, for your name is good. I will praise you in the presence of your saints."

Psalm 52:9

Begin your study by praying that God will speak to you through His Word. Today we see the depth of Saul's irreverence toward God and the breadth of his madness toward David. Remember, our study of David takes us through an actual era of history. God chronicled history as it was, not as we'd like for it to have been. Hang in there with me today. God has reasons for placing the events in His Word. He knows that we too must sometimes face horrible times.

Read 1 Samuel 22:6-23. What did Saul accuse his men of doing (v. 8)?
- ☑ conspiring against him
- ☑ not telling him about Jonathan's covenant with David
- ☑ not being concerned for him
- ☑ all of the above

You met "Doeg the Edomite" last week. Who was he (1 Sam. 21:7)?
- ☐ Saul's armor bearer
- ☐ a defector from Saul's army
- ☐ one of Saul's spies
- ☐ other: _servant : chief shepherd._

Ahimelech attempted to reason with Saul in two ways (1 Sam. 22:14-15). In the margin describe the two reasons he gave.

1. David was loyal to Saul.
a. He had inquired of God for David before.

Why do you think the king's officials disobeyed Saul's orders?
They would not kill the priests of the Lord — chosen by Go—

How many priests did Doeg the Edomite kill?   *85*

Why did David feel responsible for their deaths?

He knew that Doeg would tell Saul

I'll never forget seeing this scene in the movie *King David*. I ran to God's Word to see if the events portrayed were accurate, and to my horror, they were. At that moment, I ceased to feel pity for Saul. In my opinion, David had given him far too much credit. David gambled on the hope that Saul would never put to death an innocent priest. He was wrong.

Once again we have the great privilege of seeing the words God inspired from David's pen after David learned about the tragic slaughter. David's words of response will comprise your second and final reading assignment for today. At first glance, David may seem to be referring to Doeg, but verse 7 pinpoints Saul. The great wealth applied to the jealous king. Please read Psalm 52.

Assuming David was addressing Saul, in Psalm 52:1 what did David accuse Saul of doing?

Verse 1 strongly suggests that Saul not only had a multitude of innocent people put to death, many of them priests, but that he also bragged about it. Can you imagine the audacity? Saul reminds me of those described Jeremiah 6:15. "Are they ashamed of their loathsome conduct? No, they have no shame at all; they do not even know how to blush." Have you ever sat slack-jawed over someone who didn't even blush over something appallingly shameful? Me too. Scripture suggests that not all shame is inappropriate.

In your opinion, when would blushing be entirely fitting?

From verse 5, what was David counting on from God?

Surely God will bring you down to everlasting ruin

Psalm 52:7 tells us something vile about the ego of King Saul. How did the righteous say he "grew strong"?
- ☐ by ignoring others
- ☐ by building up an army
- ☐ by trusting God
- ☑ by destroying others

Have you ever known anyone who made him or herself feel bigger or better by putting others down? ☐ yes ☐ no If so, what did you believe those actions said about the person?

Putting others down to build ourselves up is perhaps the ultimate sign of gross insecurity. Thankfully, most people with such insecurity don't have the kind of power Saul had to physically destroy people. However, if we allow our insecurities to govern our lives, we become destroyers just as certainly as did this insane king.

Reread Psalm 52:8. Remember, David was still on the run in the forest of Hereth (1 Sam. 22:5). How did he contrast himself to the wicked?

a flourishing olive tree in the house of god.
I trust in god's unfailing love for ever & ever.

Take note, my friend! Even on the run, not knowing where his next meal would come from, David knew that compared to Saul, he was "like an olive tree flourishing in the house of God." Do you see what David did in the face of unimaginable horror? When he received the news of the slaughter of innocent people, David responded in four ways to the tragedy.

1. He placed blame where it should have been: on Saul, on evil.
2. He reminded himself that God will repay evil (v. 5).
3. He placed his hope solely in God (v. 9).
4. He reminded himself that God is good (v. 9).

When was the last time you were stunned by the depravity of humanity?

How did you sort through your feelings about the situation?

I will never forget seeing the first reports from the Oklahoma City bombing back in 1995. I am not naive, yet I could not fathom how anyone could be so heartless and depraved and, like Saul, lacking appropriate shame. I cried for the children who had been lost or injured; then I tossed and turned most of the night. Two years prior to the tragedy, I had been asked to speak at a conference of 4,500 women from the Oklahoma City area. The conference would take place the day following the bombing. I kept thinking that perhaps we would cancel the event or perhaps many would not attend.

I begged God to be clear with me and not let me say a word on my own.

The event was not canceled. Only one person who registered did not come. She was unaccounted for in the rubble of the Federal Building. Never in my entire ministry have I been more frightened that I might give the wrong message. I begged God to be clear with me and not let me say a word on my own. My text was different than Psalm 52, yet the points He sent me to make were almost identical to the ones we've noted above.

1. God is not the author of destruction.
2. God will repay evil.
3. Our hope must be in God.
4. No matter how bad things look, God is good.

In the face of unimaginable horror, we must cast our imaginations on Christ, our only hope. His Word will be our anchor when our faith is tossed like the waves.

How can each of the following Scriptures help you sort things out when tragedies like the ones we've considered today occur?

John 10:10 *The thief comes only to steal & kill & destroy, I have come that they may have life, and have it to the full.*

Lamentations 3:33 *for he does not willingly bring affliction or grief to anyone*

Lamentations 3:59 *Lord, you have seen the wrong done to me. Uphold my cause.*

Psalm 100:5 *For the Lord is good & his love endures forever, his faithfulness continues through all generations.*

David could not have survived the guilt or the pain of Saul's horrendous actions had he not cast himself on God and His Word. We must do the same. Keep having faith even in the face of unexplainable evil or disaster. You will be richly rewarded for your faith even when others scorn you for still believing. God is the only hope in this depraved world. He who promised is faithful.

DAY 3

Count Your Many Blessings

TODAY'S TREASURE

"I will sacrifice a freewill offering to you; I will praise your name, O Lᴏʀᴅ, for it is good." Psalm 54:6

Begin your study by praying that God will speak to you through His Word. We will learn that David did more than hide as he sought to escape the crazed King Saul. David took every possible opportunity to defend his people, even when he was repaid with betrayal.

Melissa played virtually every sport available to girls in her school. I've anxiously watched her play softball, basketball, and volleyball, often with my heart in my throat. But nothing exhausted me like watching her run track. My muscles were more sore than hers the next day. We may have a similar experience today. David will run so many places that we may be exhausted just watching from the bleachers. Like the One he sometimes prefigured, David often had "no place to lay his head" (Matt. 8:20). Read 1 Samuel 23.

What did David do before he defended the people of Keilah?
- ☐ He met with Jonathan.   ☑ He inquired of the Lord.
- ☐ He asked his men for advice.   ☐ Other: _____

How did David's men react to his instruction from God?
- ☐ They were jubilant.   ☑ They were afraid.
- ☐ They were angry.   ☐ Other: _____

Why do you think David asked the Lord a second time in verse 4?

He did not expect the resistance from his men & wanted to make sure he is doing God's will

Do you think David was wrong to ask a second time? Why or why not?

No. God knows the heart & is patient.

What contrasting information do you discover in verses 7 and 14?

V7 Saul claimed that God would deliver D in his hand

V 14. Day after day Saul searched for him, but God did not give D - his hands

How do you know God could not possibly have been on Saul's side based on all you've learned about Saul? Respond in margin.

The Spirit of God has left S. & an evil spirit took hold.

Tucked into the priestly ephod were the sacred lots. Casting the lots was nothing like throwing dice. These lots were ordained by God as a means by which He would guide His people in making decisions that were not specifically addressed in the written Word at that time. You and I enjoy the privilege of completed revelation. God's Word is now written in its entirety. We have no need of sacred lots. We just need lots of study. (As I revised this study, I could have deleted that last statement to appear more sophisticated with age, but the truth is, 16 years later, I'm still the queen of puns.)

What two answers from God did David receive through the ephod?
- ☑ Saul would pursue him.
- ☐ Jonathan would provide shelter for him.
- ☑ The citizens of Keilah would give David over to Saul.
- ☐ David would be victorious.

Why do you think God might have sent Jonathan to David at this time?

V16: to help D. find strength in God.

Why did David flee from Horesh in the Desert of Ziph?
- ☑ The Ziphites told Saul he was there.
- ☐ David's men deserted him there.
- ☐ David ran out of food and supplies.
- ☐ The Lord told him to flee.

How was David rescued just in the nick of time?

The Philistines attacked

Have you noticed how the colors of God's faithfulness appear brighter when the backdrop of our lives looks bleak and gray? This chapter shows God's faithfulness shining brightly against the bleak backdrop of David's life. Consider two specific evidences of God's faithfulness to David based on 1 Samuel 23.

1. God reconfirmed His directions to David. David's men reacted fearfully when he gave the order to fight the Philistines. Rather than shame them for questioning the word he had received from God, David went back to God and reconfirmed His direction. God rebuked neither David nor his men. God knew David felt great responsibility to his men. If he misunderstood God, many lives could be lost. David did not ask God a second time because he doubted God but because he needed to be certain.

In the same way, you or I might ask God to reconfirm His direction, not because we doubt God's Word but because we question our understanding. To doubt God in the face of clear direction is the sin of disobedience, but to double-check our understanding and interpretation of God's will is prudent.

Have you ever moved too quickly in a direction you believed God was sending you and later realized you were hasty and might have misunderstood? ☐ yes ☐ no   If so, briefly describe what happened.

When was the last time you "double-checked" God's direction in your life?

Did you feel faithless for asking a second time? ☐ yes ☐ no

David's example reminds us that doubting God and doubting that we understood God are two different things. Look at a second evidence of God's faithfulness to David.

2. God sent David a minister of encouragement. Jonathan went to David and "helped him find strength in God" (v. 16). God used Jonathan to reconfirm His calling on David's life. David had been betrayed by the people he tried to help. When we have been betrayed repeatedly, we risk becoming paranoid and cynical. We could convince ourselves that no one can be trusted. God was reminding David not to turn his back on trust. In effect, God was saying, "You can trust Me to fulfill what I promised you, and you can trust Jonathan not to turn his back on you."

Have you been betrayed more than once? ☐ yes ☐ no   Do you still believe that people can be trusted, or have you come to expect most people to betray you? Briefly explain your answer.

When was the last time God sent you a minister of encouragement to help you find strength in God?

We have the blessing of studying several psalms that coincide with David's experiences. I wish I could invite you to expect a coinciding psalm at every venture, but God's Word only tells us the occasions of a few of the psalms. I invite you to relish the ones we have.

Our second reading assignment will be the words God inspired David to write after the Ziphites told Saul his whereabouts. Read Psalm 54.

How did David ask God to save him (v. 1)?
☐ by His outstretched arm   ☐ by His goodness
☐ by His love   ☑ other: *by your name*

We see once again that prayer is not only for God's sake. It often acts as a reminder for our sake. Of what did David remind himself in verse 4?

Surely God is my help; the Lord is the one who sustains me.

In Psalm 54:6 what did David vow he would do?
☑ sacrifice a freewill offering   ☐ get revenge on Saul
☐ stay faithful forever   ☐ tell of his salvation

David seemed to have as many names for God as he had needs.

David began Psalm 54 with the words, "Save me, O God, by your name." We will see David call on God by a multitude of names before we conclude this series. A name meant far more than individual identification to the Hebrew people. A name represented the person's character. David seemed to have as many names for God as he had needs. Why? Because God was everything to him. One of my favorite ways David referred to God is the little word "my." In Psalm 62:6-7 he said, "He alone is my rock and my salvation; he is my fortress … my mighty rock, my refuge." Circle every appearance of "my" in the preceding sentence. Aren't you glad his God can be yours and mine as well?

No wonder, in spite of his human frailties, David was a man after God's own heart. The psalm concludes with David vowing to sacrifice a freewill offering to the Lord.

According to Deuteronomy 16:10, which presents the freewill offering in conjunction with the "Feast of Weeks," how was it to be proportioned? The offering was according to the ...

- ☐ age of the individual
- ☐ tribe of the individual
- ☐ need of the individual
- ☑ blessing God gave the individual

Counting our blessings when we're betrayed, wrongly accused, and hunted by ruthless men is a different worship than counting our blessings in the safety of Sunday worship. David responded to his helpless estate by giving a freewill offering to God in proportion to His blessings. He left us a wonderful example.

In what ways might we be helped by counting our blessings when we could far more quickly count our calamities?

No better time arises to count our blessings than when we're tempted to believe we have none. We've much to learn from God's ways in the life of David.

At this point in your study of David's life on the run, in what ways is God equipping David to be the most important king He would ever anoint over His people prior to His own Son? Respond in the margin.

To rely on God alone.

We often want to be called of God, then ushered painlessly into a position of service and honor, miraculously possessing the character our callings require. God doesn't work that way. Our appointments are not about glamour. They're about glory. God's glory.

God often works the same sequence in us that He worked in David:
1. He calls us.
2. He prepares us.
3. He uses us.
4. He prepares us some more.
5. He uses us some more.

The tricky thing about God's preparation is how He prepares us—even through trials. We find ourselves saying, "I'm not sure what I was expecting, but I never would have expected this."

Painless or painful, enjoyable or distasteful, God always works to prepare us to serve Him, but He rarely prepares us in ways we expect. Why must we experience such preparation? Because any work we've grown accustomed to is usually a work completed. As soon as we've learned one lesson, He brings another. He will continue to work in us until we see His face, because that, beloved, is the ultimate moment for which we're being prepared.

Make no mistake. Jesus will be worth it. Remember, He thought we were worth it too.

God always works. How is He working on you?

DAY 4
A Chance for Revenge

TODAY'S TREASURE

"He [David] said to his men, 'The LORD forbid that I should do such a thing to my master, the LORD's anointed, or lift my hand against him; for he is the anointed of the LORD.'" 1 Samuel 24:6

Begin your study praying that God will speak to you through His Word. Today we will behold an interesting turn of events. In our previous study, we considered God's unwavering devotion to prepare His children for His service. He doesn't simply place us in impressive positions. He prepares us until we can be unimpressed with positions altogether. Today we will see some of the fruit of God's preparation in David. In those caves God succeeded in chiseling character into the heart of David. Read 1 Samuel 24.

How many men went with Saul to look for David?   *3,000*

What caused David to be conscience-stricken in verse 5?
  ☐ He plotted to take Saul's life. ☐ He refused to forgive Saul.
  ☐ He took Saul's spear.   ☑ He cut off a corner of Saul's robe.

Why did David believe he should not lift a hand against Saul?
for he is the anointed of the Lord.

What evidence can you find to support the statement that though David assured Saul he would not harm him, he did not absolve him of wrongdoing?
1/2/15 *May the Lord judge between you & me, and may the Lord avenge the wrongs you have done to me.*

What did Saul acknowledge to David in verse 20?
I know that you will surely be king.

Do you think David believed he could trust Saul after their encounter? Why or why not?
No, he did not go with Saul.

Amazing! David resisted revenge after all Saul had done to him. After all the lives he had taken. I just returned from my fourth trip to the Holy Land and once again looked upon the eerie cave where this very event is thought to have occurred. I still find the story stunning. Mind you, David wasn't even sure Saul had the sense to spare the life of his own son (Jonathan) and daughter (Michal). He certainly had no idea how Saul would respond to David's mercy, but David knew that God cut his conscience to the quick when he damaged the corner of Saul's robe. David's men must have thought he was crazy. David apparently chose to risk man's disapproval over God's, regardless of the consequences. David's change of heart offers four evidences that he was greatly influenced by the Holy Spirit.

1. David's conscience was immediately stricken. One of the most important jobs of the Holy Spirit is to convict of sin (John 16:8). When the Holy Spirit dwells in a person, He uses the individual's conscience as the striking ground for conviction. David wasn't just having a guilty conscience. The Spirit of God was pricking his conscience. He evidenced the work of God in his stricken conscience by saying, "The LORD forbid that I should do such a thing" (v. 6). He was suddenly aware that his actions were displeasing to God. You and I may want to minimize David's sin against Saul because Saul's offense against David seems so much worse. We tend to view sin in relative terms. David's standard for measuring sin was not the wickedness of Saul; it was the holiness of God.

2. David met conviction with a change in behavior. The Holy Spirit always does His job, but we don't always do ours. If we do not fully yield to the Spirit's influence, we will often fight conviction. One sure measurement of our proximity to God, whether near or far, is the length of time lapsing between conviction and repentance. David responded to his Spirit-stricken conscience with an immediate change of behavior. His immediate response to conviction is proof that David was intimate with God at this point in his life. Remember, the same Holy Spirit who anointed David with His presence also dwells in New Testament believers. As we draw nearer and nearer to God, our sensitivity to conviction and our discernment of wrongdoing will increase. If we are filled by His Spirit, conviction will be met with a change in behavior.

3. David exercised great restraint. To me, this fact screams the influence of the Spirit like no other. He had the perfect chance to get revenge and he didn't take it. And who would have blamed him? He could easily have argued that his actions were in self-defense.

Such a level of restraint could only have been supernatural. Second Thessalonians 2:6-7 refers to the restraining work of the Holy Spirit. He is the One who holds us back when we are tempted to get revenge. The Holy Spirit promotes God's cause in our lives. God clearly states, "Do not take revenge, my friends, but leave room for God's wrath, for it is written: It is mine to avenge; I will repay" (Rom. 12:19). The Holy Spirit works restraint in us when we are tempted toward revenge; and if we are fully yielded to the Spirit, we will obey.

A moment's revenge is not worth the cost in alienation from God, not even the revenge we've been waiting for and feel so justified to seize. Perhaps all of us have encountered a window of opportunity to finally "get back" at a well-deserving foe only to be hit by a strong dose of Spirit-stricken conscience.

> David apparently chose to risk man's disapproval over God's, regardless of the consequences.

Have you ever been there—finally arrived at your chance to get a little justice and God wouldn't let you have it? Boy, I have. If you recall an example, describe it. Just make sure you don't share names or anything that would cause another person to be dishonored.

4. David respected God more than he desired revenge. Consider 1 Samuel 24:6 again. Once more, why did David pledge not to lift a hand against Saul?

David withdrew from taking the life of Saul out of respect for God, not Saul. The Holy Spirit is the undeniable influence when the cause of God is more important than our own. When Christians face the opportunity to get revenge, the issue is not another's guilt or our justification. The issue is the will of God. God did not require David to agree with Saul or to lie down under his feet like a doormat. He did, however, require David's obedience to His methods of dealing with a man who was out of God's will.

Remember several days ago when I quoted Jeremiah 6:15 to you concerning those who don't even know how to blush? Look up the verse for yourself and see what God assures us He will do. Write it in the margin. God had not yet sought to remove Saul from his place of leadership and establish David on the throne. The timing was not right. David's incomparable respect for God kept him from making a tragic and costly mistake.

In the home, church, or workplace has God ever called you to remain in a situation though you had lost respect for someone under whose authority God had placed you? ☑ yes ☐ no

Would you be willing to surrender to the power of the Holy Spirit, the Great Restrainer? ☑ yes ☐ no

Could you honor that person out of respect for God? ☑ yes ☐ no

Would you write a prayer of commitment in the margin to allow the restraining work of the Holy Spirit?

If you are willing to honor a person out of respect for God, you can be assured that God will honor you. Several times I've been required to honor a person out of honor to God. The temptation to lash out was almost unbearable at times, but the Holy Spirit was always in me, promoting the restraint of God out of respect for God.

A very strange thing has happened almost every time I've been obedient to God in this area. He has restored my respect for the person I had come to resent. God is always faithful. The results of your obedience may differ, but the blessing of your obedience is guaranteed.

How do these two Scriptures encourage you to exercise restraint?

Ecclesiastes 3:17 *God will bring into judgement both the righteous & the wicked.*

1 Peter 3:9 *Repay evil with blessing.*

> Let the Holy Spirit perform His restraining work. Someday you'll be glad you did.

Remember, the momentary opportunity for revenge might not only be a temptation from the evil one but a test from God. Be ready in advance. No doubt the time will come when you will face a window of opportunity to get back at a person who has wronged you. The only way to get through a window God doesn't open is to break it yourself. This is one window sure to leave you injured. Don't do it. Let the Holy Spirit perform His restraining work. Someday you'll be glad you did.

DAY 5

A Surly Man and a Smart Woman

TODAY'S TREASURE

"Even though someone is pursuing you to take your life, the life of my master will be bound securely in the bundle of the living by the LORD your God. But the lives of your enemies he will hurl away as from the pocket of a sling." 1 Samuel 25:29

Have you stopped to pray and read Today's Treasure? Don't miss it. Read it aloud. What a wonderful verse! "Bound securely in the bundle of the living … hurl away as from the pocket of a sling." I not only love what is inside God's Word, but I also love the way He says it. Don't you?

Let's study the context of this marvelous verse. Our previous lesson left our protagonist in the stronghold while the king whose life he had graciously spared returned home. David obviously did not trust Saul's admissions and kind words to be evidences of a changed heart. David returned to the stronghold in spite of Saul's emotional pleas. Tears are not always signs of repentance. Something can make us very emotional without making us change. We will discover that David made a wise assumption. Today we will study 1 Samuel 25 and enjoy a brief respite from the tormented King Saul. Our chapter today introduces us to some new figures in the life of David. Read 1 Samuel 25:1-22.

The first verse records a very significant event: the death of Samuel. Based on our study of this fascinating man, offer several reasons why you believe his death was a tremendous loss to Israel.

The big & last prophet that guided Israel before they chose to have a king. Walked closely w. God. Heard the voice of God.

The remainder of the chapter makes no further mention of Samuel. In one simple verse we read of his death. Under the worst of circumstances, Samuel was the best of men. He was a rare gem, faithful to the end. My life certainly didn't start like Samuel's, but I pray with all my heart to end it faithfully as he ended his. Don't you?

The chapter proceeds with a description of a character who was nothing like Samuel the prophet. Let's consider the story of Nabal and Abigail. Start by contrasting the two of them according to verses 2 and 3.

Abigail: intelligent & beautiful. Nabal: surly & mean

Which one of the following paraphrases best describes Nabal's response to David's request?

☐ I'm too busy.   ☐ I can't spare the supplies.
☐ Whose side are you on?   ☑ Why should I?

David didn't have the same patience with Nabal that he had with "the LORD's anointed." How did he plan to respond to Nabal's rudeness?

☑ slay every male in Nabal's family   ☐ kill Nabal
☐ set their property on fire   ☐ other: _____

Not all mates are perfectly suited for one another, are they? Scripture certainly proved that Nabal was indeed "surly and mean" and Abigail was a wise woman. Before we have too much fun applying this lesson to the couples we know, the Word of God also records several instances of faithful husbands and spiteful wives. We might not want to tally scores.

A good buddy of mine told me something years ago that I think about every time I hear this famous couple in Scripture mentioned. She said when she read this account, she finally had a name for her husband. "Oh, Lord," she lamented, "I am married to such a Nabal." She said she had the strangest feeling that God said to her in response, "But he is married to no Abigail." We laughed and laughed, but we also knew it could have been the absolute truth.

Our first reading assignment concluded with David preparing for war. He took four hundred men with him. All he really had to have was a sling and a few smooth stones. I'd say Nabal's about to be a fable.

Read 1 Samuel 25:23-44. How did David respond to Abigail's approach?

Praise be to the Lord

Thinking back on David's first claim to fame in the nation of Israel, what do you think Abigail might have been trying to accomplish when she used the terminology, "But the lives of your enemies he will hurl away as from the pocket of a sling"?

remind him of his help from God in conquering Goliath.

Try to put yourself in Abigail's position. How do you think Abigail might have felt when she returned home to a party and a drunken husband?

||||||||||||||||||||||||||||||||||||||||||||||||||||||||||||||||||||||||||||||||||||||||||||||||||||||||||||||||||||||||

Write a brief obituary for Nabal that might have appeared in the *Moan Morning Herald*. Think creatively! You could have a blast with these in your small group.

In verse 39 David recorded a wonderful lesson for any of us dealing with wicked, dreadful people, whether in business or in personal relationships. Have you ever dealt with anyone who was "surly and mean"? ☐ yes ☐ no

Do you see any principles in 1 Samuel 25:39 that you could apply in dealing with difficult people? ☑ yes ☐ no   If so, list them below:

He has kept his servant from doing wrong
Praise be to the Lord who has upheld my cause.

Not all stories have happy endings, but this one certainly does. What happened to Abigail?

Became David's wife

I do love a good romance. Isn't God's Word better than any novel? I see just one little problem. David went a bit overboard in the marriage department. We could be a little bit understanding about his broken vows to Michal; after all, Saul had given his wife away to "Paltiel son of Laish." The hopeless romantic in us could say, "Bless his heart" on that one and could be thrilled he had a new bride. But then, who was Ahinoam (v. 43)? I thought we had been with David every minute. When did he come up with her?

Sometimes we can thank God not only for what He wrote in His Word but also for what He did not. We don't need to know any details. We'll just try to celebrate Abigail's good fortune, although I'm not sure how happy you can be sharing your man with another wife. Some things we may never understand; however, one principle is definitely ours to claim no matter what we see happen in the weeks to come: Polygamy was not the will of God. Genesis 2:24 says that "Man will leave his father and mother [not father and mothers] and be united to his wife [not wives], and they will become one flesh." You just can't be one flesh with two spouses.

Right now you may be struggling with a few questions. I found myself wondering, *Did God tolerate David's actions? Did God make exceptions to His first commands regarding marriage in the lives of His kings?* Our dilemma calls for a brief consideration of a third reading assignment.

The following verses are sure to clear away some of the clouds of confusion, so give today's lesson a few more minutes. Read Deuteronomy 17:14-20.

Why were kings told not to multiply wives?

V17 *his heart will be led astray.*

According to verses 18 and 19, how did God ensure that each king would consider His specific commands?

V18 *he is to write for himself on a scroll a copy of this law + he is to read it all the days of his life.*

David knew that God intended him to be the next king of Israel. Already he had disobeyed one of God's specific commands for kings. He had taken more than one wife. As always, God's commands are for our sake, not for His. Kings had been commanded by God not to take "many wives." The King James Version says, "Neither shall he multiply wives to himself" (v. 17). The word *many* or *multiply* is the Hebrew word *rabah*. It means to increase, multiply, have more. The Word of God is clear from the second chapter of Genesis that two wives is "more" than God planned. God's reason was clear. Those who multiply wives would have hearts led astray.

At this point in our study we can take a moment to inhale deeply and smell trouble brewing. God's Word will once again prove authentic. Eventually David's heart will be led astray. God presented the consequence as a promise, not a possibility. We will unfortunately be witnesses when his straying heart ruptures like a volcano. Until then, we'll praise the God of David who still has a fresh supply of mercy every morning, prompting hearts to ache when they are prone to stray. May we take God at His Word and not have to learn everything the hard way!

COMPLETE YOUR

BETH MOORE LIBRARY

BETH MOORE's collection of LifeWay Women Bible studies covers relevant topics from believing God to loving difficult people. Each in-depth study helps guide you on your journey to find the answers to life's toughest questions. **How many have you done?**

Go to **lifeway.com/bethmoore** to see the full list and complete your Beth Moore Bible study library.

Download a free Beth Moore Bible Study Resource Poster at lifeway.com/bethmoore

LIFEWAY.COM/BETHMOORE | 800.458.2772 | LIFEWAY CHRISTIAN STORES

The words of Psalm 27 flow from the pen of a man in a deadly battle he did not choose. Read Psalm 27. Compare Ephesians 6:10-12.

Ps: 119:175 iron in your soul.
2 Tim. 4:7-8. I have fought the good fight.

"Kalos" means good, honorable & beautiful.
make tribulation out of irritation.
Eph 6 : struggle - hand to hand.
Ps 24: confidence.
V6. have my head exalted.

How to Have a Heads-Up on Our Enemy

don't hit the snooze butta.

1. __Wake__ __up__. In the context of days of darkness, the apostle Paul wrote: "__Wake__ __up__, __O__ __sleeper__, rise from the dead, and Christ will shine on you" (Eph. 5:14).

1 John 4:4

2. __Look__ __up__. What have we __exalted__ ? Compare Psalm 27:1,10; 1 Samuel 22:1-5; and 2 Corinthians 10:3-5.

Stronghold

• A stronghold was a man-made __fortress__ and a __high__ place of __hiding__ beyond normal reach.

2 Cor 10:3-5
Eccl. 8:1

Joshua 4:6-10

3. _____Stand_____ _____up_____ (Eph. 6:10-14).

evils "schemes"
(6:11)

- _____Methodeia_____ means "_____method_____"; the following or pursuing of an orderly and technical _____procedure_____ in the handling of a subject."[1]

- "Everyone who competes in the games goes into strict training. They do it to get a crown that will not last; but we do it to get a crown that will last forever. Therefore I do not run like a man running aimlessly; I do not _____fight_____ like a man _____beating_____ _____the_____ _____air_____" (1 Cor. 9:25-26).

4. _____Dress_____ _____up_____ (Eph. 6:11).

Put on the whole armor of God
with humility.

1. Spiros Zodhiates, gen. ed., *The Complete Word Study Dictionary, NT* (Chattanooga, TN: AMG Publishers, 1992), 954.

Tragic Ends and Faithful Friends

Day 1
A Case of Overkill

Day 2
The Living Dead

Day 3
Alone with God

Day 4
The Death of Israel's Giant

Day 5
A Fallen Friend

DAY 1
A Case of Overkill

TODAY'S TREASURE

"David thought to himself, 'One of these days I will be destroyed by the hand of Saul. The best thing I can do is to escape to the land of the Philistines.'" 1 Samuel 27:1

Our fourth week will no doubt stir some deep emotions in our hearts. We may not always be able to relate to David's extreme circumstances, but we can easily relate to his feelings. We will see David, because of Saul's efforts to kill him, panic and go to live with the enemy. We will witness his great distress and learn from his example how to respond when we feel completely alone.

David's doubts and fears did not exempt his name from the heroes of faith listed in Hebrews 11. You and I can also experience times of defeat and still live lives of faith. This week we will encounter the God who was David's sustaining force through his bleak circumstances. We begin our fourth week with a difficult look at the life of David and one we can probably relate to on a lesser level. We will move forward from our glance at his encounter with Nabal and Abigail in chapter 25 to a very low point in his life in chapter 27.

Don't miss reading any part of 1 and 2 Samuel, even if God does not lead us to center a study on a particular chapter or portion. Read 1 Samuel 26.

Check any of the following statements that describe the events recorded in this chapter.

- ☑ The Ziphites told Saul where David was hiding.
- ☑ Abishai wanted to kill Saul, but David would not allow it.
- ☑ David took the spear and water jug near Saul's head.
- ☐ Saul retaliated by taking Abishai captive.
- ☑ Saul told David he would not try to harm him again.

Read 1 Samuel 27. The Philistines were one of the greatest foes of Israel. Why would David settle in their land? Respond in the margin.

To get out of Saul's reach.

Who went with him?   ☐ 6,000 men   ☐ Jonathan   ☑ 600 men

In response to David's request, Achish gave him the town of Ziklag for his settlement. How long did David remain in Philistine territory?

- ☑ one year and four months   ☐ two years
- ☐ six months   ☐ four months

Did David's practice in the land of the Philistines seem excessive or uncharacteristic to you in any way? ☑ yes ☐ no If so, how?

Brutality of killing everybody

In your own words, what did Achish say to himself about David?

He has power over David.

Did God command David to raid the Geshurites, Girzites, and Amalekites and leave not a man or woman alive? ☐ yes ☑ no

My mind was filled with questions after first seeing 1 Samuel 27. What had happened to David? Why was he taking up an alliance with the Philistines? Why was he on a rampage with every surrounding village? Did you have a few of the same questions? I believe two verses hold the keys for understanding David's uncharacteristic actions.

What had David concluded at this point (v. 1)?

One of these days I will be destroyed by Saul.

Exactly why did David leave no one alive (v. 11)?

They might inform on us.

Life on the run obviously took its toll. Fear, frustration, and exhaustion apparently caused David to experience hopelessness, perhaps even depression and panic. Possibly he was driven to the point of paranoia. The result was a literal case of overkill. You see the downward spiral of his mood at the first verse of the chapter: "One of these days I will be destroyed by the hand of Saul."

He fought everyone with a vengeance, with the exception of his two clear enemies.

David was facing what seemed to be the inevitable. Death appeared imminent. He was convinced he would ultimately be destroyed by a madman. He believed his only option was to escape to the land of the Philistines. David knew firsthand that Saul was scared of them. David surmised he would at least be safe for a while if he lived among the Philistines. He felt like giving up, but he couldn't because everyone had become an enemy in his eyes. Therefore, he fought everyone with a vengeance, with the exception of his two clear enemies: Saul and the Philistines.

No doubt, David was right to keep his hands off Saul, for he was the Lord's. We have no way of knowing how God responded to his alliance with the Philistines. To be sure, God had an opinion. However, He kept the matter between Himself and David at this time, just as He has graciously done with me when I did not respond favorably to difficult circumstances.

Look at a psalm scholars believe David penned at this time in his life. Perhaps we will gain some insight into the feelings he was experiencing. His feelings may have caused him to make either the wrong choices or the right choices for the wrong reasons. Read Psalm 10.

Why do you think David might have felt as if God was far away and hidden in times of trouble? Respond in the margin.

Which of these words are ways David characterized his enemy (v. 2)?
☑ arrogant ☑ scheming ☐ dishonest ☐ mighty

In which of these ways did David characterize himself as the victim?
☑ weak ☐ afraid ☑ sick ☑ grieved   *innocent, helpless, faithless, oppressed.*
afflicted.   *v14*

See what happens when we focus more on our battles than on God? Our enemy appears bigger, we appear weaker, and God appears smaller. Beware: long-term battle can cause vision impairment if eyes focus anywhere but up.

In your own words, what did David apparently believe Saul was saying to himself in Psalm 10:6? *Nothing will shake me, I'll always be happy & never have trouble.*

What did David believe Saul was saying to himself in verse 11?
God has forgotten; he covers his face & never sees.

Complete verse 13: "Why does the wicked man revile God? Why does he say to himself ' *He won't call me to account* '"?

What must the victim do according to verse 14?
☐ ask God to destroy his enemy ☐ fast and pray
☐ find refuge and wait ☑ commit himself to God

In the margin name three actions God takes for His children (v. 17). *hear, encourage, listen*

We may have a difficult time relating to David's exact dilemma and his outrageous responses, but we can certainly relate to his feelings. When was the last time you felt like David? Consider the following questions and briefly give examples when your answer is yes.

Have you ever battled an enemy so hard and so long that you felt like giving up or doing something rash?

Have you ever felt powerless over your real enemy and lashed out at someone who was completely innocent?

Have you ever gone through a season of your life when you were highly suspicious of virtually everyone and trusting of virtually no one?

When was the last time you felt God was hiding Himself?

A woman who feels powerless and out of control in her marriage can be overly controlling in her parenting.

David's most obvious problem was that he felt so powerless and out of control in one area that he wielded an inappropriate amount of power and control in another. We are also capable of responding destructively when we harbor similar feelings. A woman who feels powerless and out of control in her marriage can be overly controlling in her parenting. If she feels overpowered by her boss, she can be overcontrolling toward her husband.

Many dreadful results can occur from unchecked feelings of powerlessness. Tragic numbers of girls who were abused as children try to gain a feverish control of their bodies through anorexia nervosa, a form of self-starvation. Many have controlled themselves to death. We are wise to reemphasize a rule of thumb we learned in our first considerations of Saul's jealousies: We can't just trust our feelings. We must entrust our feelings to God.

God has not forgotten. He has seen your battles. He has gathered your tears and blotted your brow. He knows those who have treated you unfairly and when you're almost ready to give up or give in. Keep telling Him. Stay in His Word. Keep claiming His promises. God assured David over and over that he would be king, but David let conflict cloud his calling. We need not despair. We must stand in God's Word when the battles get tough and resist the temptation to panic. We also can be guilty of our own version of overkill.

Conclude by reading the following verses. Paraphrase them into your own words of encouragement. May they be a blessing to you today.

Galatians 6:9-10 *Let us not become weary in doing good ... as we have opportunity, let us do good to all people ...*

1 Peter 4:19. (Compare Peter's exhortation with David's in Ps. 10:14.)

Offer hospitality to one another without grumbling.

DAY 2
The Living Dead

TODAY'S TREASURE

"Samuel said to Saul, 'Why have you disturbed me by bringing me up?'
'I am in great distress,' Saul said. 'The Philistines are fighting against me,
and God has turned away from me. He no longer answers me, either by
prophets or by dreams. So I have called on you to tell me what to do.'"
1 Samuel 28:15

Begin your study by praying that God will speak to you through His Word.
Today we are going to study a very peculiar encounter in Scripture and one
without precedent. We may share some puzzling moments, some difficult
moments, and some humorous moments. God is sovereign. He is Lord over
the living and the dead.

Psalm 115:3 is the perfect introduction and theme for our lesson today.
Read this marvelous verse and paraphrase it in the margin.
Our God is in heaven; he does whatever pleases him
Every time you have a question today regarding how or why something
happened, think of this wonderful multipurpose verse. Read 1 Samuel 28.

According to verse 3 Saul had previously "expelled the ___*mediums*___
and ___*spiritists*___ from the land."

Which one of the following best describes Saul's response when he saw
the Philistine army?

☐ confusion ☐ fury ☐ intimidation ☒ terror

When the Lord did not answer Saul by "dreams or Urim or prophets,"
what did Saul ask his attendants to do? *Find me a woman
who is a medium so I may go & enquire of her.*

What did Saul want the woman from Endor to do for him?

☐ foretell the outcome of his battle with the Philistines
☐ tell him why God would not answer him
☒ consult a certain spirit and bring him up
    Samuel

Why do you think the woman might have cried out at the top of her voice when she saw Samuel? Respond in the margin.

V12. She realized that Saul will kill her (his deception)

In what ways did the woman at Endor describe the man in the vision, convincing Saul it was Samuel? Choose any that apply.

- ☑ He was old.
- ☐ He was angry.
- ☐ He was holding a scroll.
- ☑ He was wearing a robe.

According to the prophet Samuel, why did God refuse to answer Saul?

V19 Because you did not obey the Lord.

What two prophecies did Samuel issue to Saul?

- ☑ The army of Israel would be handed over to the Philistines.
- ☐ David would take Saul's life with his sword.
- ☑ Saul and his sons would die the next day.
- ☐ David would reign over Judah.

God's occasional refusal to respond to the pleas of someone in His Word often strikes a humanitarian chord in us. At first we may wonder why God would not answer Saul since Saul first inquired of Him before he sought a spiritist.

Does God seem a little unfair to you at first in His lack of response to Saul? Why or why not?

Saul was seeking his own interest, not God's

God neither responds haphazardly nor withholds an answer without regard. Why is God silent at times? Isaiah 59:1-3 gives us one valid explanation for God's occasional silence—one that certainly applied to Saul at this time.

Read all three verses carefully then mark each of these statements either true or false based on what you've read.

- ___F___ The arm of the Lord is too short to save.
- ___T___ The ear of the Lord is not too dull to hear.
- ___F___ Iniquities can never separate a person from God.
- ___T___ God can choose not to hear the unrepentant sinner.

Unconfessed, unrepented sin can easily be the reason for God's silence in our lives. Remember, Saul continued in disobedience to God. He relentlessly sought the life of an innocent man and even attempted to spear his own son. He had the priests of the Lord slaughtered and gave approval to an entire town being wiped out. We've seen some regrets, but we've never seen him truly turn from wickedness to righteousness. Notice that Isaiah 59:2 does not say God *can't* hear, but that He *won't*.

In your opinion, what is the difference between can't and won't hear?

can't – impossible to
won't – chooses not to

I can vividly remember times in my life when God seemed silent and I realized He was waiting on me to confront and confess certain sins in my life. His silence suggested, "I will not go on to another matter in your life, My child, until we deal with this one."

Have you ever experienced the silence of God only to realize He was waiting for you to confront an issue of sin? ☑ yes ☐ no

One prayer God surely will hear even when we've been rebellious and sought our own way is the prayer of sincere repentance. The prayer for deliverance from sin must precede the prayer for deliverance from our enemies.

Isn't it interesting that Saul set out on a journey to seek that which he himself had expelled from the midst of Israel? He certainly didn't have a difficult time finding a spiritist either, suggesting that when we don't take God too seriously, others don't take our leadership too seriously.

Taking a few steps backward in our Christian walk is not very difficult. Christians used to call it "backsliding." I wish the only direction existing for a Christian was onward to maturity, but unfortunately some of our footprints in the sand look a lot like figure eights!

What does God's Word say about spiritists and mediums (Deut. 18:10-12)?

Anyone who does those things is detestable to the Lord.

Saul knew God's Word. Early in his reign he did what God's Word commanded. After his regard for God shrunk and his flesh abounded, he sought the very thing he once had considered wrong. We've done the same from time to time. We've felt convicted to get rid of something or to cease a certain practice; then, when our regard for God began to shrink and our regard for our own flesh began to grow, we were out the door hunting it down.

Can you think of a few personal examples? Let me make a few suggestions: Have you ever given up R-rated movies under the direct influence of the Holy Spirit and found yourself at a later date with a ticket and popcorn in your hand, heading into a movie you formerly wouldn't have watched? Have you ever given up gossip magazines because God had convicted you toward purity of mind, but you found yourself throwing one into your grocery basket again? At one time were you very sensitive about saying hurtful things to or about others, but now it doesn't bother you much anymore?

In the margin share an example of a time when, by the prompting of the Holy Spirit, you abstained from something only to return to it later.

We've all been there. Seeking what we once cast from our lives is an evidence of backsliding. Beware of backing up, or like Saul, we may dig up a dead person—our old sin.

How does James 4:17 apply to Saul and to us?

Anyone who knows the good he ought to do & doesn't do it, sins.

No doubt, God had His own agenda the day Saul sought the witch of Endor. You almost have to chuckle as the witch almost jumped out of her skin at the sight of Samuel. Either she was an imposter or she was expecting a demonic imitation. She not only knew that God alone could have stirred Samuel from the dead, but she also knew that God probably would not have bothered unless the king himself was the inquirer. God had a point to make, to be sure.

The vision of Samuel was not for the simple intent of humor, but it still affords me a snicker. I have to smile over the way Saul knew it was Samuel. "'An old man wearing a robe is coming up.' … Then Saul knew it was Samuel." No doubt Saul had seen Samuel in that same old garb a thousand times! Among Samuel's many wonderful attributes, we never discovered an eye for fashion. Samuel's robe rang a familiar bell in Saul's mind with good reason!

Look back at 1 Samuel 15:27. Why might that old robe have seemed familiar to Saul?

Saul tore the hem of S's robe!

Saul might have asked the spiritist, "Do you happen to see a tiny little tear in the robe?" Neither Samuel's clothing nor his mood had changed. "Why have you disturbed me by bringing me up?" I didn't get the feeling this was a joyful reunion, did you? I think what Samuel wanted to say was, "Now what?"

Let's be careful how much application we draw from this lesson about the dearly departed. God did something very rare that day. He gave Saul a vision of Samuel raised momentarily from the dead so He could smack Saul in the face with His sovereignty. We cannot conclude from this encounter that we'll be wearing the same clothes eternally (Hallelujah!), that our loved ones can ask God to let us appear to them after we're dead, or that it's OK for us to seek to talk to the dead.

We arrive at God's sovereign purpose for supernaturally intervening. The encounter ends with the harsh news of the imminent death of Saul and his sons. I find myself hoping even Saul's life had an ultimately happy ending. When Samuel said, "Tomorrow you and your sons will be with me," we do not know what Samuel meant. He may have simply meant, "You are about to die." Or he may have meant Saul and his sons would join Samuel among the redeemed. I'd like to think that Saul and his sons took the opportunity to settle business with God, knowing of their imminent demise. Sometimes the most merciful thing God can do in a rebellious person's life is let him know he is going to die so he can beg the mercy of God.

Sometimes the most merciful thing God can do in a rebellious person's life is let him know he is going to die so he can beg the mercy of God.

DAY 3

Alone With God

TODAY'S TREASURE

"David was greatly distressed because the men were talking of stoning him; each one was bitter in spirit because of his sons and daughters. But David found strength in the LORD his God." 1 Samuel 30:6

Begin your study by praying that God will speak to you through His Word. Today our emphasis switches from Saul back to David. When we last saw David, he had entered an alliance with Achish, a Philistine and the son of the king of Gath. Read 1 Samuel 29:1–30:6 and answer the following.

What two arguments did the Philistine commanders make against David to keep him out of battle?

☑ David might turn against them during battle.
☐ Achish showed favoritism to David.
☐ The battle would be too risky for David.
☑ David might attempt to regain Saul's favor.

What did David and his men discover when they returned to Ziklag?

☐ Ziklag had been raided.
☐ Ziklag had been burned.
☐ Their wives and children had been taken captive.
☑ all of the above

Describe the response of David and his men according to 1 Samuel 30:4.

They wept aloud until they had no more strength to weep.

Reread verse 6 carefully. Why would the men want to stone David?

each one was bitter in spirit because of his sons & daughters

David was greatly distressed over the blame his men cast on him. He responded by finding "strength in the LORD his God."

In the margin list things you can think of that David might have done to find strength in his God.

*prayer,
recalling God's actions
in his life,
remember!*

When we've suffered a loss, we often look for stones to throw—and someone at whom to throw them.

I'd like to draw a few points from the verses we've just considered. The passage paints perfect portraits of human nature.

1. Hurting people often find someone to blame. When we've suffered a loss, just like David's men we often look for stones to throw—and someone at whom to throw them. Notice that David also suffered the loss of his family. He didn't know if he would ever see them again. He had taken many lives. I'm sure he assumed his enemy would not blink an eye at taking the lives of his wives and children. David cried the same tears the other men cried, but because they needed someone to blame, they focused their anger on him.

2. Nothing hurts more than our children in jeopardy. Many things hurt and cause us to search for stones to throw, but, as in verse 6, nothing has the potential to cause bitterness in spirit like matters involving our children. They are our Achilles' heel, aren't they? Someone can treat our child unfairly and we're ready to pounce. We almost can't help living by the philosophy: If you want to make an enemy out of me, just mess with my kid.

Can you imagine how many poor decisions have been made when parents have hastily thrown the stones of retaliation in behalf of their children? We are so tempted to intervene. Sometimes intervention may be appropriate. But whether or not it's appropriate to get involved beyond the necessary emotional and spiritual support, no stones are allowed.

David's men ultimately arrived at a place of reason. They chose not to act at the peak of their emotions—a wise response for all of us.

3. Nothing helps more than finding strength in our God. Sometimes no one offers us encouragement or helps us find strength. We'd better be prepared at times to strengthen ourselves in the Lord. Knowing how to encourage ourselves in the Lord is essential. The New International Version says: "But David found strength in the LORD his God." Others can help and be encouraging, but this kind of strength comes only from the Lord.

Reflect on this principle a moment. In what ways can you encourage yourself in the Lord? Respond in the margin.

Without a doubt, my most precious and painful times in this Christian experience have been times when I was all alone with God. Such times forge an unforgettable, inseparable bond. Don't miss the opportunity. I am convinced that God sometimes stays the encouragement of others purposely so we will learn to find it in Him.

Have you ever been angry at someone for not being as supportive as you would have liked? ☑ yes ☐ no

If so, could it be that God wanted you to find strength in Him by yourself? Would you be willing to forgive the person you believed failed you and consider what God wanted from you?

If so, please write your request for God's help and insight.

Read 1 Samuel 30:7-31, and answer the following questions:

How did David make the decision to pursue the captors?

Consulting the ephod + calling on Abjiathar.

Why did 200 men stay behind?

to exchausted to cross the ravine.

What was the raiding party doing when David saw them?

eating, drinking & reveling

How long did it take for David and his men to fight them?

2 days.

When the victorious group returned, conflict erupted over the plunder.
What was David's apparent reasoning why they must all "share alike"?

V23: The Lord has given it to them.

Let's share a few words of application based on our second reading assignment as we conclude today's lesson.

1. Assured victory does not mean easy wins. God told David in advance he would "certainly overtake them and succeed in the rescue" yet we see references to exhaustion (v. 10), hard work (v. 17), a nonstop, 24-hour battle (v. 17), and four hundred escapees (v. 7). God was absolutely true to His word. The end was exactly as God had promised, but what we often don't count on is the means. God often gives us a victory that requires blood, sweat, and tears. Why? Because He is practical. When He can bring about a victory and strengthen and mature us all at the same time, He's likely to do it.

God revels in overcoming and undergirding all at once. You see, God's idea of victory has virtually nothing to do with plunder. It has to do with people. What comes out of a battle isn't nearly as important as who comes out of a battle. That day God not only worked a victory through David but He also worked one in David. The man after God's own heart came out of battle with grace and mercy and a little better grasp of God's sovereignty. God gave him the opportunity to participate firsthand in the fight.

2. We don't have to win big to win. No wholesale slaughter resulted. Quite the contrary, four hundred men got away, yet God called it a victory. David could have been furious with himself because he let some guys get away. Instead, he chose to focus on the ones he brought home: their families, his family. If your family has come out of a serious battle intact, fall on your face and praise your faithful God. The victory is yours.

We constantly fight an unseen enemy. God has assured us the victory, but He has told us to take an aggressive stand against the evil one, covering ourselves in His armor. We're going to win, but victory is going to take blood, sweat, and tears—His blood, our sweat, and tears from both of us.

When was the last time God brought you victory but the battle was difficult?

Describe what God accomplished in you through the difficult battle. Thank Him not only for what came out of the battle but who!

DAY 4

The Death of Israel's Giant

TODAY'S TREASURE

"When the armor-bearer saw that Saul was dead, he too fell on his sword and died with him." 1 Samuel 31:5

Begin your study by praying that God will speak to you through His Word. Today we close the portion of our study of King David recorded in the Book of 1 Samuel. Some Scripture lessons are hard to swallow while others make us laugh. God, in His infinite wisdom, tucked something to learn inside every one. We must come to a place of important closure today before we proceed to our next book of the Bible. Read 1 Samuel 31.

First Samuel 31:1 records the victory of the Philistines over Israel. Based on God's promise to Israel in Deuteronomy 11:22-25, why do you think Israel lost the battle?

disobedience to god.

What request did Saul make of his armor bearer?
- [ ] guard Saul with his life
- [x] kill Saul with his sword
- [ ] guard Saul's sons' bodies
- [ ] run and get help

Why do you think the armor bearer would not kill Saul? Record several possibilities if you can.

He was the king - God's anointed.

What was Saul's final action?
- ☐ He mourned the death of his sons.
- ☐ He cried out to God.
- ☑ He killed himself with his own sword.
- ☐ None of these.

What did the Philistines do with Saul's body?
- ☑ stripped off his armor
- ☑ cut off his head
- ☑ hung him on the wall of Beth Shan
- ☑ all of these

War is hard stuff, even when you're only a spectator. Today's reading is especially difficult because we feel we've come to know the people who perished. We're not well-acquainted with Abinadab and Malki-Shua, but we feel we've come face to face with the good, the bad, and the ugly in Saul and with the tender and beloved in Jonathan. My heart aches at their difficult end.

I wonder if Jonathan had heard that David was on the other side. Did Jonathan look for David's face before he threw his spear for fear he'd harm his friend? Did Jonathan wonder if David intended to keep the covenant they had made even if Jonathan perished that day? Was he afraid? Did tears blur the sight of his brothers' bodies nearby? I find myself wanting to know more, not ready to find his name missing from the page. He was the kind of friend we all want—the kind of friend David needed.

And what about Saul? Critically wounded and hardly able to move, Saul urged his armor bearer to take his life. Saul knew the history of the Philistines. He knew they made sport of their prize captives. The armor bearer must have stood frozen as he watched the wounded and bleeding king muster his last bit of strength to fall on his sword.

"When the armor-bearer saw that Saul was dead." He had pledged to protect his king to the death. He had done it. His job was over and for one armor bearer, there would be no other. He would die with his king.

The Philistines did not need Saul alive to mock him. They cut off his head, surely in memory of their slain giant, and impaled his body on the wall of Beth Shan. The valiant men of Jabesh Gilead heard the news and "journeyed through the night to Beth Shan." They removed the bodies and burned them. Two possibilities might explain the practice of cremation so rare among the Israelites: They were trying to remove all evidence of mutilation, or they were burning away the touch of the unclean hands.

The men of Jabesh Gilead performed a brave and loving act. Certainly the bodies were well-guarded. They could have ended up impaled right beside the bodies they came to rescue. Why would they take such a chance? Allow me to refresh your memory about a very vital scene.

> Jonathan was the kind of friend we all want—the kind of friend David needed.

Reread 1 Samuel 11:1-11. In your own words, why did the people of Jabesh Gilead owe honor to Saul?

He rescued them from the Amewheles.

May our memories of kindness be long and of offenses be short.

The men of Jabesh Gilead paid a tribute to a king who started well. They showed their gratitude, even after 40 years. May we accept and imitate their example. May our memories of kindness be long and of offenses be short. It's not too late to say thanks. Owe somebody a favor? How much better to repay it before you stand with them under the shade of a tamarisk tree.

Is there anyone you've never thanked appropriately for kindness done in your behalf? ☐ yes ☐ no   If so, how could you show your appreciation?

Saul saved the people of Jabesh Gilead, and the people remembered. Their refreshed memories and subsequent acts of gratitude were appropriate. Reflecting on things worth remembering deepens our relationship with our Savior. The Scripture references below mention several things we need to remember.

Match each verse with the appropriate reminder.

4 A. Psalm 77:11	1.	It is more blessed to give than to receive.
3 B. Psalm 89:47	2.	Thank God when you remember a fellow believer.
5 C. Psalm 119:55	3.	Remember how fleeting life is.
1 D. Acts 20:35	4.	Remember the miracles of God long ago.
2 E. Philippians 1:3	5.	Remember the Lord's name at night.

Scripture often records God remembering His children. Each time, recorded close by is a subsequent action in their behalf. Consider a few examples:
- "God remembered Noah ... and the waters receded" (Gen. 8:1).
- "He remembered Abraham, and he brought Lot out" (Gen. 19:29).
- "God remembered Rachel ... and opened her womb" (Gen. 30:22).

Remembering should also provoke appropriate actions in us. Review the matching exercise you completed above. Choose any one of the reminders and reflect on an action you could take in response.

A good memory often leads the way to a good response. In the midst of a tragic scene, a group of heroes emerged, all because they had good memories. No doubt God's heroes are those who never forget His faithfulness. May we be counted among them.

DAY 5
A Fallen Friend

TODAY'S TREASURE

"Saul and Jonathan—in life they were loved and gracious, and in death they were not parted. They were swifter than eagles, they were stronger than lions." 2 Samuel 1:23

Begin your study by praying that God will speak to you through His Word. Today we conclude our study of the relationship between David and Saul. We've pictured the slain body of the first king of Israel, critically wounded by the Philistines, fatally pierced by his own sword. Nearby lay the body of his armor bearer.

As I worked on this study, somehow I could not shake the thought of the bodies strewn on Mount Gilboa—the tragic king and his three sons. But somehow, my mind kept returning to the armor bearer who checked the pulse of his captain and when he discovered none, took his own life. His part in the scene beckons me to reconsider his life.

I'm not sure our current society has much to compare to the calling of an armor bearer. Perhaps the closest we can come would be to study the lives of the Secret Service agents who guard the president. Recall the comparison we drew between ourselves and Jonathan's armor bearer on week 1, day 1. We are the armor bearers of God with one big difference: We don't just bear it; we wear it. As I kept thinking about that role and the body of the armor bearer next to his king, God spoke a Scripture into my heart. It was Galatians 2:20.

Read Galatians 2:20 and explain what you think it means.

I have been crucified with Christ & I no longer live, but Christ lives in me

Our old body of sin, the nature that must seek its own way, the person who is hopelessly depraved and resigned to failure, hangs limp on the cross. Raised in its place is the Spirit of the Living God poured into a temple of flesh so that God's presence will remain among men. The armor that once we could only carry in our hands is now fitted for us and we rise from the dead—warriors. Oh, that we would not cling to the things of our old body of sin. It is nothing but a decaying carcass. I have been crucified with Christ. I no longer live but

Christ lives in me. I must rise, turn away from the old things of death, take on His armor, and fight the good fight.

Write Romans 6:6 on a card and plan to memorize the verse.

For we know that our old self was crucified w. his

Paul assured us that our old self has been crucified with Christ. He intended that we no longer be slaves to sin.

Read 1 Peter 2:16 and paraphrase the verse.

Live as free men, but not to use your freedom a a cover-up for sin; live as servants of God.

In a society replete with disposable razors, diapers, contacts, contracts, and marriages, the word permanent is like a lost treasure.

The word *servants*, which Peter was urging as the position of all who are in Christ, is the Greek word *doulos*. It means "a slave, one who is in permanent relation of servitude to another, his will being altogether consumed in the will of the other."[1] Sounds like an armor bearer to me, doesn't it to you? Sacrificing his will, his agenda, for the agenda of his master? The word *permanent* describes the kind of service God desires us to offer. In a society replete with disposable razors, diapers, contacts, contracts, and marriages, the word *permanent* is like a lost treasure.

Do you see your role of servant of the Living Lord as absolutely and utterly permanent? I'm not talking about your salvation. I am talking about servanthood. Can you say without a doubt, "I don't know where I will live in 20 years, whether I'll still have my spouse, my health, a job, godly friends, or a growing church, but I can promise you one thing: I will be actively serving God"? If, with some sense of confidence, you can say those words, you are rare. You understand something of the role of a true *doulos*, a sold-out servant.

From the following Scriptures, what do you learn about servanthood that parallels the life of a loyal and true armor bearer of God?

Galatians 1:10 *If I were still trying to please men I would not be a servant of God/Christ's*

Romans 14:4 *To his own master he stands or falls. And he will stand, for the Lord is able to make him sta*

What does 1 Corinthians 4:1 list as one of our privileges as *doulos* of God?

entrusted w. the secret things of God.

Read Matthew 10:39. In your opinion, which of the following statements best paraphrases this verse?

☐ To love God is to lose your life.
☑ To lay down your life for Christ's sake is to find His.
☐ To find yourself is to lose everything else.

With our role as God's servant/armor bearer more deeply clarified, we will turn our attention to the first chapter of 2 Samuel. We pick up today exactly where we concluded our previous study. Read 2 Samuel 1:1-16.

According to verse 2, how long a period of time passed before David learned of Saul's death? ☐ a long while   ☐ two days   ☑ three days

What lie did the Amalekite tell about Saul's death?

That Saul requested him to kill him

How did David and his men respond to the news about Saul and Jonathan?

Tore their clothes, mourned, wept, fasted.

What gave David a unique right to ask the question in verse 14?

He was the Lord's anointed.

Have you ever heard the saying, "He lies when the truth is better"? If a literal example of this expression ever existed, this is it. Few people living in the Middle East would have failed to hear rumors of Saul's pursuit of David. Many must have followed them as closely as a faithful watcher of a modern soap opera. People love conflict. We love reading about it and hearing about it. We revel in the sagas of the rich, famous, and miserable. We often enjoy conflict.

When the men were returning home after David had killed the Philistine, the women met King Saul with singing, dancing, joyful songs, tambourines, and lutes. As they danced, they sang: "Saul has slain his thousands, and David his tens of thousands."

Those women started a jealousy that cost both men dearly. "Saul was very angry; this refrain galled him. 'They have credited David with tens of thousands,' he thought, 'but me with only thousands. What more can he get but the kingdom?' And from that time on Saul kept a jealous eye on David" (1 Sam. 18:8-9).

Many days later, as the deceitful Amalekite lay slain at David's feet, that little song caused another casualty. At least one opportunist was hoping he'd find favor with David by claiming he had taken the life of Saul. He was dead wrong. Read 2 Samuel 1:17-27.

In David's song of lament, why did he not want word of Saul's death and the deaths of his sons told in Gath and Ashkelon?
    ☑ The daughters of the Philistines would be glad.
    ☐ The Philistines would be warned of David's vengeance.
    ☐ The news would result in mutiny.

What were David's apparent feelings toward Jonathan in his lament?

love for a brother.

In David's song of lament, his words suddenly turn from the refrain of the assembly to the grief of a single heart: "I grieve for you, Jonathan, my brother." The Hebrew word for *brother* in this verse was `ach. It means "a brother, near relative. `Ach is any person or thing which is similar to another. It is generally a term of affection."[2] One was a shepherd, the other a prince, yet so alike were they that they were "one in spirit" (1 Sam. 18:1). They were brothers.

David called his friend's love for him "wonderful." The Hebrew word used for *wonderful* is *pala* (2 Sam. 1:26). It means "to be separate, be distinguished, be singular, be extraordinary, ... be miraculous, be astonishing."[3] Clearly, we see from the definition that David was distinguishing the sacrificial nature of this friendship from anything else anyone had ever demonstrated to him. So determined was Jonathan that David be king, a position that Jonathan stood to inherit, Jonathan committed his entire life to that end. David found it "astonishing."

I know what it's like to lose a best friend. My buddy and I were absolutely inseparable. We dressed alike, cut our hair alike, shared a locker, and had endless spendovers. I had lots of boyfriends as a teenager, but I only had one best friend. Her name was Dodie. One day she dropped by the house to pick me up for a bite to eat. My parents would not let me go because we were preparing to leave town. Dodie never came back. Within half an hour, I heard the blood-curdling screams of an ambulance. I can hardly share it even today. I still visit her grave. I still ache for our friendship.

David grieved the tragic loss of life that took place on Mount Gilboa. His thoughts must have been consumed with how differently he wished it had all happened. Not coincidentally, the next chapter begins with the words, "In the course of time, David. ..." We share a moment of his grief when we see the words, "In the course of time." Some things just take "the course of time." Nothing else works. You can bet some lonely hours filled that "course of time." Some tears. Some regrets. Some endless replays. Some anger. Some confusion. But it did finally pass. Not the ache but the pain. Blessedly, thankfully "in the course of time."

Have you ever experienced a loss only time could heal? If so, how much time passed before you started to sense God's healing?

we are created out of relationship (Trinity) for relationship w. God + other peop

1 Sam 30:6
vgl " 22:16

We can pattern our own relationships after those of Christ Himself:

that Christ died to save — we are now the body of C.

The <u>World</u> <u>Witness</u>. (John 3:16)

Heb 10:24-25 The <u>72</u> <u>Service</u> (Luke 10:1-2)

Local body of bedr

Matthews — disciples → means learner.

The <u>12</u> <u>Discipleship</u> (Matt. 20:17)

Gethsemane — oil press.

The <u>3</u> <u>Transparency</u> (Matt. 26:36-38)

17:1-13

a little further. V39.

<u>1</u> <u>Intimacy</u> (Matt. 26:38-39)

We can go so far with God in the fellowship and comfort of close companions, but a time comes when each true follower is summoned <u>further</u> <u>still</u>.

1. Further still … when you are overwhelmed with <u>sorrow</u> (Matt. 26:38).

Circle, surround.

The Greek term *perilypos* means "grieved <u>all</u> <u>around</u>, intensely sad."[1]

"It suggests a sorrow so deep it almost <u>kills</u>."[2]

dread is not sin.
when is dread distrust? when it's premature & distractive.
cup.

2. Further still ... when you desperately need to wrestle with the *will*
   of God (Matt. 26:39). (Compare Matt. 26:27-29 and Isa. 51:22.) *cup of God's wrath.*

3. Further still ... when nobody else *gets* *it*.
   (Compare Matt. 26:38,41.)

John 15:9
John 18:10-11

4. Further still ... when the most serious matters of your life
   need *settling* (Matt. 26:50-54). *Intimacy between Christ & God.*

5. Further still ... when life can't be the same but the pain
   can *bring* *gain*.

God is strong willed, not strong whimmed.

Pain has a purpose in my life.

1. James Strong, *Strong's Exhaustive Concordance of the Bible* (Peabody, MA: Hendrickson Publishers, n.d.), #4036.
2. Donald A. Carson, "Matthew" in *The Expositor's Bible Commentary*, vol. 8 (Grand Rapids, MI: Zondervan, 1984), 543.
Note: Beth read from *John for Everyone* by N. T. Wright. Published in 2004 by John Knox Publishers.

The Long-Awaited Throne

Day 1

Settling Down

Day 2

Things That Bring Change

Day 3

Suspicious Minds

Day 4

The Shepherd King

Day 5

Turning Mourning into Dancing

DAY 1
Settling Down

TODAY'S TREASURE

"David also took the men who were with him, each with his family, and they settled in Hebron and its towns. Then the men of Judah came to Hebron and there they anointed David king over the house of Judah."

2 Samuel 2:3-4

Begin your study by praying that God will speak to you through His Word. Our fifth week ushers us into a pivotal season of David's life. The man anointed by the Holy Spirit many years before was about to occupy the promised throne. The crown did not come easily. God used the struggles leading to the throne to prepare His chosen king. We will discover an important equation evidenced in David's life as well as in ours: Time + Conflict = Change.

David had a number of difficult lessons to learn before he could adequately shepherd the people of God. May the events we study this week deepen our reverence for God and equip us to serve the flocks He has given us.

Last week's lesson in 2 Samuel 1 concluded as David received the tragic news of the death of Saul and his sons. David's life was destined to change dramatically. At least 15 years had passed since Samuel went to the home of Jesse and anointed the young shepherd. Reflecting on all the events of his life must have been mind-boggling for David. He was forced to grow up in a hurry and learn to make harsh decisions. David, a thinker, revealed his introspective, insightful spirit in the psalms.

We can see ample evidence of a man after God's own heart as we too reflect on the years between his anointing and the death of his predecessor. He had taken some wrong turns and some right turns, but he took virtually every step crying out to his God. As chapter 2 unfolds, David is 30 years old. Let's see what transpires "in the course of time." Read 2 Samuel 2:1-7.

Why did David go to Hebron?

God told him.

What did David send messengers to tell the men of Jabesh Gilead?
- ☑ of David's appreciation for their kindness to Saul
- ☑ to encourage them to be strong and brave
- ☑ that David had been anointed king over the house of Judah
- ☑ all of the above

Can you identify times when you proceeded in a direction because of a hunch rather than the confirmed will of God?

How greatly we could profit if we would take to heart David's example in the first verse of today's study. David inquired of God before he took a single step forward in his inevitable journey to the throne. Did you notice that David kept asking until he had a specific answer from God? He did not want general directions. He wanted to know God's exact will for his life. David wasn't interested in simply getting to the throne. He wanted to get to the throne God's way.

In retrospect, can you identify times when you proceeded in a certain direction because of a hunch rather than the confirmed will of God? I certainly have. At times I have asked God's direction, then assumed my first hunch was His will for my life. I'm learning to be more patient and allow God to be more specific if He wishes. No matter how long we may wait for direction, we are wise to ask before we advance.

How is God's presence specifically prioritized in the following verses?

Exodus 33:15-17 *If your Presence does not go with us do not send us up from here,*

Luke 24:48-53 *Stay in the city until you have been clothed with power from on high.*

God probably won't speak to us from the clouds nor can we toss the Urim and Thummin and get a divine answer, but we have something they did not have: His written and completed Word. God will speak specifically to us through Scripture if we learn how to listen. God has taught a method to me that never fails. It may take time, but it always works. The method I use consists of four general steps:

1. I acknowledge my specific need for direction. Example: "Lord, I have been asked to serve on the pastor's council. I need to know whether or not this council is Your will for my life at this time." I almost always write my question in a journal so that I can keep a record of God's activity in the specific matter.

2. I continue to pray daily and study His Word.

3. I ask Him to help me recognize His answer. He usually helps me recognize His answer by bringing His Word and the Holy Spirit He has placed within me into agreement over the matter. In other words, I resist reading into my situation everything God's Word says. I specifically ask Him to confirm with His Word and His Spirit what He desires to apply to my life. One or two weeks later I might be studying a particular passage of Scripture and His Holy Spirit will draw my attention to it and remind me of my question. The Spirit almost seems to say, "Look, Beth, that's it!"

4. I ask for a confirmation if I have any doubt. You might ask, "What if the Holy Spirit still hasn't given you an answer when the deadline comes?" I usually assume the answer is no.

What works for you? How do you most often receive specific direction from God?

When David inquired, God instructed him to go to Hebron. The region of Hebron has a rich biblical history. It has been occupied almost continually since around 3300 B.C. Hebron is located in the hill country of Judah about 19 miles to the south of the city of Jerusalem. Some very important people and events are connected with Hebron.

Read each reference below and fill in the blanks.

Genesis 13:18: _____Abraham_____ settled in Hebron and built an _____altar_____ to God.

Genesis 18:1-15 (Mamre is in Hebron): God spoke to Abram through three visitors and told him Sarah _____will have a son_____.

Joshua 14:13-14: Joshua gave _____Caleb_____ Hebron as an _____inheritance_____ in the promised land because he _____followed the Lord, the God of Israel, wholeheartedly_____.

God chose to write some very rich history on the map of Hebron, not the least of which we'll begin to consider in today's study. Reread 2 Samuel 2:3. "David ... with his family ... settled in Hebron." *Settled.* Nice word, isn't it? One that extends the invitation to rest a while and put down a few roots.

Have you ever felt unsettled? Can you remember a time when you longed for a place to belong and grow a few roots? ☑ yes ☐ no If so, briefly describe when and why.

USA

Your life may presently seem unsettled. Perhaps your husband's job keeps you on the move or you're living in an apartment with half your things in storage, waiting on a permanent home. You may even be new to the area, and you can't seem to feel at home. Whatever the reason, you just may feel unsettled.

In what ways could Psalm 119:19,54 be an encouragement to you whenever you feel unsettled?

19: I am a stranger on earth, do not hide your commands from me

54: Your decrees are the theme of my song wherever I lodge.

107

David had been on the move constantly for years. The Word of God abiding in Him had probably been his only comfort. After settling in Hebron, "The men of Judah came … and there they anointed David king over the house of Judah" (2 Sam. 2:4). What a significant moment in the life of our subject. At last, his private anointing years earlier became public. He was anointed king over "the house of Judah," his first step to reigning as king over the entire nation of Israel.

What do you think David felt as he was chosen to be king? Write three words that describe what you think he was feeling.

We do well to consider how God spoke to and led in the lives of Abraham, Moses, David, and many others in Scripture. Like them, we may be asked to abandon our lives to God long before we assume the position for which He called us. Over 15 years had passed. What better time for David to have uttered the words of Psalm 145:13!

Write Psalm 145:13 in the margin with a deepened appreciation as you consider it from David's perspective.

Few experiences offer the opportunity to reflect on the past like finally settling down and establishing some roots.

I asked you earlier if you ever felt unsettled. Describe how it felt to finally settle into a home, job, church, place of service, or relationship after a long season of unrest.

Were you able to see and acknowledge God's faithfulness even after such a long season of unrest? ☑ yes ☐ no

David no doubt wished that God would fast forward a few of his years of unrest, but he knew God's faithfulness would appear "in the course of time." From the moment David became king over the house of Judah, he began his official works of diplomacy. He applauded the men of Jabesh Gilead for their "kindness to Saul" (2 Sam. 2:5) and pledged his favor to them. But not all could be accomplished by words of diplomacy and pledges of protection. The entire nation of Israel would ultimately have to be under his authority. Much like Joshua, the land was to be David's, but he had to take some of it by force.

[Handwritten margin note:] Your kingdom is an everlasting kingdom, and your dominion endures through all generations. The Lord is faithful to all his promises and loving to all He has made.

DAY 2

Things That Bring Change

TODAY'S TREASURE

"The war between the house of Saul and the house of David lasted a long time. David grew stronger and stronger, while the house of Saul grew weaker and weaker." 2 Samuel 3:1

In our previous lesson, the "house of Judah" anointed David as their king, and we saw our protagonist take his first giant step toward his God-given destiny as king over all Israel. Although this kingdom was given to David by God, David would have to take it from the old aristocracy.

Over the next few lessons we will consider the overthrow that enabled David to reign over all Israel. You will encounter many names in 2 Samuel 2–4. You may become confused unless you give your reading full attention today. Some of these names become very important figures in David's kingdom, so we will attempt to identify the main players.

During your reading for days 2 and 3 you'll encounter several names of important figures in David's kingdom. Use the margins to jot down the name and helpful information about that character. This list will be a helpful resource throughout the remainder of our study, so give it your best effort.

The pacifist in me would like to skip the bloody details of the civil war in Israel. The Bible teacher in me knows we shouldn't. Old regimes rarely crumble without bloodshed. Consider the demise of Nazi Germany. New regimes rarely arise without bloodshed. Consider the American Revolution. Rich history is written on the pages of 2 Samuel depicting the end of an old regime and the beginning of the new. Just like America's history, Israel's history was often written in blood. Read 2 Samuel 2:8–3:5.

Abner, Ishbosheth

Joab

Abishai, Azahel.

In the margin write the names of the characters you encounter in the passage. Note items of identifying information.

Yesterday began with an equation. Write the equation from page 105:

Time + *conflict* = *change.*

How does 2 Samuel 3:1 support the equation *Time + Conflict = Change?*

*long time   war between   David stronger
                houses of David   Saul weaker
                + Saul.*

You noticed David's additional wives. According to Deuteronomy 17:17, David's heart was certain to be led astray. Polygamy was an extremely common practice among Eastern kings. However common, the nation of Israel had been told not to "imitate the detestable ways of the nations" (Deut. 18:9). David's actions were acceptable to men during this ancient era, but they were not acceptable to God. The consequences of David's actions would eventually begin to catch up with him. Until then, we have many other names to consider.

One of the most important names today has been Ish-Bosheth. You may have been surprised to see him identified as one of Saul's sons. He is not listed in the beginning of Saul's reign in 1 Samuel 14:49 but appears in a final list of sons in 1 Chronicles 8:33, indicating that he was born after Saul became king. Obviously Abner, commander of Israel's army, became the man in the power seat after Saul's death. He placed Ish-Bosheth (also called Esh-Baal), Saul's youngest son, in authority. We are told that he reigned for only two years. We will learn how his authority came to a sudden end.

Second Samuel 3:1 shows how *time* plus *conflict* equals *change*, "the war … lasted a long time. David grew stronger … while the house of Saul grew weaker." We've fought some pretty tough battles in our journeys—battles with temptations, strongholds, doubts, fears, addictions, and compulsions. Some of them have waged for years. No matter what the cause of our battles, time will pass and change will come. Just like David and the house of Saul, we will either grow *stronger* or *weaker*. We cannot remain the same after a severe and long battle. We rarely stay the same in times of war. We can't always choose our battles, but we can certainly make choices to affect our outcome. We want to learn to make choices that will cause us to grow stronger rather than weaker.

One of the most repeated themes in David's life and ours is warfare. The battles of David came as a result of the ultimate overthrow of an old authority.

What does Ephesians 2:1-3 describe as the source of much of the warfare we experience? *Satan; Ruler of the kingdom of the air*

The Word of God makes us aware of three different enemies we have as Christians. Each of these unite under our old authority and seek our allegiance.

Galatians 5:15-16

Sinful nature

Ephesians 6:12

Spiritual forces of evil

1 John 2:15-16

love of the world.

Look up each of the references in the margin, and write a one- or two-word summary of each of our three enemies.

We will fight these enemies to varying degrees for the rest of our lives. Sometimes we become discouraged because we see no progress, but we can be assured that *time* plus *conflict* will equal *change*. We want to change for the better so our battles will not be in vain. God obviously wanted us to learn from David's approach to warfare because He included so many of David's psalms addressing the subject. Your second reading assignment consists of a psalm written by David and dedicated to anyone facing a battle. Read Psalm 20:1-9.

Fill in the blank according to verse 1: "May the LORD _answer_
you when you are in distress."

According to 1 John 2:20, how could Psalm 20:6 apply to Christians?

we are all anointed of God & know the truth.
The Lord saves his anointed, he answers him.

What parallel can you draw between Psalm 20:6 and Romans 8:34?

Christ Jesus at the RH of God is interceding for us.

When we trust in the name of the Lord our God, what will be the ultimate
results of our battles according to Psalm 20:8?

They are brought to their knees & fall,
but we rise up & stand firm.

Fill in the blank according to Psalm 20:9: "Answer us when we _call_."

Compare verses 1 and 9 of Psalm 20. God is so anxious to answer us when we
are in distress, but an answer requires a plea for help. In other words, we must
call out to Him in order for Him to answer us.

Meditate on this truth for a moment: God could rescue us with or
without our cry for help. Why do you think He wants us to call on Him
before He rescues us? Respond in the margin.

David continually called on God to fight his battles for him. Consequently,
David always knew whose hand had brought the victory. The battles God
allowed David to fight were means toward a divine end. We cannot pick fights
or choose our own battles and expect God to get involved and fight for us. But
when God ordains or permits our battles to be used to accomplish a divine
end and we depend on God through every sweep of our sword, we will grow
stronger instead of weaker.

Are you aware of ever picking a fight that was not the will of God? Really
think about it. ☐ yes ☐ no   If so, when was it and what was the outcome?

Today we've had our attentions drawn to our three enemies: (1) Satan
and the evil principalities, (2) the world, and (3) our old sin natures. Are
you aware of presently being in a battle with any one of the three right
now? ☐ yes ☐ no If so, which one? _____

What have you learned today to help you in your battle with this enemy?

DAY 3

Suspicious Minds

TODAY'S TREASURE

"Abner said to David, 'Let me go at once and assemble all Israel for my lord the king, so that they may make a compact with you, and that you may rule over all that your heart desires.' So David sent Abner away, and he went in peace." 2 Samuel 3:21

Begin your study by praying that God will speak to you through His Word. Today we continue studying events leading to David's reign over the entire nation of Israel. Judah was first to anoint David as their ruler—a fitting union since David was from the tribe of Judah. Today we will get to know a little more intimately some of the historical figures you recorded in the margins yesterday. Read 2 Samuel 3:6-21.

Refresh your memory by identifying Ish-Bosheth and Abner.

Ish-Bosheth: *son of Saul*

Abner: *head of Saul's army.*

The Bible offers no evidence to support Ish-Bosheth's accusation of Abner. Consider verses 6 and 7 carefully. Why do you think he might have made such an accusation?

Abner had been strengthening his own position in the house of Saul.

How did Abner respond to the accusation?

☐ paid no attention   ☑ transferred his allegiance to David
☐ killed Ish-Bosheth   ☐ confessed

What one thing did David demand of Abner before making an agreement? ☐ surrender   ☑ Michal   ☐ kill Ish-Bosheth   ☐ a red BMW

Time and conflict forced a change once again. Ish-Bosheth provides an interesting contrast to David in his approach to long-term battle. He was fighting a losing battle for at least two reasons:
  • He was fighting for a position God did not give him.
  • He did not call on the name of the Lord.

Ish-bosheth was also one of God's chosen people. If he had renounced his father's ways and followed the commands of God for David to be king, God would have looked on his heart and blessed him. Instead, he followed the sins of his father and became jealous and suspicious of someone who had been on his side. The accusations Ish-Bosheth made against Abner resulted in a complete transfer of loyalties. Abner defected and marched to the other side.

God does not tell us David's motive for wanting Michal to return to him. He certainly did not lack for female companionship. Maybe he was indignant because he won her fair and square. Maybe he wanted everything back that was rightfully his. Maybe he used her to demonstrate his political and military power. Maybe he loved her. Clearly, Paltiel loved her.

Whatever David's motives might have been, these events mark a crucial change in Israel—and in David's career. Our second reading assignment records the conflict resulting from Abner's new loyalties. Read 2 Samuel 3:22-39.

Joab made an accusation against Abner behind his back. What do you think Joab was trying to accomplish?

— He came to deceive you.

He was threatened by Abner's prominence & acceptance by David.

What insight did these verses offer you concerning David's heart?

Loyal.

Consider David's words in verse 39, "I am weak, and these sons of Zeruiah are too strong for me." I believe he may have been trying to say that in comparison they had a far greater appetite for violence and insatiable delight for blood than he did. They were ruthless. Why did David keep Joab aboard? We'll discover a few reasons in the chapters to come, but one reason is found in 1 Chronicles 2:16. Read 1 Chronicles 2:13-17.

What was David's relationship to Joab?

Zeruiah's son — nephew
(David's sister)

Read 2 Samuel 4:1-12. How did Mephibosheth become lame?

Nurse dropped him.

What do you think Recab and Baanah were expecting from David?

To be honored & rewarded.

What insights about David's heart can you draw from these verses?

does not approve of opportunistic & deceitful violence.

Violence breeds violence. No matter the country or corporation, when there is a power struggle the most important question seems to become, "Whose side are you on?" Every person seems to look out for his own neck and attempts to pitch his tent in the camp of the one who can do him the most good. Remember, God never comes to take sides. He comes to take over. Joab and Abner were both Israelites. So were Ish-Bosheth and his murderers. What a shame.

We're not likely to draw actual swords and thrust them into the bellies of our brothers and sisters in Christ, but how God must be grieved when we use the Sword of the Spirit to unnecessarily wound our brothers and sisters. The Word of God is to be used as a sword against the Evil One, not against our own brothers and sisters. Peter, one of Christ's disciples, once used his sword to cut off the ear of another. Can you think of ways we could use our Swords—our Bibles—to "cut off the ear" of others?

How can we wrongly use the Bible to cut off someone's hearing rather than invite her to listen?

Unbalanced emphasis.

When Peter wrongly used his sword, Christ quickly rebuked him, "Put your sword back in its place" (Matt. 26:52). Christ commanded that we "love one another" (John 13:34), "speak … the truth in love" (Eph. 4:15), "restore … gently" (Gal. 6:1), and "forgive" (Col. 3:13). Oh, God of heaven and earth, help us to "put your sword back in its place."

Through this study and others you may have taken, you are increasing your knowledge of the Word of God. We do not desire to gain only head knowledge. We have entered into this particular study of His Word so that our hearts might be changed. We want a heart like His. As our knowledge of the Word increases, may our knowledge of how to use the Word also increase.

Write a prayer asking God to help you use His Word appropriately as you deal with your brothers and sisters in Christ.

DAY 4
The Shepherd King

TODAY'S TREASURE

"The LORD said to you, 'You will shepherd my people Israel, and you will become their ruler.'" 2 Samuel 5:2

What an exciting day. David was about to experience the fulfillment of God's promise. As we witness a tremendous pivot in the life of David, we can assume his introspective mind was swirling with many things, filling him with all sorts of emotions. Read 2 Samuel 5:1-5.

According to verse 1, who came to David at Hebron?
- ☐ the house of Judah
- ☐ the Philistines
- ☐ several of the tribes of Israel
- ☑ all the tribes of Israel

According to verse 3, what did the elders of Israel do after David made a compact with them?
- ☑ anointed David king over Israel
- ☐ fought against all opposition
- ☐ celebrated the Feast of Weeks
- ☐ offered a sacrifice to God

Verses 4-5 offer several important numbers. Identify the following:

30 years _David's age_   40 years _reigned_
33 years _over Judah + Israel_   7½ years _in Hebron King of Judah._

Don't miss the significance of David's age when he became king. In Israel, 30 years of age was significant for several reasons. According to Numbers 4:3,21, a Levite could begin his service to the Lord as priest or servant at age 30.

What further significance does age 30 possess according to Luke 3:23?

Jesus started his ministry at about 30.

Obviously God sees significance in age 30. Although we cannot know for certain God's reasons, we can reflect on this general season of a person's life.

Why do you think 30 might be a prime time to begin serious ministry?

When I began my speaking ministry at 25, I could not begin to count the people who looked at me with furrowed brow and asked, "How old are you?" I couldn't wait until I could answer, "In my 30s!" In my ignorance, I thought age would help bring credibility. Now I know nothing is magical about any age. God is not primarily concerned about our years. He's looking for a willing, teachable spirit as He readies us for service.

David certainly could mark a significant moment on the calendar of his 30th year! In 2 Samuel 5:3, we see for the first time a title attributed to David that represents the culmination of God's promise. Turn back to 1 Samuel 16 and bask in verses 1, 7, and 12 once again. This moment is too wonderful to hurry past. God didn't choose the one Samuel expected. He chose a shepherd boy, of all things. Today we get to consider a few reasons why.

> "The LORD said to you, 'You will **shepherd** my people Israel, and you will become their ruler.' "

According to 2 Samuel 5:2, what did God call David to do in this wonderful affirmation of his commission? Fill in the blank in the margin.

A shepherd and a king have more than a little in common. On week 1, day 3, I asked you to refute the statement that God called David in spite of the fact that he was a common shepherd. God chose David in many ways because he *was* a shepherd. God often referred to Himself as a shepherd and His people as sheep. He also considered every earthly leader over His children to be a shepherd. (See Ps. 78:52-53; 100:3; 119:176; and Jer. 23:1).

Read 1 Peter 5:2-4. In what ways does God continue to draw an analogy to shepherds and sheep in our present age?

care, overseers, not greedy, eager to serve, not lording it over, being examples.

We don't have the benefit of David's experience with real sheep, but God no doubt believed David's qualifications as a shepherd would enhance his leadership. We can certainly learn from David's example.

Can you see ways God may be using you to shepherd a flock? We certainly don't have to be a pastor of a church to shepherd a flock. You may discover that God has entrusted you with several flocks. List those God has entrusted to your care for His eternal purposes.

Does today's lesson help you see your role as a more official assignment? ☑ yes ☐ no   If so, how?

Every believer is a shepherd.

Virtually all of us are leaders in some capacity. If you are a mother, Sunday School worker, preschool helper, or Christian witness in your workplace, you are a leader. From David's successes and failures, we will learn volumes about shepherding a flock. He was God's choice and our example. Find out what happened after David became king over all Israel. Read 2 Samuel 5:6-25.

What attitude did the Jebusites display toward David?

Haughty, taunting

What did David call his new residence?

- ☑ the City of David
- ☐ the Promised Land
- ☐ Bethel, the House of God
- ☐ the City of God

Why did David become "more and more powerful" (v. 10)?

because the Lord God Almighty was with him.

I love 2 Samuel 5:12: "And David knew that the LORD had established him as king over Israel and had exalted his kingdom for the sake of his people Israel." David knew! Many things must have confused David in his previous 15 years. So many things he did not know.

- Why had God chosen him?
- Why did Saul turn on him?
- Why did Jonathan have to die?
- When would God's promise of the kingdom ever be fulfilled?

David did not know how he would ever live to be king. But when God handed over the most fortified city in all Israel to David and placed favor in the heart of the king of Tyre toward him, David knew the Lord had established him.

You may be going through a confusing time right now. You may not know how God is going to use a situation in your life or why certain things have happened to you. But you can be encouraged and strengthened by recalling what you know about God in the midst of uncertainties.

Complete the following sentence as it applies to your life: I may not always know what God is doing in my life or why He works the way He does, but I always know ... *I can trust you.*

> David knew the Lord had established him.

In confusing times, recounting what we do know refreshes us. David still had many unanswered questions. He would never know for sure why God allowed certain things to happen, but he knew God had done exactly what He promised. You may never know why or how, but you can always know who is faithful.

The last verses of 2 Samuel 5 represent the fulfillment of God's promise to David as stated by Abner in chapter 3. "Abner conferred with the elders of Israel and said, 'For some time you have wanted to make David your king.

Now do it! For the LORD promised David, "By my servant David I will rescue my people Israel from the hand of the Philistines and from the hand of all their enemies"'" (2 Sam. 3:17-18).

Strangely, David had come so far, yet he was back where he started. The hand that wrapped around his weapon as he waited for God's signal to overcome the Philistines looked far different from the hand that had searched for a smooth stone many years before. The first time he ever used his hands in battle was against the Philistines. Now he stood against them once more. To a man on the run, the Philistines had been a temporary refuge. They had taken advantage of his homeless estate by enjoying his strength. To a king on his rightful throne, they were clearly an enemy once more. Perhaps God inspired David to write the words of Psalm 144:1-2 on this very day.

Write Psalm 144:1. *Praise be to the Lord my Rock; who trains my hands for war, my fingers for battle.*

God trained David for war, and only God could give him success. List every name David used for God in Psalm 144:1-2.

Rock, loving God, fortress, stronghold, deliver, shield, refuge, subdues people.

Which of these names can you most readily call God today? Why?

David knew without a doubt that God had given him the victory and subdued the people under his leadership. He still didn't know why. He simply knew who. Second Samuel 5:7 tells us "David captured the fortress of Zion, the City of David." As the city fell into his hands that day, the new shepherd-king must have thought, *You have been to me what these walls have been to this city. No other excuse exists for my safety or my success. You are my fortress.*

The names David called his God fell from the lips of experience, from things he knew. Sometimes we stand to learn the most about God from the situations we understand the least.

We began our series weeks ago with a shepherd-boy. Today we've seen a shepherd-king. He was still guarding the sheep with "integrity of heart" and "skillful hands" (Ps. 78:72). Hands prepared for war yet still for the same purpose: the protection of sheep. Same shepherd, different sheep. God's sheep.

As God said, "You will shepherd my people Israel, and you will become their ruler" (2 Sam. 5:2).

> Sometimes we stand to learn the most about God from the situations we understand the least.

DAY 5

Turning Mourning into Dancing

TODAY'S TREASURE

"David, wearing a linen ephod, danced before the LORD with all his might, while he and the entire house of Israel brought up the ark of the LORD with shouts and the sound of trumpets." 2 Samuel 6:14

Today we gather with the children of Israel on the city streets of Jerusalem as they celebrate the coming of their new king but not until we learn some difficult lessons. We will see that worship is not only the ultimate freedom and privilege but also an awesome endeavor to be taken seriously.

You may feel like you've been on a spiritual roller coaster before our study concludes today. Please pause and ask God to "give you the Spirit of wisdom and revelation, so that you may know him better" and to enlighten the "eyes of your heart … in order that you may know the hope to which he has called you" (Eph. 1:17-18). When you have finished praying, proceed to your first reading assignment by reading 2 Samuel 6:1-11.

What did David and thirty thousand men set out to do?
- ☐ subdue remaining enemies
- ☐ rebuild the city of Jerusalem
- ☐ rebuild the tabernacle
- ☑ bring the ark to Jerusalem

How did they transport the sacred vessel? *on a new cart pulled by oxen.*

What were David and "the whole house of Israel" doing as the ark was being transported?
- ☑ celebrating with all their might
- ☐ proclaiming the Word of God
- ☐ offering sacrifices to God
- ☐ falling prostrate before God

David felt what two emotions toward God after Uzzah was killed?

V 8: angry   V 9 fear

How could the ark have such devastating effects on Uzzah and such blessing on the household of Obed-Edom? Offer your personal thoughts in the margin.

Imagine becoming emotionally geared for a great celebration only to greet disaster instead. Shocking under any circumstances, Uzzah's death in the midst of such celebration must have felt like emotionally jumping off a cliff.

I'm sure we've all experienced an unexpected emotional dive. I have a friend who was left standing at the altar on her wedding day. I have another friend who was told he was being considered for a promotion, but when his boss called him into his office, he was laid off instead. Still others have joyfully expected a baby and miscarried. Devastation is always heartbreaking. Devastation when we expect celebration is almost more than we can take.

Have you ever encountered devastation when you thought you were going to experience celebration? ☑ yes ☐ no   If so, what happened to turn your celebration into devastation? Please respond in the margin.

Look again at the two emotions David felt toward God in 2 Samuel 6:8-9. Did you feel either one or both of these emotions toward God?

David felt anger and fear toward God, yet Scripture calls him "a man after God's own heart." I think one reason David remained a man after God's own heart was his unwillingness to turn from God, even when he felt negative emotions. David allowed his anger and fear to motivate him to seek more insight into the heart of God.

Attempt to follow David's example by allowing our questions and confusion to motivate us to seek God. At first consideration, the account of Uzzah and the ark is hard to swallow. God almost seems mean-spirited. In times like these, we find out whether we have based our faith on *who God is* or on *what He does*. Because His ways are higher than our ways, we cannot always comprehend what God is doing or why He makes certain decisions. When we sift His apparent activity through the standard of who He is, the fog begins to clear. Basing our faith on who God is rather than what He appears to be doing is crucial to our spiritual health. Practice this approach and see if it works.

We will first consider today's verses on the basis of *who God is*. Then we'll see if we can figure out *what He was doing*. We will practice our new perspective by considering the answers to two questions.

Lord Almighty

What is 2 Samuel 6:1-11 trying to tell us about who God is? Scan the text and in the margin record any words used to describe God.

God is not trying to tell us He is *harsh*. He's trying to tell us He is *holy*. The words represent a big difference, although sometimes our limited understanding leads us to confuse them. The key to viewing the ark correctly is in verse 2.

What do you learn about the ark of the covenant from 2 Samuel 6:2?

called by the Name, the name of the Lord Almighty, who is enthroned between the cherubim that are on the ark.

We have difficulty understanding how sacred the ark of the covenant was because we have the advantage of living after the incarnation of Christ. We can only compare it to Christ Himself, the Word made flesh to dwell among us.

Once man and woman were cast from the intimate presence of God's fellowship in the garden of Eden, God began His ministry of reconciliation that ultimately was fulfilled on the cross. Hundreds of years followed man's expulsion with no direct invitation for mankind to come and fellowship with God. At last Exodus 25:8 gives the revolutionary words God said to Moses: "Then have them make a sanctuary for me, and I will dwell among them."

What music to starving ears! In the innermost place in this sanctuary, God commanded them to build the ark of the covenant according to very specific directions. Then He said, "There, above the cover between the two cherubim that are over the ark of the Testimony, I will meet with you" (Ex. 25:22). The awesomeness, the holiness, the majesty of God dwelled right there, between the cherubim on that sacred ark. Until God was incarnate among men many centuries later in the person of Jesus Christ, the ark was the sacred center of God's glory and presence. To treat the ark inappropriately was to treat God inappropriately, not just because of what it was but who God was and is.

Now, based on *who God is,* can we draw any sound conclusions about what He was doing that day? I believe we can.

1. God was setting ground rules for a new regime. God was ushering in a new kingdom with a new king He had chosen to represent His heart. He dealt with the disrespect of man through many judges and the reign of a selfish king. With a new day dawning, God was demanding a new reverence. I believe Uzzah's outward act may very likely have been an indicator of an inward attitude. Remember, God does not look on the outward appearance but on the heart.

2. God wanted His children to be different from the world. God would not accept attitudes and approaches from His children that were no different from the attitudes and approaches of the godless. Do you remember how they attempted to transport the ark? They attempted to move it on a cart pulled by oxen. Some very important history is written in 1 Samuel 6, shedding a little light on what went wrong many years later. The Philistines had captured the ark, then after being struck with plagues, they sought to return it.

Read 1 Samuel 6:7-8. How did the Philistines transport the ark?

new cart pulled by 2 cows

Do you see what Israel did? They copied the methods of the Philistines. How careful we must be not to think that God is less holy because others seem to get away with irreverence! At times when my children had been scolded for particular behaviors, they each said to me, "But _____ does it!" or "_____ says it!" I said the same thing to my children you probably say to yours: "Those are not my children. I expect something different from you because of who you are and what you know."

We are sometimes tempted to measure our respect for God by the lack of respect surrounding us. The godless, however, are not our standard. God is. Through the pen of King David, God told us to "praise him according to his excellent greatness" not according to public opinion (Ps. 150:2, KJV).

3. God wanted His kingdom established on His Word. The Israelites made the mistake of transporting the ark by the same method as the Philistines without consulting God's designated commands for its transportation. At the time David's kingdom was established, David certainly had access to the Books of Moses, the first five books of the Bible.

Read the instructions they should have read that day: Exodus 25:10-16 and Numbers 4:5,15. How was the ark supposed to be transported?

carry w. poles inserted in the rings.

God masterfully designed the transportation of His glory to literally rest on the shoulders of His revering priests, not on the backs of beasts. Do you see any ways in which we could apply this principle to ourselves? Believers in Christ make up the priesthood today according to 1 Peter 2:9.

4. God was teaching the relationship between blessing and reverence. God revealed the relationship through the effects of the ark on Obed-Edom and his household. God desires His presence and His glory to be a blessing, but reverence for Him is the necessary channel.

Hard lessons learned well undoubtedly usher in a fresh respect and new freedom. As strange as this statement may seem, the more we learn about and the more we fear God, the more freedom we have to worship Him. We'll see this principle at work in David's life as we continue with our second and concluding reading assignment for today. Read 2 Samuel 6:12-23.

Why do you think David's attitude changed once he discovered that God had blessed the household of Obed-Edom?

wanted to share in God's blessing.

What two things did they do differently as they transported the ark according to verse 13?

carrying the ark
sacrifice a bull + calf every 6 steps.

Michal insulted David for dancing before the Lord (v. 14). Has anyone ever made fun of you or insulted you because of your outward expressions of love for God? ☑ yes ☐ no   If so, how did you feel?

Our second reading offers us the opportunity to see the following points:

1. All worship is based on sacrifice. Just as our bold approach to the throne of grace could only have followed Christ's shed blood on Calvary, David's bold approach that day in Jerusalem could only have acceptably followed the shed blood of sacrifice. David offered a sin offering first. He was acknowledging his sin and asking God to grant him and his people forgiveness based on the blood of the sacrifice (Heb. 9:22). David was not free to worship acceptably until sacrifice had paved the way.

2. Worship with abandon is an intimate experience. We see David almost oblivious to everyone around him, totally liberated in the spirit, dancing through the streets of Jerusalem "with all his might" (v. 14). Oh, I love this scene. Centuries later, a group of disciples were stunned when Mary of Bethany poured the fragrance of abandoned worship on Christ's feet (John 12:1-8).

Completely abandoned worship is often misunderstood. We don't see David practice such outward worship often. Usually his worship took the form of songs, words, and prayers, but this was a very special moment. One worth celebrating with complete abandon. The glory of God was born "in the city of David" that day.

David went home to "bless his household," but he was met with ridicule and condemnation. He did not allow Michal to quench his spirit. He responded to her with the words, "It was before the LORD." Can you almost hear him say, "How dare you! My worship was not for you; it was for the Lord!" Her scolding must have stung his heart. You can sense his reaction from the text, yet he resolved, "I will celebrate before the LORD." He seemed to be saying, "Whether or not my family does, whether or not my friends do, whether or not this nation does, I will celebrate!"

What a slice of life we've seen today. We've gone from anger to rejoicing, devastation to celebration. We would miss a certain blessing if we did not conclude today's lesson with David's words in Psalm 30:11-12.

Please write Psalm 30:11-12 in the margin.

I'm not sure we will ever be released to fully "dance" before the Lord until we've learned to wail. You'll never know the experience of being clothed with joy until you've allowed Him to remove your sackcloth. Like David, you may be angry at God for taking someone's life you cared for deeply. Perhaps you are still hurt and confused. We have no idea whether David ever fully understood Uzzah's death. We just know he was willing to wait, to study, to hear God's Word, and to approach Him again. Then came indescribable celebration. He may not have understood more about Uzzah's death, but he understood more about God, which made his loss more tolerable. God is not harsh; He is holy. He is not selfish; He is sovereign. He is not unfeeling; He is all-knowing. Like David, we need to come to know Him and respect Him and like David, we will love Him more.

David was not free to worship acceptably until sacrifice had paved the way.

You turned my wailing into dancing; you removed my sackcloth & clothed me with joy, that my heart may sing to you and not be silent. O Lord my God, I will give you thanks forever.

123

viewer guide | session six

v18: Sat before the hand - unique in scripture.
Divine deal between God & D.

Host crucial moment in OT - Brueggeman.
7.8 e.o.

You 15:1 the word of the Lord - 1st time in scripture that th "word of the lord comes to a man"

Expansion of A.C.

Luke 1:32-33 ~

YY Oh Sovereign Lord.
first used in Abrahamic Cov

PART 1

David's "So Far"

God had brought David all the way from the pasture to the establishment of the ___Davidic___ Covenant. This covenant is the God-ordained expansion of the original ___Abrahamic___ Covenant.

- Note the first-time reference to God as "___Sovereign Lord.___ ___Adonai Yahweh___" (Gen. 15:2).
  See 2 Samuel 7:18,19,20,22,28-29.

- God promised Abram, "I will make you very fruitful; I will make nations of you and ___kings___ will come from you" (Gen. 17:6).

- **The Abrahamic Covenant:** The promise of the ___land___.

- **The Davidic Covenant:** The promise of the ___leader___.
  Note 2 Samuel 7:23-24.

1 Sam 4: 10-12. Thus far the Lord has helped us. 'that day'

PART 2
Our Own "So Far"

Focus on 2 Samuel 7:28. Three bone-deep beliefs keep us moving forward:

1. " _You are God_ !" We can know we've come "so far" when we can
   make the shift from _our_ plans for God to _God's_ plans for us. *have to relinquish control.*

2. "Your words are _trustworthy_." We can know we've come
   "so far" when we begin to want most what God has _already_
   offered us.

   We cannot trust the words of God if we do not know it.

3. You have promised " _good things_ " to me.
   We know we've come "so far" when we grow convinced that God
   only _does_ _us_ _good_.

   Eph 1:3

   - God's _will_ for us is good (Rom. 12:2).
   - God's _purpose_ for us is good (Phil. 2:13).
   - God's _work_ in us is good (Phil. 1:6).
   - The _hope_ God has given us is good (2 Thess. 2:16).
   - The _works_ God created us for are good (Eph. 2:10).
   - The _fight_ God called us to win is good (1 Tim. 1:18-19).
   - The _fruit_ God produces in us is good (Jas. 3:17).
   - The _gifts_ God gives us are good (Jas. 1:16).
   - God equips us with _everything_ good (Heb. 13:21).
   - God works all things together in our lives for _the good_ (Rom. 8:28).

A Man After God's Own Heart

Day 1
Humble Beginnings

Day 2
Compulsory Praise

Day 3
A Virtuous Man

Day 4
Room in the Palace

Day 5
Shunned Sympathy

DAY 1
Humble Beginnings

TODAY'S TREASURE

"The LORD declares to you that the LORD himself will establish a house for you." 2 Samuel 7:11

This week highlights many of King David's virtues. We'll glimpse qualities God may have seen when He looked in David's heart and chose him to be His servant. We will discover more of what being a man or a woman after God's heart really means. David's reign begins with integrity and administrative adeptness. Let's revel in a chapter dedicated solely to the best of King David!

Last week concluded with David's celebratory dance through Jerusalem as the ark entered the city. Today's study unfolds with the confetti swept from the streets, the merchants back to work, the children back in class, and the king on his throne. After what seemed like an endless struggle, "the king was settled in his palace" (2 Sam. 7:1). Please read 2 Samuel 7:1-17.

Fill in the blank: "The king was settled in his palace and the LORD had given him _____ from all his enemies."

What concern did David share with the prophet Nathan (v. 2)?

In your opinion, which of his virtues did David display when he expressed concern about a dwelling place for God?

The chapter unfolds with the king settled in his palace receiving some well-deserved rest. Sometimes God offers us rest we do not accept. When was the last time you accepted God's invitation to receive a little rest? And have you noticed how the body rests more readily than the mind? We may seize the opportunity to put our feet up for a while, but the mind stays in overdrive.

I think David had a little difficulty getting his mind to rest. Certain thoughts occurred to David "after ... the LORD had given him rest" (v. 1). You and I have had similar experiences. Sometimes we are so busy we can't even think. All sorts of plans seem to pour like a waterspout when things get settled.

Ever been horror-struck by your own audacity? This was one of those times for David. Life was calm. Enemies subdued. Perhaps he was sitting on his throne when his eyes were unveiled to the splendor around him. The one

who found refuge in a cave was now encased in a palace. He looked around and thought, *What's wrong with this picture?* He responded with shock: "Here I am, living in a palace of cedar, while the ark of God remains in a tent" (v. 2).

Perhaps several virtues could be noted in David's sudden reaction to his surroundings, but let's not miss the virtue of humility so present in his life at this point. He summoned the prophet Nathan the moment the thought had occurred, as if lightning would strike if he didn't.

God issued several wonderful and significant promises through the prophet Nathan in verses 9-16. Some were to David personally. Others were to the nation of Israel as a whole, and several were to David's "offspring."

Record the promises under the appropriate headings.

To David	To Israel	To David's offspring

These promises capture a wonderful moment between God and His chosen king. We get a fresh glimpse of their highly reciprocal relationship and behold the elements of their everlasting covenant. The prophet Nathan emerges as a new figure in Israel's history. God sovereignly raised prophets to serve as His voice to Israel. God apparently never intended for civil leaders to have absolute and unquestioned authority. They were to listen to the voice of God through His Word and through His prophets. All persons have someone to whom they must ultimately answer—parents and children alike, employees and employers alike, kings and kingdoms alike. God calls prophets to issue His Word, not the messages leaders want to hear. Samuel prophesied to King Saul. Nathan served as the prophet in the royal court of David.

King David sought Nathan's counsel, revealing another important virtue: accountability. David didn't consider himself above reproach or the need for advice. David's statement assumed the question, "What am I to do about the ark?" His sudden sense of audacity drew him to accountability.

James 5:16 directs us to an important form of accountability. Do you confess your faults and seek counsel when you feel you have offended God? ☐ yes ☐ no If so, do you receive godly counsel? ☐ yes ☐ no

Sometimes even a fellow believer can offer wrong advice. We are wise to make sure a fellow believer's advice agrees with God's Word. Notice Nathan's initial response to David: "Whatever you have in mind, go ahead and do it, for the LORD is with you." God used David's concern as a teaching tool for both David and Nathan. He taught them a lesson on making assumptions.

Perhaps we would be wise to heed as well. God was teaching an important lesson through each man. To David God said, "Don't assume that every bright and noble idea in a godly man's mind is of Me." Good ideas and God's ideas are often completely different. To Nathan God said, "Don't assume that a leader I have chosen is always right." The Lord can be "with" a man while a man can make a decision "without" God.

Do you see how important these two lessons are for us to learn too? Have you ever found yourself in a difficult situation after wrongly making either of these two assumptions? If so, explain briefly in the margin.

In our next unit we'll discover a primary reason why God wanted to dissuade Nathan from thinking David's actions were always right. God was preparing Nathan for a time when he would have to confront and rebuke David. Thankfully, at this point the hearts of both men were right toward God. Their motive was right even if their move was wrong.

God's message to His new king was so rich, so revelational. He began with a gentle rebuke we must remember every time we have a good and noble idea: "Are you the one to build me a house to dwell in?" In other words, "Have I appointed you to do that?" God reminded David that He is fully capable of appointing a servant for specific tasks. If we are seeking Him through prayer and Bible study, we will not likely miss His appointments. We need to wait on Him even when we have a great plan.

Isaiah 40:31

Waiting on the Lord brings at least two wonderful results. Read each of the margin verses and record the result. Note in Isaiah 40:31 the word "hope" in the NIV is "wait" in KJV. Consider this verse from the KJV.

When we wait on God, He gives supernatural strength and accomplishes the inconceivable. Did you notice how God gave David the vision for the temple but his offspring was to build it? God can entrust a vision or an idea to us that may be ours to pray about and prepare for, but not participate in directly.

Isaiah 64:4

As I read 2 Samuel 7:6-7, I saw another wonderful principle at work. To me, God seemed to be saying, "As long as My people are on the move, I'm on the move! You can't tie Me down as long as My people are mobile!" Isn't He wonderful? The "tent" to which God was referring was the Old Testament tabernacle designed by God to move with the people. That's God's way. You can't leave home without Him.

Fill in the following blank according to John 1:14: "The Word became flesh and made his _____ among us."

The Greek word for *dwelling* is *skenoo*. It means "to encamp, pitch a tent … to tabernacle."[1] God was pitching a tent so He could be where His people were, so that one day they could be where He was. Praise His name!

> "David, you won't build a house for Me. I'm going to build a house for you."

The climactic point in God's message to David comes in verse 11. Allow me to paraphrase: "David, you won't build a house for Me. I'm going to build a house for you." What overwhelming words. We want to do so many things for God, then they suddenly pale in comparison to the realization of all He wants to do for us. Romans 8:32 says, "He who did not spare his own Son, but gave him up for us all—how will he not also, along with him, graciously give us all things?"

Have you recently become aware of something God wants to give you or do for you? ☐ yes ☐ no If so, what is it?

Are you accepting what God is offering you? ☐ yes ☐ no If not, in the margin explain what is stopping you.

David discovered what we often discover: You can't outgive God. God draws His message to a close by issuing what is often called the Davidic Covenant. He issues His promise in the form of a declaration (vv. 11-16). Notice that the blessings and cursings of God on David's son might be conditional (v. 14), but God's kingdom covenant was completely unconditional. The covenant rested on God's faithfulness, not man's.

Interestingly, many years later David reflected on an additional reason why God did not choose for him to build the temple. In 1 Chronicles 28:3 David said: "God said to me, 'You are not to build a house for my Name, because you are a warrior and have shed blood.'" God chose to have His temple built during a reign characterized by peace. I am touched by the mercy of God toward His beloved David. He did not snatch the privilege from him in judgment. Rather, He allowed David's son to receive the honor.

What could be better than being appointed to do a marvelous task for God? For me it would be for my child to do a marvelous task for God. I would happily forfeit participation in the great things of God for my children to inherit the opportunity. God finally assured David, if I may paraphrase again, "You have the right idea. It's just the wrong time. A house will be built for My name but not now, and not you. Your son will build My house." If I were David, I would have been unable to contain myself.

We will soon see that David was completely overwhelmed. Our eyes will get to penetrate more deeply into the heart of David as we behold his response to God's gracious promises in our next study.

Compulsory Praise

TODAY'S TREASURE

"How great you are, O Sovereign LORD! There is no one like you, and there is no God but you, as we have heard with our own ears." 2 Samuel 7:22

Today we camp on Scripture that stole our hearts in week 5. I want you to get a chance to respond to similar promises of God over your own priceless life. Ask God to grant you a double portion of His presence today and to let you revel in David's response as readily as if you had said the words yourself.

We've looked at the personality of David from many different angles. Few Scriptures will allow us to dive into the depth of his passionate soul more deeply than these. We'll taste a morsel of one of David's greatest virtues: While others were prone to wander, he was prone to worship. Today's verses are so rich that I will combine the commentary with the questions rather than asking a set of questions then adding commentary. Read 2 Samuel 7:18-29.

In the margin fill in the blanks according to 2 Samuel 7:18.

"Then King David went in and _____ _____ the LORD."

Have you ever responded like David when someone told you something you knew was an answer from God and you wanted to run and sit before Him? ☐ yes ☐ no If so, when?

Moments like those represent an indescribable intimacy in your relationship with God. When those moments occur, you can't even explain how you feel. Your only response is to go and sit before the Lord.

When I am overwhelmed by something God has done for me or said to me, I often find that I have to sit a moment and wait for my heart to write words on my lips. Sometimes I weep for a while before I can begin to speak. David might have done the same thing. So intimate were the words God spoke to him through Nathan that he left the messenger's presence and went straight to the One who sent the message.

In the margin paraphrase David's words in verse 18.

I have asked the same question more times than I could count, but not for the reasons you might assume. Yes, for reasons I will never understand, God has given me opportunities for ministry in this season of my life, and I praise Him for that. Yet the moments that most often move me are extremely intimate and private. Because they are so personal, I probably will never share in a testimony some of the most wonderful things God has done for me. What David was feeling was not about grand positions—it was about personal petitions.

We each have countless opportunities to be overwhelmed at the goodness of God. Can you glance back at your life and say, "Oh, God, we've come so far!"? Or do you have the tendency to only focus on how far you have to go? Right now, please praise Him for how far you've come and entrust the rest of your journey to the One who brought you this far.

After saying, "Who am I … that you have brought me this far?" David said, "And as if this were not enough in your sight, O Sovereign Lord, you have also …" (v. 19). How like God to keep giving and giving. David was stunned by God's words of prophecy over his family. What more precious promise could God have given David than to assure him He would remain with his offspring long after David was gone? What peace we can have in knowing God will bless our children.

Read 2 Samuel 7:22 aloud just as you believe David must have said it. Then read aloud starting at verse 18 and ending with verse 22.

Did you sense a different emphasis, a rising tone, in verse 22? As if David was suddenly overcome, he broke out in compulsory praises. "How great you are, O Sovereign Lord!" Have you ever experienced David's kind of praise?

At times our praises are planned. For instance, in my quiet time I always plan to have a time of praise and worship. The words and reasons change but praise and worship are necessities to my daily time with God. At times our praises, though unplanned, are as quiet in our spirits as a whisper—times when we quietly, reverently acknowledge His worthiness. At other times praise is absolutely compulsory—when we would burst if we did not praise; when whispers are hard to contain; when hands are difficult to stay; when knees seem to bend by themselves; when spirit, soul, and body join in compulsory harmony, "How great You are, O Sovereign Lord! There is no one is like You!"

Over two thousand years ago a group of disciples were compelled to praise Christ. Some of the Pharisees said, "Teacher, rebuke your disciples!" How did Christ respond to the Pharisees in Luke 19:40?

That's compulsory praise. Every now and then we enjoy a moment void of doubt and full of mystery, when we're overwhelmed with humility yet stunned with possibility. Moments when we realize with every one of our senses that He stands alone. "No one—no mate, no child, no preacher, no teacher, no ruler, no principality, no one is like You." Nothing is quite like suddenly realizing that nothing is like Him.

Read 2 Samuel 7:23-24 carefully. In the margin list every distinction David extols about Israel in these two passages.

Israel—I love the sound of the syllables. I love their history. But most of all, I love their peculiarity. Their very identity was in their set-apartness. We often try so hard to blend in. We sometimes resent that God has ordained His people to seem strange to the rest of the world, yet our identity is in our peculiarity.

According to 1 Peter 2:9, we are also a peculiar people on purpose and for a purpose. Have you felt a little peculiar lately because of who you are in Christ? ☐ yes ☐ no   If so, in the margin briefly explain why.

If David could speak to us from heaven, I am quite certain he would tell us to celebrate our peculiar position in Christ. He would also probably tell us to praise a faithful, covenant-keeping God.

Why did David want God to keep His promises (2 Sam. 7:25-26)?

Our human nature is self-serving and ambitious. God desires to purify all other motives of ambition in us except the ambition that God would use us to draw attention to Himself and His great name. God's Spirit influences us to transfer personal ambitions to the ambition of His exalted name and character.

Do you struggle with personal ambition? ☐ yes ☐ no   How can you pursue excellence in your job, service, talents, or activities for His name rather than your own? Respond in the margin.

How do you think David found courage to offer God his prayer (v. 27)?

I believe David referred to his petition for God to establish his house forever. He would never have presumed to pray this prayer without first knowing God's will. David concluded with the words, "Now be pleased to bless this house." In other words, "Go ahead and do as You've so generously promised." David believed God and prayed in accordance and anticipation.

Psalm 106:12 says, "Then they believed his promises and sang his praise." Quite possibly David "believed his promises" then "sang his praise." After all, he was accustomed to singing God's praises. I imagine that David might have ended this intimate time with God in a song of praise. No congregation. No instrument. No hymnal. Just the three-part harmony of his spirit, soul, and body presenting an unscheduled compulsory concert before the ear of God.

I challenge you to do the same as your last assignment. God doesn't care if you have perfect pitch or none at all. Just sing Him a song … whatever He brings to mind. Any familiar chorus will do. Go ahead! You may feel silly at first, but you will soon be ushered into a precious moment of praise. Tell Him you believe the promises He has made you; then sing. Sing Him a love song.

DAY 3
A Virtuous Man

TODAY'S TREASURE

"David reigned over Israel, doing what was just and right for all his people." 2 Samuel 8:15

We're studying virtues of the "man after God's own heart." On day 1 we saw authentic humility. David was filled with horror that he lived in a palace while the ark of God dwelled in a tent. We also saw a sense of accountability as David immediately sought the prophet Nathan when he feared he may have offended God. On day 2 we met the virtue that surely captivated the heart of God: David's undeniable propensity to worship. Today we add several more virtues as worthy examples for us to follow. Our reading is quite different from our two previous lessons. We return to the battlefield as the nation of Israel was once again established as a formidable power. When the dust of war settles, several important virtues will emerge. Please read 2 Samuel 8:1-18.

Write in one sentence what you believe to be the point of this chapter:

David spared one-third of the Moabite army and left 100 of the Zobahite chariot horses mobile. Why do you think he left any alive? Offer your thoughts in the margin.

What did David do with all the gold and silver he had acquired from the nations he had subdued?

Enjoy the words of verse 15 while you can. Describe David's leadership at this point in his reign.

We've seen virtues of David presented as subtle themes in God's shadow. Now God directly pinpointed some of David's virtues, allowing him to take a momentary spotlight. Remember the thoughts on ambition yesterday? I believe God allowed David to be entirely successful at this point in his reign because He could trust David to exalt the name of the Lord. The psalms constantly testify of David's ambitious desire in battle to bring glory to God.

My then four-year-old nephew, Chris, was bickering with his cousins over which video to watch and Chris didn't get his way. He burst into tears and said, "I don't want to watch that old thing! It's nobody's favorite!" What he really meant was the movie wasn't *his* favorite. Our entire extended family still quotes him when we don't want to eat at a particular restaurant, play a particular game, or do a particular activity. Of all the chapters we've studied, as Chris once said, this one is nobody's favorite.

Though our hearts may not be drawn to 2 Samuel 8, this chapter undoubtedly represents the zenith of David's career. God had given him success. David had it all: fame, fortune, power, and position. For just a little while, David handled the unabashed blessings of God with brilliant integrity. Let's seize the moment. We can glean the following virtues from our reading today:

1. A spirit of cooperation. In 2 Samuel 7:10-11 God promised David He would give the nation of Israel rest from her enemies. David did not sit on the throne and simply wait for God to fulfill His promise. He obeyed God's beckoning to the battlefield to participate in the victory.

When God assures us of a promise, He desires we respond by assuming a posture of cooperation in the fulfillment of that promise. Other times God directs us to sit still and wait. Wisdom involves learning to know the difference. Whether God tells us to sit, stand, or move, He calls us to respond with a spirit of cooperation. Christ, the coming King, did more to exhibit a spirit of cooperation than anyone who ever lived. Each name listed in the "Hall of Faith" in Hebrews 11 represents a spirit of cooperation. The study of David's life inevitably invites the student to ask herself some difficult questions. Keep in mind, I never ask you a question I have not asked myself first.

> Whether God tells us to sit, stand, or move, He calls us to respond with a spirit of cooperation.

Where do you believe you fit on the following scale in reference to a cooperative spirit toward God?

UNCOOPERATIVE ⟵――――――――――⟶ VERY COOPERATIVE

Have you exhibited a spirit of cooperation with God recently?
☐ yes ☐ no   If so, briefly explain in the margin.

Join me in asking God to make each of us keenly aware when we do not offer Him a spirit of cooperation.

2. A ray of hope. David did not annihilate his enemy and simply leave the nations destroyed. First, God didn't tell him to do so. Second, I believe his God-given motive was to bring the other nations to a place of subservience rather than a place of nonexistence.

How did the Moabites and Arameans respond similarly to defeat (2 Sam. 8:2,6)?

Psalm 9:11

David wrote the Scriptures that appear in the margin. Read each one and record David's intentions toward the nations.

King David lived in a harsh and cruel time. That he would measure people with a line and kill two-thirds of them naturally offends our modern sensibilities. Commentators' suggestions mitigate some of the harshness: That those killed were Moabite soldiers or that the reprisal was because the Moabites slaughtered David's family entrusted to their care. Clarke's commentary even

Psalm 9:20

suggests: "Death seems here to be referred to the cities ... we may conclude that two-thirds of the cities, that is, the strong places of Moab, were erased."[2]

We must remember that David lived before the time of Christ. He did not have the advantage of the completed revelation. We cannot judge him by modern standards. What we remarkably do see is that David had a concern for the spiritual welfare of the nations. That concern was a giant step forward for a man of his day. David left a remnant among the nations. David exhibited hope for the nations to bend their knees to the King of all kings.

Psalm 22:27-28

3. A literal dedication to God. At this point David had never confused the source of his strength. Any rewards he immediately dedicated to the Lord. If he was praised for his successes, he quickly gave the praise to God. If he was exalted for his successes, he lifted the name of God even higher. When he was surrounded by splendor, he wanted God to have something more splendid. When he returned with gold, silver, and bronze, he dedicated them immediately to the Lord. The Hebrew word for *dedicate* in this passage is *qadhash*, meaning "to hallow, dedicate, consecrate to God, declare as holy, treat as holy; to sanctify, purify, make oneself clean; to be pure."[3]

Read the definition several times; then consider how much *dedication* has to do with *purity*. If we immediately dedicate all our successes to God—verbal praises, positions, or paychecks—how will purity be a factor?

David immediately dedicated the treasure he received to God. Centuries later, Christ also dedicated the treasure He had received to God. You are the gold and silver—the treasure Christ received because He exhibited a spirit of cooperation and hope when He agreed to die on the cross. Read John 17:9-11.

What did Christ do with the treasure His Father had given Him?

In the margin name several kinds of treasures God has given you and the ways you have dedicated these treasures to God.

4. Justice and righteousness. The definitive verse of 2 Samuel 8 says, "David reigned over all Israel, doing what was just and right for all his people" (v. 15). Consider the two virtues of justice and righteousness together because God often treated them as a pair, somewhat like fraternal twins rather than identical.

According to 2 Samuel 8:15, David did what was fair (just) and what was right. Jeremiah 22:3 describes several specific examples of justice and righteousness. List them below:

Justice and righteousness bring a specific response in the heart of God. Identify the response by filling in the blank in the margin Scripture.

In Acts 13:22 we have the perfect opportunity to highlight the description God placed on David. How is David described?

☐ my chosen king   ☐ a man after my own heart
☐ the shepherd of Israel   ☐ the king of the nations

God delivered a marvelous prophecy about the Messiah, Jesus Christ, in Jeremiah 33:15. Write the verse below. Then circle the similarities between David's reign and Christ's reign.

> "'Let him who boasts boast about this: that he understands and knows me, that I am the LORD, who exercises kindness, justice and righteousness on earth, for in these I _____ declares the LORD.'"
> **JEREMIAH 9:24**

Second Samuel 8:15 describes the moment David most clearly and completely fulfilled his calling. For a season, the kingdom of David reflected the kingdom of the supreme King of all kings, yet to come—Jesus, the Christ, the sovereign Victorious. These were the glory days of David's kingdom. God had given him the keys to the kingdom: *justice* and *righteousness*—keys to a kingdom that will never end. We will consider one last virtue based on our reading today.

5. The wisdom for administration. The wise king knew that growth meant a greater need for administration. As the eighth chapter concludes, we see one of the first orders of business: the delegation of authority and responsibility. In 2 Samuel 8:16-18 we find the various positions David filled. He had obviously learned an important lesson in his initial leadership of the distressed, indebted, and discontented (1 Sam. 22:2). A leader needs help.

Moses did not learn so easily. Thankfully, he had a wise father-in-law who offered him some life-saving advice when he saw the people gathered around him from morning until night. "What you are doing is not good. You and these people who come to you will only wear yourselves out. The work is too heavy for you; you cannot handle it alone" (Ex. 18:17). A good administrator knows when and how to delegate!

Whether or not we realize it, most of us are in administrative positions in the home, workplace, or church. Are you overloaded right now? If so, what are some ways you can delegate some responsibilities?

Even if we can't see how we are hurting ourselves by taking on excess responsibilities, we need to seriously consider the harm we may be doing to those around us. Jethro specifically said that Moses' unwillingness to let others take some of the responsibility was not only hurting him but also hurting others.

What are some ways that carrying too much responsibility might hurt those you are trying to serve? Respond in the margin.

Administration was another of David's royal virtues that directly reflects the coming King of kings. As Chief Administrator, Christ will delegate many responsibilities of the kingdom to those who reign with Him (Rev. 5:10; 20:6).

We have grasped David as a man after God's own heart more this week than ever before in our study. We've seen Christ's own heart illustrated over and over. No one was more humble. No one held Himself more accountable to God. No one revealed a greater heart for worship. No one had such a depth of cooperation with God. In all these ways David provides a picture of Jesus. Christ dedicated His every treasure to God, His Father, and will return for us when the Father nods. He will rule in justice and righteousness. As Chief Administrator, He will delegate the responsibilities of the kingdom to the faithful on earth. The characteristics God saw and loved so much in David are those most like His Son. God has one specific bent toward partiality: He loves anything that reminds Him of His only begotten Son. To be more like Christ is to be a man or woman after God's own heart.

We have several more virtues to behold on days 4 and 5. I look forward to meeting you there. Thank you for your dedication to God's Word. May His Word make us more like His Son.

DAY 4

Room in the Palace

TODAY'S TREASURE

"David asked, 'Is there anyone still left of the house of Saul to whom I can show kindness for Jonathan's sake?'" 2 Samuel 9:1

Today we continue to study the virtues of the man God chose to be king. We've caught glimpses of humility and a desire for accountability. We've seen him worship with abandon. We've noted a spirit of cooperation and felt the breezes of his hope brush against our faces.

Through David, we catch momentary glimpses of Christ, not just a man after God's own heart, but a man with God's own heart. How wonderfully typical of a proud and loving father. Through the Old Testament, God raised up men for the specific purpose of revealing wonderful secrets about His beloved Son. As if He could only go so long without talking about His Son, the Old Testament is filled with portraits capturing sudden snapshots of Christ.

God sometimes used Old Testament figures like Isaac, Moses, and David to say, "My Son is like this." David had moments when he resembled God's Son—times when God might have said, "See this guy? His heart reveals what My Son is like." Today we will have the pleasure of seeing a tender aspect of David's heart. Join me as we study with a spirit of anticipation. Read 2 Samuel 9:1-13. Read verse 1 carefully.

What emotions do you think David might have been feeling that caused him to ask this question? List your thoughts in the margin.

Whose kindness was David wanting to show according to verse 3?
☐ Jonathan's ☐ Saul's ☐ God's ☐ Ahithophel's

How did Ziba describe the son of Jonathan?

What two ways did David want to show kindness to Mephibosheth for the sake of his father, Jonathan?
☐ to eat at his table ☐ to be second in command
☐ to restore Saul's land ☐ to give him a Hebrew wife

According to verse 8, what do you think Mephibosheth was feeling?

Correct the statement in the margin based on verse 11. Draw a line through the error and write the correct words.

Don't you love God's Word? How I praise Him that His Word is not just a book of rules and regulations, do's and don'ts. The Bible is a book of the heart. Realize God's Word reflects God's ways as you read a story like the one we've read today. His heart must be so tender. Our previous lesson spotlighted the zenith of David's reign. God gave unparalleled success. David was famous throughout the land, both hailed and feared for being the foremost example of God's power on earth. Now we travel from his public feats to his private feelings.

David knew well the familiar feeling we all know as loneliness. You heard his loneliness as he said, "Is there anyone still left of the house of Saul to whom I can show kindness for Jonathan's sake?" David had conquered kingdoms and subdued enemies. He had servants at his beck and call. All was momentarily quiet and peaceful—and he missed his best friend.

Mephibosheth ate at David's table like one of his honored guests.

God fulfilled Jonathan's wish and gave David everything, but Jonathan wasn't there to share it. David sought the next best thing. Ziba, a servant of the house of Saul, told him about Jonathan's son Mephibosheth. Ziba's choice of words is interesting. "There is still a son of Jonathan; he is crippled in both feet." His choice of words and timing intimates that he suspected the son's handicap might disqualify him from anything the king sought.

In the encounter between David and Mephibosheth we see several characteristics of God displayed. Consider with me the following virtues of God.

1. His loving-kindness. Notice: David was searching for someone of the house of Saul to whom he could show *God's* kindness, not his own (v. 3).

How does God first describe Himself in Exodus 34:5-6 when He proclaimed His name, the LORD to Moses?

The Lord is first of all *kind*. Compassionate. He desires to deal with us first in *mercy*. If we refuse to accept His mercy, He often deals with us in the way He must; but He is above all *kind*. As a man after God's own heart, David was tender. His heart was full of loving-kindness, and he was anxious to pour it out on a willing vessel.

2. His initiation of the relationship. "Where is he?" David inquired and summoned Mephibosheth immediately. Note he did not seek David. David sought him. David was the king. What could he possibly have needed? He had everything. But he *wanted* someone to whom he could show God's kindness.

Luke 19:10

Read the three Scriptures in the margin. Note how David's action in seeking Mephibosheth pictures God's action in seeking and loving us.

John 15:16

God is always the initiator of the relationship, always looking for someone who will receive His loving-kindness!

3. His complete acceptance. David did not hesitate when Ziba informed him of Mephibosheth's handicap. In the Old Testament people considered physical imperfection shameful, but David summoned Mephibosheth exactly as he was. How reflective of God's heart! Many wait until they can get their act together before they approach God. If only they could understand, God calls them just the way they are; then He empowers them to get their act together.

1 John 4:19

What does Matthew 9:12 tell you about the heart of God?
- ☐ God helps those who help themselves.
- ☐ Jesus came to minister to the broken and the hurting.
- ☐ The self-inflicted must find their own remedies.
- ☐ The healthy ones first discover God.

Picturing the scene when David met Mephibosheth brings me to tears. Imagine the king sitting on the throne, surrounded by splendor. His brightly adorned servants open the door, and before him stands a crippled man. The Word says, "When Mephibosheth son of Jonathan, the son of Saul, came to David, he bowed down to pay him honor." With crippled legs he crept before the king, then he bowed before him. Can you imagine the difficulty for a handicapped man to get down on his knees, press his forehead to the floor, as was the custom, then rise up? Mephibosheth was obviously humiliated. "What is your servant, that you should notice a dead dog like me?" (v. 8).

Have you ever felt like Mephibosheth? I have. Surely everyone who has ever accepted Christ as Savior has crept before Him, crippled from the fall of sin, overcome by our unworthiness against the backdrop of His Majesty's brilliance. "To the praise of the glory of his grace, wherein he hath made us accepted in the beloved" (Eph. 1:6, KJV)!

4. His calming spirit. As Mephibosheth practically came crawling before the king, David exclaimed, "Mephibosheth!" He knew him by name … just as Christ knows us (John 10:3). David's next words were, "Don't be afraid." How many times have we seen those words come from the precious lips of our Lord? "It is I. Don't be afraid."

- To the Twelve as He sent them forth, "Don't be afraid" (Matt. 10:31).
- To a bunch of scaredy-cats in a storm, "Don't be afraid" (Matt. 14:27).
- To the three overcome by His glory, "Don't be afraid" (Matt. 17:7).
- To the father of a dying child, "Don't be afraid" (Mark 5:36).

How very Christlike David was in this moment.

5. His delight in restoration. David's first desire was to restore Mephibosheth. "I will restore to you all the land that belonged to your grandfather" (v. 7). He had been so hurt by the fall. He had lived with such shame. The king could hardly wait to see Mephibosheth's shame removed and his life restored. David knew about restoration. He penned the words, "He restores my soul" (Ps. 23:3). Perhaps the most grateful response we could ever offer God for our restoration is to help another be restored.

I was nearly overcome when I looked up the name *Mephibosheth* and found that it means "shame destroyer" or "image breaker."[4] What a precious portrait of our Savior! He has been my shame destroyer and my image breaker!

6. His desire for another son. Mephibosheth came stooped as a servant before the king. The king came to make him a *son.* He was family—invited to sit at the king's table to partake of his fellowship as one of his own. Imagine the sight when Mephibosheth first limped to the table set with sumptuous delights, surrounded by festive activity, and sat down, resting his crippled legs at the king's table. Hallelujah! We are like Mephibosheth. No matter how many sons the Father has, He still wants more to conform to the image of His first and only begotten, virgin born.

Delight in writing 1 John 3:1 in the margin.

That's us, all right. One day, when we sit down to the ultimate wedding feast, the lame will be healed, the blind will see, the restored will leap and skip with ecstatic joy! We will be surrounded by the ministering servants of heaven! He is a God of loving-kindness just searching for someone with whom to share it. Not just the moment when we first bow before Him and acknowledge that He is king, but every single time we sit at His table. Joint heirs. Sons. Daughters. He is the shame destroyer. The lover of the lame.

   I would never have learned to walk with God on healthy feet had I not experienced sitting at His table as a cripple. My emotional and spiritual healing has come from approaching God in my handicapped state and believing I was His daughter and worthy of His love.

I believe God has used His Word to cause you in some way to relate to Mephibosheth. Glance over the ways David's actions picture the virtues of God. In the margin note how this lesson has described you.

Isn't God wonderful?

DAY 5
Shunned Sympathy

TODAY'S TREASURE

"David thought, 'I will show kindness to Hanun son of Nahash, just as his father showed kindness to me.'" 2 Samuel 10:2

Today we conclude our focus on virtues of David. We will unearth other virtues later, but we will not focus on them as an entire unit. Read 2 Samuel 10:1-19.

For what reasons did David want to show kindness to Hanun?
   ☐ His father had died.
   ☐ He had been kind to David.
   ☐ His kingdom had been destroyed.
   ☐ His father had been kind to David.

The Ammonite nobles led Hanun to believe David had sinister motives. What do you think Hanun was trying to accomplish by treating David's men as he did?

From verses 9-12 describe Joab's leadership in a word.

Who joined the battle according to verse 17?

The account of this battle contains many virtues of David, each further representing the God who chose him and placed His Spirit on him. I would like to highlight three outstanding evidences of God's character at work in David.

1. An active sympathy for the suffering. David knew better than anyone that a crown did not make a person void of feelings or oblivious to losses. Though Saul was not his father and had often treated him with malice, David had grieved his death. David's throne had been seasoned with bittersweetness because of the tragedy prompting it. Likewise, Hanun was assuming the throne of the Ammonites but at the cost of his father's life.

David believed in showing kindness, especially to those who had shown him kindness. If those who had been kind to David were not alive, he sought their offspring so he could show kindness in return. He attempted such an act toward the incumbent king of Ammon, desiring to express heartfelt sympathy. David had experienced devastation. He had also been in need of sympathy.

Read David's words in Psalm 69:20. What happened when he had looked among men for sympathy?

Have you ever needed a sympathetic ear or gesture from another person but were unable to find it? ☐ yes ☐ no   If so, when?

Sometimes not finding what we feel we need from others can ultimately bring us benefit. Two direct benefits can result if we are willing.

First, we can become more sympathetic when others are in need. We can become far more sensitive and caring. "Live in harmony with one another, be sympathetic, love as brothers, be compassionate and humble" (1 Pet. 3:8).

Have you had an experience that caused you to become more sympathetic to others? ☐ yes ☐ no   If so, what was the experience and how has it affected your personal opportunities to minister to others? Write about it in the margin.

Second, we can reach out to a sympathetic God. David exhibited the character of God as he extended sympathy to someone who had experienced loss. You can depend on a sympathetic God in your need. David knew the disappointment of reaching out to others for sympathy and not receiving it, but he learned from his experience that God is always compassionate and sympathetic.

Psalm 103:13

Psalm 116:5,15

Psalm 145:9

David penned each of the margin verses. Under each, list how he described the sympathetic heart of God.

God is always sympathetic, but His sympathy is not always accepted. David experienced something similar as his extension of sympathy was rejected by Hanun. The Ammonite nobles attempted to make the new king feel foolish for trusting David's motives. "Do you think David is honoring your father by sending men to you to express sympathy" (2 Sam. 10:3)? A possible paraphrase might be, "Are you some kind of gullible idiot?"

Hanun responded by humiliating David's men. By cutting off their garments and half their beards, he was symbolically making them half the men they were. I see an important similarity between David's rejected sympathies, expressed by the humiliation of his delegates, and God's rejected sympathies expressed by humanity's rejection of Christ. God's most glorious extension of sympathy to a dying world was Christ, His Son.

According to Hebrews 4:15, how is Christ able to sympathize with us?

God sent Christ as the delegate of His sympathy to the misery of men somewhat like David sent delegates of sympathy to Hanun. Christ was also met by those who stirred up misunderstanding among the people, just like the Ammonite nobles. Ultimately, His message of sympathy was rejected by the very ones to whom it was first extended, and Christ hung on a cross in complete humiliation. For those who have received Him, Christ remains our sympathizer, ever ready to lead us to a door of escape from temptation or a door of mercy when temptation has turned to participation.

Do you allow God to extend sympathy to you in your pain or loss, or do you tend to reject His efforts? Remember, Christ is the extension of God's sympathy to you. Allow Him to minister to you in your need.

Let's consider two more outstanding evidences of God's character.

2. A fierce protectiveness toward his own. David sent messengers to meet the men so they would not be publicly humiliated. In effect, he threw a cloak around their exposed bodies and formed a plan to spare their dignity.

I'm not sure we can understand what this humiliation meant to a Hebrew. The thought of being exposed in such a heartless manner would be humiliating to anyone, but to a Hebrew, such humiliation was virtually a fate worse than death. They were a very modest people. Their enemy preyed on one of their worst nightmares. In our present society, many excuse their vulgar participations in pornography by saying, "I simply exercise an appreciation for the human body." Nakedness is something to be shared and enjoyed strictly in the confines of marriage. David fiercely protected the dignity of his men. God is even more protective of us. In a beautiful soliloquy, God responds to the shame Israel has suffered in Ezekiel 16:8-14 by saying:

I spread the corner of my garment over you and covered your nakedness. … I bathed you with water and washed the blood from you and put ointments on you. I clothed you with an embroidered dress and put leather sandals on you. I dressed you in fine linen and covered you with costly garments. I adorned you with jewelry … and I put a … beautiful crown on your head. … You became very beautiful and rose to be a queen. And your fame spread among the nations on account of your beauty, because the splendor I had given you made your beauty perfect.

Ever since Satan exposed shame in the garden of Eden, God's redemptive plan has been to cover it and relieve man of shame's chains. He did so by His own blood. David revealed qualities of his Father, God, when he immediately responded to the shame of his own people with a plan to restore their dignity. He evidenced the protectiveness of God.

3. Vengeance toward the enemies of his people and mockers of his mercy. David did not just formulate a plan to spare the dignity of his men. He took on their enemy himself. God also takes on our enemies when we've been shamed.

Lamentations 3:58

How do each of the margin verses prove God's defensiveness toward those who hurt or shame His children?

Isaiah 35:3-4

Let me assure you, God can take on your enemy with far more power and might than you ever could. When someone persecutes you, your Father takes the oppression very personally, especially when you are ill treated for obeying Him, as David's men were. The battle is the Lord's!

Matthew 18:6-7

God has extended mercy to every member of the human race. He sent His delegate of sympathy for our sin to hang on a cross as the divine remedy. Those who reject His mercy and mock His motives will be punished sooner or later if they do not repent. Pray for your enemies. Pray they will accept God's delegate of mercy toward them. Pray for a willingness to be a vessel of God's mercy in their lives. A battle is coming and all captives will be kept eternally.

Do you see that any one of us could be a man or woman after God's own heart? God is looking for qualities that remind Him of His Son. These qualities are developed in us at no small cost, just as they were in the life of David; but the pleasure of God is profoundly, indescribably worth it!

As you conclude today, take a moment to reflect on this week. Which one of David's virtues has been most outstanding to you? Why?

Let's recap the virtues we've noted in this unit. David was humble, accountable, and worshipful. He was cooperative, hopeful, dedicated, and just. He was a righteous king and an effective administrator. He was an initiator of relationships: kind, loving, accepting, restoring, and welcoming. He was sympathetic, protective, and defensive against the wrongs done to his people. We've seen David at his best, exhibiting the characteristics of the Holy Spirit within him. His heart was patterned after his God's. For a time, he was the greatest king who ever lived—the apple of God's eye.

If we're smart, we'll find ourselves thinking …

If that can happen to ___David___, it can happen to ___anyone /me___

Psalm 19 is a song hailing the revelation of God …

• through ___nature___

This portion of Scripture presents what one commentator calls "the paradox of ___inaudible___ ___noise___."[1]

• through ___Torah___

• to man's ___innermost___ ___self___.

Our responses to the intimate revelation of God requested in Psalm 19:11-14 set guards on the walls of our lives:

1. ___love___ the ___Word of God___.

2. ___heed___ the ___warning___.

"God's Word warns us of danger and directs us to hidden treasure. Otherwise how will we find our way? Or know when we ___play___ ___the___ ___fool___?" (Ps. 19:11-12, The Message)

3. Seek the *discernment*

   "The words related to *shagah,* 'to err,' suggest some act of turpitude perpetrated through *distraction* under the effect of anger, alcoholic intoxication, or the *passion* of love and hatred."[2]

4. *de-vault* the *fault*.

5. Fear willful sin.
   - Willful sins are either on *purpose* or driven by *pride*.
   - Rule (Hebrew term *masal*) means "to rule, reign, govern, have dominion, *manage*"[3] (Ps. 19:13).

Consider *meditation* as "the *musical* soliloquy sung in my heart."[4]

1. Peter C. Cragie, "Psalms 1-5" in *World Biblical Commentary,* vol. 19 (Waco, TX: Word Books, 1983), 181.
2. Samuel Terrien, *The Psalms* (Grand Rapids, MI: William B. Eerdmans Publishing Co., 2003), 213.
3. Warren Baker, gen. ed., *The Complete Word Study Dictionary OT* (Chattanooga, TN: AMG Publishers, 1994), #4910.
4. Terrien, 214.

The Wages of Sin

Day 1

Up on a Rooftop

Day 2

Contrasts in Character

Day 3

"You Are the Man!"

Day 4

Painful Pleas

Day 5

No Relief Like Repentance

DAY 1
Up on a Rooftop

TODAY'S TREASURE

"One evening David got up from his bed and walked around on the roof of the palace. From the roof he saw a woman bathing. The woman was very beautiful, and David sent someone to find out about her."
2 Samuel 11:2-3

Week 6 took us to the heights of David's reign and to the breadth of his character. This week will painfully prove the depths to which one can fall after reaching such heights. Against God's warning, David multiplied wives and grew accustomed to having all he wanted. We'll see the outcome of his eroding self-control. David sinned grievously against the Lord but finally arrived at a place of complete repentance.

We live in a society offering little encouragement toward restraint. God's Word will speak frankly to each of us about the necessity of self-control. Through many chapters of Scripture we've seen the qualities of David extolled. Now in two short verses we see him tumble headlong into the pit of sin. Join me as we step out on the roof of an ancient Hebrew home to catch a fresh breath of spring air. Read 2 Samuel 11:1-5.

What was David supposed to be doing in the spring?
- ☐ celebrating the Passover
- ☐ building the temple
- ☐ going off to war
- ☐ taking a census

1.

In the margin list the three actions David's temptation turned into (vv. 3-4).

2.

The sin between David and Bathsheba had numerous repercussions. What was the first result according to verse 5?

3.

- ☐ Bathsheba was humiliated.
- ☐ She became pregnant.
- ☐ Uriah learned of their betrayal.
- ☐ She was shunned by her family.

Few things frighten me more than this testimony of David's life. We too could be persons of character and integrity yet destroy our ministries and ourselves through the choice to gratify our sudden lusts. Like David, a few short verses could record our downfall. Don't be drawn into their sin by romantic—and false—notions. We cannot afford to justify their behavior through sympathy. In our culture we justify immoral behavior with the excuse that two people were "in love." David and Bathsheba were not in love. They simply chose to act in a dishonorable and destructive way. We could speculate that he was intoxicated by her beauty mixed with an opportunity to display his power. She may have been enamored with his wealth and prestige.

We can't lend this scene the sympathies we're tempted to offer "victims" of passion in romance novels. This trashy romance is down in the bottom of the barrel. Down with all the sticky stuff. Where the stench is—the place we find ourselves when the line between wanting and getting erodes.

We may wish we could get everything we want until we look at David and Bathsheba. In the gap between wanting and getting we must flex the muscle of self-control to protect ourselves. David rose to a position where his every wish was someone else's command. He ceased to hear a very important word—one without which integrity cannot be maintained. The word is *no*.

Have you recently had to say no to yourself for something you really wanted but knew you shouldn't have? ☐ yes ☐ no

How difficult is it for you to say no?

Like most of us, David probably could say no rather easily to some things but had great difficulty saying no to others. How badly he wanted what he shouldn't have obviously regulated the difficulty.

For the sake of review, in Deuteronomy 17:17 which of the following did God command the rulers of His chosen nation not to do?
 ☐ take many wives ☐ send their armies to war without them
 ☐ serve other gods ☐ all of the above

In the midst of all his integrity in the other areas of his life, "David took more concubines and wives in Jerusalem" (2 Sam. 5:13). God clearly stated the consequences of multiplying wives in Deuteronomy 17:17.

What was the consequence?
 ☐ The king would surely die. ☐ The king would lose his kingdom.
 ☐ The king would suffer. ☐ Other: _____

Proverbs 4:23

Just as God warned, David's heart had gone astray. For a season the heart so much like God's wandered to an abyss of no resemblance. A heart out of God's hands never fails to fall into danger. The Word of God makes over five hundred references to the heart, but in two God uses the words "above all."

Jeremiah 17:9

What does God tell us "above all" about the heart in the two verses that appear in the margin?

These two verses easily relate together. In the margin combine the two concepts into your own one-sentence statement.

David, the man of God, the Lord's anointed who enjoyed God's complete provision, took what did not belong to him and cast himself headlong into scandal. He believed his own cheating heart.

We don't have the luxury of considering the events between David and Bathsheba a rarity. Unfortunately, many people of God allow their hearts to wander and fall into adultery. The threatened institution of marriage in our day, in the church and out, beckons us to confront the actions of King David. His actions can teach us not only how adultery can happen but how to prevent or avoid it. Let's consider a few places David went wrong.

1. He was in the wrong place at the wrong time. "In the spring, at the time when kings go off to war ..." (2 Sam. 11:1). David had been an effective administrator and delegator, but he had exceeded the wise bounds of delegation. He left himself with little responsibility and idle hands. David handed Joab a baton he should have kept for himself. David should have been leading his troops just as the other kings were leading theirs. He was obviously restless. "David got up from his bed" (2 Sam. 11:2). Sadly, he had delegated so much responsibility that he left himself open to boredom and temptation.

2. He failed to protect himself with a network of accountability. At one time David had been sensitive to the thought of offending God. He sought the counsel of prophets and allowed himself to be held accountable. We've reached a season in David's life when he was answering to no one, apparently not even God. All of us need to be surrounded by people who are invited to hold us accountable and question the questionable.

We discussed the matter of accountability in our previous unit; we are now seeing some of the repercussions of living without it. No one questioned David's actions, yet they knew he was wrong. We don't need those kinds of associates, do we? I want people in my life who love me enough to offend me if necessary and help me not to fall.

In the margin note who in your life you are certain would question the questionable. Then note ways you could strengthen your guard by greater accountability.

David grew accustomed to wanting and getting. What a dangerous habit! This time he went too far. He took something belonging to someone else, and no one called his hand on it. But God held him accountable.

3. He was lonely. David allowed himself to be placed so high on the throne that he found himself all alone. The words of 2 Samuel 9:1 hint at David's loneliness and lack of peers as he cried, "Is there anyone still left of the house of Saul to whom I can show kindness for Jonathan's sake?" Dave Edwards once said, "All rebellion begins in isolation."

Have you experienced isolation? ☐ yes ☐ no If so, what form of rebellion or disobedience to God crept into your isolation?

How can we avoid making the same kind of mistake? The following four precautions will keep us from being trapped in sin as a result of loneliness:
- Be careful to fulfill the responsibilities God has given.
- Deliberately set up a network of accountability partners.
- Avoid lengthy periods of isolation, if possible.
- Be aware of the progressive nature of sin.

For the remainder of the lesson we will allow our attention to focus on the fourth safeguard. I believe we have all experienced the progression of sin, and 2 Samuel 11:1-5 illustrates three progressive areas of sin in David's life.

Step 1: He sinned in thought. David saw the woman bathing and concluded she was beautiful. Sight turned into desire. The seed of sin was first sown in his mind, just as it is first sown in our minds. If the sin of the mind is not confessed and repented, it virtually always gives birth to the next stage. The meditation of David's mind turned into the conversation of his mouth.

Step 2: He sinned in word. God knows that our meditations (the focus of our thoughts, what we think and rethink) will ultimately turn into conversations. That's why He tells us to meditate on Him and His Word!

Think how often sin not squelched in the mind makes its way to the mouth. If we begin thinking about adultery and do not allow God to halt the thoughts, we'll start talking about it in one form or another just as David did. The talking invariably draws us closer to action. Temptations rarely go from the mind to the deed. The second stop is usually the mouth.

David's method certainly wasn't subtle. He saw Bathsheba and allowed wrong desires (the participation of his mind), then he summoned someone and expressed his interest (the participation of his mouth), then sent someone to retrieve information. These two steps enticed a third.

Step 3: He sinned in deed. David flirted with adultery in thought and word, stopping at neither venue to repent and ask God for help. Action followed. David committed adultery and set in motion a hurricane of repercussions.

I've approached my time of confession and repentance for years by categorizing my sins according to each of the three areas we've addressed. In my prayer time, I ask God to bring to my mind any sins of *thought, word,* or *deed.* Virtually everything will fall into one of those three categories. David's example shows how often the three areas unite as participants in grievous sin.

We must learn to allow God to halt sin in the place it begins—the thought life. We're wise to aggressively confess the sins of our thoughts. Our thought-life sins are so numerous that their familiarity tends to make them less noticeable. Our minds may fuel jealous thoughts, sudden lusts, quick criticisms, and harsh judgments without ever regarding them as sin.

A heightened awareness of wrong thoughts will work greatly to our advantage. Getting in the habit of confessing sin in the thought life is not to constantly remind us what wretches we are but to remind us what victors we are. Confessing wrong thoughts stops sin in the first stages, before it comes out of our mouths and then directs our actions. If I allow God to halt sin before it takes one step out of my mind into word or deed, the only person hurt will be me. Once sin progresses from the mind to mouth and deeds, we've involved others. The repercussions and chastisements escalate.

Unchecked thoughts usually progress. Our minds can't be "fairly pure." Purity comes with a radical attitude toward the thought life. God looks out for our best interest when He commands us to love Him with our whole minds.

> If wrong thoughts give way to wrong words, often giving way to wrong actions, how can we begin safeguarding ourselves from wrong actions?

As you conclude, please write the following Scriptures on a card you can carry with you and memorize. Let them become staples in your prayer time to guide you through purity of thought, word, and deed before God.

Psalm 139:23-24 (thoughts)
Psalm 19:14 (words)
Psalm 15:1-2 (deeds)

None of us is beyond the sin of adultery. Two kinds of people are in greatest danger: Those who think they could never be tempted and those presently being tempted. May we cast ourselves on the mercy of God and find help in our time of trouble. *Big* trouble.

DAY 2
Contrasts in Character

TODAY'S TREASURE

"Uriah said to David, 'The ark and Israel and Judah are staying in tents, and my master Joab and my lord's men are camped in the open fields. How could I go to my house to eat and drink and lie with my wife? As surely as you live, I will not do such a thing!'" 2 Samuel 11:11

Yesterday we saw David's sin begin in his thought life and end up in the conception of an innocent child with another man's wife. We may see the greatest evidence of his faraway heart today as he reacted to the news of Bathsheba's pregnancy. Let's begin reading 2 Samuel 11:1-27.

Why did David bring Uriah home?

Have you ever felt someone was faking an interest in you for an ulterior motive? ☐ yes ☐ no   In what ways was David probably faking interest?

URIAH
Evidences of
Strong Character

> In 2 Samuel 11:1–17, a stark contrast becomes evident in the character of Uriah and David. In the margin list as many evidences as you can find of Uriah's strong character and David's flawed character.

How did David involve Joab in his grievous sin?

DAVID
Evidences of
Flawed Character

Consider the words of verse 25, and describe David's heart at this point.

Verse 27 concludes: "But the thing David had done displeased the LORD." You may be familiar with these passages, but did you find yourself secretly hoping the story had changed this time? Imagine how the Father's heart is wounded when we behave so unlike one of His children. He was no doubt grief-stricken by David's sin, even though He saw it coming. Considering the events we've read today, David's heart was obviously further away from God than we imagined. If David were accused of a faraway heart and tried in a court of law, how much evidence would there be to convict David? As members of the *jury*—not the *judge*—consider four evidences of David's faraway heart.

    1. David resisted many opportunities to repent of his sin and lessen the charges against himself. Most of us have been carried away by an overwhelming and sudden craving of the flesh, but we've often cried out for help before sin was heaped on sin. Other times, we've thrown ourselves into a revolving door of sin, just like David, and continued in a destructive cycle.

After his sin with Bathsheba, how might David have behaved with repentance and integrity?

In the margin respond to the question: Why do you think David didn't stop and repent? You might consider the answer by asking, "Why have I not at times stopped and repented in the earlier stages of sin?"

After he committed the act of adultery, even though the consequences of the pregnancy were already at work, David could have fallen on his face before God, repented, asked for mercy, and begged God to help clean up the mess he had made. Throughout his encounters with Uriah, he had many opportunities to consider his actions and recant. He didn't.

David had God's Spirit in him. You can be sure the Spirit was doing His job of conviction! Sadly, David had quenched the Spirit to such a degree that he was able to resist repeated conviction. Little should frighten us more than realizing the Holy Spirit's conviction has grown so faint we hardly sense it. We are dangerously far away when we can sin with little conviction.

2. David was unmoved by Uriah's integrity. His faraway heart was unaffected by an encounter with authentic integrity.

How had David once shepherded his people (Ps. 78:72)?

Uriah's integrity should have spurred such a sense of loss in David that he could not bear to remain so far from the Father. David surely recognized integrity. For most of his life, his character had been replete with it! When I confront godly character, I never fail to think, *I want to reflect character like him, Lord!* or, *Please, God, make me an example like her!* unless my heart is so far away it can do nothing but despise the confrontation.

If Uriah were on trial for integrity, there would be ample evidence to convict him. Just as David resisted continuous opportunities to turn from sin, Uriah resisted continuous opportunities to turn from integrity.

3. David tried to cover his own sin. Most of us have tried to cover our sin at one time or another.

Have you ever gotten tangled in a web of sin while you tried to cover the first one? ☐ yes ☐ no   What emotions did you feel during this season?

Who is blessed according to Psalm 32:1?

Whom did God inspire to write Psalm 32?

The word *covered* in the original Hebrew is *kasah* and it means "to cover, conceal, hide; to clothe; … to forgive; to keep secret; to hide oneself, wrap oneself up."[1] When we try desperately to cover up our sinful ways, we are bound for disaster as sin perpetuates. Only through repentance will God "cover" us and "clothe" us with His loving forgiveness. Only when we run to Him in the nakedness of our sin will He wrap us up with "garments of salvation" and a "robe of righteousness" (Isa. 61:10). David was trying to cover his tracks. God wanted to cover his *sins*. The latter means life. The former means death—to something or someone.

4. He involved many others in his sin. Apparently David never stopped to consider the position in which he was placing others. We too can become so self-absorbed that we do not care what we are asking from others. We can be unmoved by the compromises of others on our behalf. Intense selfishness accompanies a faraway heart. In fact, one accurate way to measure our intimacy with God is to see where we fall on the chart of selfishness. The measuring stick might look something like this:

A heart far away from God	A heart near God
←	→
characterized by extreme *selfishness* and *self-absorbency*	characterized by the marked *selflessness* of Christ

Take a moment and ask God to reveal to you where you might be on this chart. Be sensitive to the positive or negative tendencies He may point out through His Holy Spirit over the next few days.

David navigated his way to the negative extreme of this spectrum. In David's selfishness, he involved a servant in his plans; he invited Bathsheba to a season of guilt and grief; he attempted to entice Uriah to compromise his values; he involved Joab in his sin; and he had Uriah killed. Most importantly "the thing David had done displeased the LORD" (2 Sam. 11:27). Still he did not repent. We may rightly conclude David had ample evidence to convict him of a faraway heart. The results were tragic.

What are we to do with this information and the sting of our own failures reawakened in our hearts? First Corinthians 10:11-12 gives us several reasons why God has given us accounts like David's.

In my research I found a section out of a worn, yellowed book called *The Making of a Man of God* by Alan Redpath. I would like to conclude with his words and vow never to forget them. I hope you'll spend some moments in prayer after you read it. Thank you for staying true to God's Word even when it paints pictures that aren't pretty. God's Word is always for our good.

> David was called "a man after God's own heart." That was the caliber of the man, the height to which he had risen. He had become king of all Israel, and he had defeated all his enemies. He had risen now to the peak of his life and career—when suddenly the devil tripped him up.
>
> Oh, from what heights of blessing it is possible for a man to fall! To what depths of sin a man can descend, even with all that spiritual background! The higher the pinnacle of blessing, authority, and publicity he has attained by grace, the deeper and more staggering can be his collapse. There is never a day in any man's life but that he is dependent upon the grace of God for power and the blood of Jesus for cleansing.[2]

Amen. Pray for yourself; then pray for someone you know who is being mightily used by God.

"These things happened to them as examples and were written down as warnings for us, on whom the fulfillment of the ages has come. So, if you think you are standing firm, be careful that you don't fall!"

1 CORINTHIANS 10:11-12

DAY 3
"You Are the Man!"

TODAY'S TREASURE

"David burned with anger against the man and said to Nathan, 'As surely as the LORD lives, the man who did this deserves to die! He must pay for that lamb four times over, because he did such a thing and had no pity.' Then Nathan said to David, 'You are the man!'" 2 Samuel 12:5-7

Our last chapter ended with some solemn, hair-raising words: "But the thing David had done displeased the LORD" (2 Sam. 11:27). Our next reading begins to assess the cost of a few moments of carnal pleasure. Read 2 Samuel 12:1-14. Note that Nathan used an analogy involving sheep.

Which were David's responses to Nathan's analogy?
- ☐ believed the man deserved to die
- ☐ became angry
- ☐ commanded the man pay four times
- ☐ all the above

Good news (v. 13)

At what point did David admit his sin?

How did Nathan respond to David with good and bad news? Record your answer in the margin.

Bad news (v. 14)

The scene unfolds with Nathan sent to confront David's sin. We need to be careful not to confront for any other reason. We need to resist self-appointed confrontation with a fallen brother. Galatians 6:1 records one of those reasons.

According to Galatians 6:1, who should restore a fallen brother and why should he be careful? Respond in the margin.

If you have ever confronted someone without being appointed by God, how did you know God had not appointed you?

Have you ever tried to help restore someone only to find yourself tempted as well? ☐ yes ☐ no   If so, what were the circumstances?

Nathan was God's man for the job, but he still needed the protection and leadership of God as he confronted the powerful, persuasive king. He probably dreaded his appointment like the plague, but he was obedient to the will of God. Virtually a year had passed since David's initial sin with Bathsheba. We know the baby had been born, but we do not know exactly how old he was.

The time is so important because no sign of repentance had yet occurred. David appeared to be moving on with his life as if nothing had happened, but how do you suppose his sin affected his relationship with God? Had he simply picked up where he had been? Hardly! Most of us have had seasons of unrepentance when we outwardly attempted to go on with life as if we had not sinned against God. However, our unwillingness to repent has internal effects.

Have you ever had a season of unrepentance in your Christian life? ☐ yes ☐ no If so, what kind of internal effects did your unwillingness to repent have? Respond in the margin.

David wrote exactly how he felt during his season of unrepentance. Take a moment to look at what David was going through during the course of that year as recorded for us in Psalm 32:3-5.

What obvious toll did David's unwillingness to repent have on him?

How were your experiences similar?

I believe Psalm 32:3-5 describes a malady we might call *sin sickness*. I have to confess, I know what it's like to be sin sick. During periods when I refused to repent, I felt sapped of strength and sick all over. I groaned in my sin. Thankfully, the seasons of my sin and rebellion were the most miserable periods of my life, worse than any uninvited suffering I've ever experienced.

Have you found the misery of your unrepentant heart to exceed the misery of difficult circumstances? ☐ yes ☐ no Why do you think the misery of sin might be worse?

God graciously forgave me once I repented, and He forgot my sin; but I am thankful He did not allow me to forget my sin.

Have you ever noticed God helps us accept His forgiveness, but He does not make us forget our sins? ☐ yes ☐ no Why do you think He does not remove the memory of our sins? Respond in the margin.

Psalm 32:3-5 teaches an important truth. Spiritual illness (unrepentance) can lead to emotional illness (groaning, heaviness) and physical illness (bones wasted, strength sapped). Don't misunderstand. Certainly not all emotional and physical illness is caused by an unrepentant heart, but a refusal to repent takes a serious emotional and physical toll. I know. I've been there.

The prophet Nathan used a good preaching method to confront David. He used an illustration familiar to his hearer and drove the illustration home with the Word of God. His method struck an immediate chord with David.

Sometimes the further we wander outside God's will, the more we judge others and the less we show mercy. David was ready to fine the man "four times over" and kill him—until he found out he was the man. What was God trying to accomplish? I believe He wanted David to recognize the *grace* of God in the midst of the grave consequences of his sin. God wanted David to recognize he deserved to die. Bathsheba also deserved death, according to Hebrew law. So did Joab for setting up another person's death. God allowed David to sit as judge over his own life and pronounce a death sentence on himself so his Heavenly Father could grant him the undeserved gift of life. No doubt, David never forgot that moment.

God rebuked David through the prophet Nathan by saying in effect, "I anointed you, delivered you, gave you Saul's kingdom and all that belonged to him. If you had needed more, I would have given it. But you didn't ask Me for things I longed to give to you. You took something that wasn't yours."

David, through his behavior, wounded the heart of God by despising His Word. The Hebrew word *despised* is *bazah* which means "to disesteem ... to scorn."[3] David's disesteem cost him dearly. As the chosen king of Israel, the man revered for having the hand of God on him, David was the most well-known, highly feared figure in the entire world. Through him God was teaching the nation Israel and the heathen nations about Himself. David's heinous, progressive sin did a terrible thing. It gave "great occasion to the enemies of the LORD to blaspheme" (v. 14, KJV).

The word *blaspheme* is *na'ats* and it means "to revile, scorn, despise, reject; to condemn, to deride."[4] Listen to the rest of the definition and consider how serious this cycle of sin was in David's life: "It contains the idea of disdain for one who formerly received favorable attention and then rebelled." What other nations saw in David caused them to cast their eyes on David's God. Though many had not turned to the God of Israel, He had captured their attention and respect. David's actions caused the nations to lose their respect for God.

David placed God in an excruciating position. As God's foremost teaching instrument, even the eyes of the heathen nations were on David. God was teaching the way to the Messiah through His chosen king. Through David's victories, God taught something of Himself. Now, through David's failures, God would reveal something more of Himself. God's actions regarding David's sin teach the very foundation of all salvation—God will forgive the sinner, but He will still judge the sin.

God allowed David to pronounce a death sentence on himself so He could grant him the undeserved gift of life.

159

DAY 4
Painful Pleas

TODAY'S TREASURE

"Then David comforted his wife Bathsheba, and he went to her and lay with her. She gave birth to a son, and they named him Solomon. The LORD loved him." 2 Samuel 12:24

For the remainder of week 7 and through all of week 8 we will continue to see David during the most difficult season of his life. Some of the events will not be fun to study, but they overflow with vital life lessons. The nuggets of gold we will dig from the painful caverns of the coming chapters will captivate us until the winds of victory blow in our faces once again. Pause right now and ask God to tender your heart to His Word. Read 2 Samuel 12:15-25.

In what ways did David respond to his child's sudden illness?

Imagine yourself in David's position after his painful loss. Read his immediate responses in verse 20. In the margin describe which response would have been most difficult for you and why.

What was David's sustaining belief through his grief (v. 23)?
☐ He would have other children.
☐ He would be with his child after his own death.
☐ His sin would finally be absolved.

What was God's attitude toward David and Bathsheba's second child?

Nathan had hardly turned the doorknob to leave before David's child fell ill. David had been warned that his son would die, and still he "pleaded with God for the child" for seven days. When the child died, the servants were terrified David would do something desperate. They were stunned when David received the news, got up, washed his face, changed clothes, and went into the house of the Lord and worshiped.

Did David waste his time pleading with God over the life of the child? After all, God's message through Nathan was painfully clear. As we attempt to determine whether David's efforts were wasted, we have the privilege to peek at just a little of the intense intimacy David shared with God. When he fell on his face before God, the prodigal returned home to the place he belonged. He was bankrupt in soul, demoralized, and terrified, but he was back. Too many months had passed since he had last entered the indescribable place of God's presence, but he still recognized the Father.

Through David's crisis, he was reminded of all he knew of God's ways. David did not plead with God out of ignorance or naïveté but out of his intimate knowledge of God. God does indeed hear our prayers and reserves the right to relent if the change does not compromise an eternal necessity.

Need proof? Read the verses in the margin and note the circumstances.

Exodus 33:3,15-17

Isaiah 38:1-5

David knew something about his God that we need to realize as well. God did not create man in His own image to be unaffected by Him. More than any other creature, we are products, not of His head, but of His heart. Numerous times in Scripture God responds to the needs of His people with the words, "I have heard your cry." I would despair of life if I believed God is unaffected by our cries. The God of Scripture is One who feels.

Draw lines matching these verses to God's emotional responses.

Psalm 95:10	grief
Zephaniah 3:17	deeply moved, troubled
John 11:33	delight
Ephesians 4:30	anger

Unlike us, God is never compromised by His feelings, but He does care deeply. When David heard he would live but his child would die, he probably begged God to allow him to die instead. Can you imagine God being unaffected by a parent's painful pleas? You may be thinking, *But, Beth, God did not do what David asked. David's prayers didn't change a thing. Where is grace? Where is mercy? What changed?* Let's consider a few of the things that changed.

1. David's painful pleas forced him back to a crucial place of depending on God. Somewhere along the line, David had mistaken the power of God as his own. He had so often been told he could do anything, he started to believe it. God demands we depend on Him because only He can keep us safe. When we depend on Him, He takes care of us. When we seek security in other places, He is obligated to turn us back toward home. When we refuse the less painful nudgings of the Holy Spirit, we risk more drastic measures. Tragedy caused David to depend on God. God's judgment seems harsh until we reconsider David's many transgressions. He multiplied wives and concubines, took another man's wife, and took the man's life all with no willingness to repent.

Don't conclude from today's lesson that the loss of a child must be chastisement on sinful parents. God is not mean-spirited. Remember, David was the king of God's holy nation and had continued to rebel against God in spite of the Holy Spirit's urgings.

2. David's pleas would satisfy his spirit in the many months of mourning to come. As he grieved the loss, he needed to know he had done everything he could to prevent the child's death. David did not want his child to die because he did not ask God. (See Jas. 4:2.)

In your relationship with God, do you feel freedom to bring the desires of your heart to Him in prayer? ☐ yes ☐ no How do you usually respond if He does not give you the desire of your heart?

3. David's pleas ultimately ensured his survival through the tragedy he and his wife would suffer. David's pleas returned him to intimacy with God. The return positioned him to make it through such loss with victory. David's restored relationship to God enabled him to comfort his grieving wife. When tragedy hits, if we cast ourselves on the Savior and rely on Him for the very breath we draw, we will one day get up again. We will even have the strength to comfort another mourner. Perhaps most difficult to fathom, we will have the strength to return to worship.

I'm glad Scripture does not record the scene when David first returned to public worship. The moment belonged to God and David alone. I cannot hold back the tears as I imagine how quickly David's words turned to sobs. I can picture him standing there acknowledging through wails of grief his God's sovereignty and loving-kindness.

Do you remember ever returning to the Lord in worship after a painful loss you believe He could have stopped? ☐ yes ☐ no If so, in the margin describe some of the feelings you experienced at that time.

You may view your return to worship as one of the most difficult and painful experiences of life. I suspect David would concur, but his return restored his sanity. His rediscovered relationship with God became the pillar to hold him up through the painful repercussions of his sins.

4. David's pleas touched the heart of God to respond. God loved this man—just as He loves us. The one He loves He must discipline (Heb. 12:6). But does God's heart ache as He disciplines? I believe the answer is yes. Beautiful evidence of the Father's tender heart toward David emerges in this tragic account. God could not give David what he asked because He had to perform an eternal work and teach an eternal lesson. But He did something else: "Then David comforted his wife Bathsheba, and he went to her and lay with her. She gave birth to a son, and they named him Solomon. The LORD loved him; and because the LORD loved him, he sent word through Nathan the prophet to name him Jedidiah" (2 Sam. 12:24-25).

Out of grace God removed the curse on the sinful union of David and Bathsheba. Their union had been wrong. Their motive was wrong. Even when David found out Bathsheba was pregnant, he tried to manipulate a way for her to stay out of his life. But now we see them drawn together by terrible tragedy. God removed the curse of their marriage and brought a child from their union. *Jedidiah* means "beloved of the Lord."

"The LORD loved him." God loves you. His chastisements can be painful, but God never turns His back on us. He will discipline but not forsake us. He will always seek to draw us back to a place where He can bless us once more.

DAY 5

No Relief Like Repentance

TODAY'S TREASURE

"Cleanse me with hyssop, and I will be clean; wash me, and I will be whiter than snow. Let me hear joy and gladness; let the bones you have crushed rejoice." Psalm 51:7-8

Between confronting sin and restoring fellowship must come the bridge between those two vital works—contrite confession. We have the blueprint for the bridge of confession fresh from the heart of a grieving king. Psalm 51 will be a fitting conclusion to our study of David's infamous transgressions.

Read Psalm 51 aloud with some of the passions of its poet. In five words or less, what was David's theme in this chapter?

David's sin had injured many people. Why do you think he said, "Against you, you only, have I sinned?"

1.

In the margin list the six requests David made in verses 10-12.

2.

Why do you think the two results listed in verse 13 were dependent on God's granting David's six requests?

3.

This psalm invites the vilest of sinners to drink from the fountains of forgiveness. Consider these specific phrases from each of the first 13 verses.

4.

Verse 1: "Have mercy upon me, O God." So great was David's need for cleansing, so urgent his plea, he began his prayer with no introduction and no high praises.

5.

What does Isaiah 59:1-2 tell you that sin can cause?

6.

David recognized that until he expressed repentance, words would be wasted.

"According to your unfailing love; according to your great compassion." David knew his God was complex and multifaceted. In his history with God, David had called on His sovereignty, His might, His deliverance, His intervention. But at this moment, David called on the God of love and compassion. Only on the basis of covenant love could David dare ask for mercy.

Verse 2: "Wash away all my iniquity and cleanse me from my sin." Don't miss the most important emphasis in this statement: the word "all." What a wonderful word! The mercy of God is enough to cover all our sins. Few things in life are as fresh and thrilling to me as that moment when I know God has heard my repentant cry and I am completely clean.

Describe your feelings when you know God has cleansed you from your sin.

Are you able to accept that all your confessed and rejected sins have been completely forgiven? ☐ yes ☐ no   If not, what do you think holds you back from accepting God's complete forgiveness?

Verse 3: "For I know my transgressions." Psalm 51:3 proves David could not ignore his sins. Are you in David's position right now? Are you carrying the weight of past sin? Is the guilt and remorse more than you can bear? Do you have a sin you can't seem to give up? You can't live with it but can't bring yourself to live without it? Satan screams: "To give it up will be far more painful than living with the guilt." Refuse to hear another of Satan's lies. The freedom of Christ is worth the surrender of absolutely anything. Relief, not remorse, awaits the repentant.

If you're afraid to give up something you know is wrong, tell God about it. Confess your fears. Let Him encourage you and fill you with His Word.

If you are struggling, write a prayer expressing your feelings and asking for His help.

Verse 4: "Against you, you only have I sinned." For those of us who have known God and experienced His presence, the biggest heartbreak over sin is the realization that we have offended Him. God takes our sin personally. When we don't confess, we scoff at the cross. A man who lived many centuries before David also had an opportunity to sleep with another man's wife.

Read Genesis 39:6-10. What is the man's name? _____

Write the one question he asked his pursuer.

Verse 5: "Surely I was sinful at birth." David recognized something of the depth of his inclination to sin. With a fresh sense of shock he seemed to be saying, "Sin is as much a part of me as the flesh and blood that makes up my body. It's my heritage! Oh, God, have mercy on me!"

Since your salvation, have you ever come to the stunning realization of your own depravity apart from Christ? ☐ yes ☐ no   What impact did this "poverty of spirit" have on you? Respond in the margin.

Verse 6: "Surely you desire truth in the inner parts." God is our one and only source of transforming truth. Deep inside in the secret places we are most vulnerable to lies.

What have we learned over and over again from Jeremiah 17:9 about the nature of the heart? The heart is ...
- ☐ deceitful above all things
- ☐ jealous and cold
- ☐ to be despised and ignored
- ☐ a trustworthy guide

Virtually every external sin results from the internal practice of believing a deceitful heart. Only God can sow truth in our hearts; only we can let Him. God can always be trusted to tell us the truth, but sometimes we don't want to hear the truth. According to John 8:32, truth sets us free.

Have you ever found truth to be painful but liberating? ☐ yes ☐ no If so, what did you learn?

"You teach me wisdom in the inmost place." The inmost place is where experience turns into wisdom! Wisdom is knowledge applied. Head knowledge alone is useless on the battlefield. Truth stamped on the heart makes one wise.

   Verse 7: "Cleanse me with hyssop." For the people of the Old Testament, hyssop carried a powerful ritual and symbolic message.

Read the first mention of hyssop in Exodus 12:22-23. Why do you think David referred to hyssop in his prayer of repentance?

> As a freshly forgiven sinner, I am cleansed, forgiven, and absolutely purified of sin.

"Wash me and I will be whiter than snow." When I feel weighed down by sin and guilt, I feel spiritually dingy and dirty. The image of snow speaks volumes to me at those times. As a freshly forgiven sinner, I am whiter than snow. I am cleansed, forgiven, and absolutely purified of sin.

   Satan lies to you. He tries to convince you that you are covered by guilty stains even when you repented long ago. Let God sow truth in your inner parts! Know the truth so you can recognize a lie!

   Verse 8: "Let the bones you have crushed rejoice." This line is perhaps my favorite in Psalm 51. I know exactly what the psalmist was talking about. Do you? David mixed the pain of confessing and turning from sin with the pleasure of restored fellowship. God sometimes uses circumstances and discipline to figuratively break our legs from continuing on the path of sin. Only the repentant know what it's like to dance with joy and gladness on broken legs!

Can you think of a time you rejoiced after finally being broken by God? ☐ yes ☐ no   If so, what caused your rejoicing even though the process was painful?

Verse 9: "Hide your face from my sins." With a sudden realization of his own depravity, David could not bear for God to look. He was filled with shame, Satan's signature of approval. Allowing God to open our eyes to sin is not only painful but also embarrassing. Once we look, we don't want God to see. We must accept that He's already seen our sin, still loves us, and wants to forgive.

   Verse 10: "Create in me a pure heart." The Hebrew word for *create* is *bara*. Also used in Genesis 1:1, the word "refers only to an activity which can be performed by God" and describes "entirely new productions."[5] David was admitting his need for something only God could do. Pure hearts never come naturally. In fact, a pure human heart is perhaps God's most creative work.

Verse 11: "Do not … take your Holy Spirit from me." To David, the removal of God's spirit was a fate worse than death. He said in verse 4, "You are … justified when you judge." When we compare his plea in verse 11, David seems to be saying, "Do whatever you must; just don't take your Holy Spirit from me!"

Based on his experience with Saul, why do you think David pleaded with God not to remove His Spirit?

Verse 12: "Restore to me the joy of your salvation." Most of us have borrowed these precious words from time to time. Sometimes our prayers seem to go unanswered because, in our misery, we beg for our joy to be restored without the obedience of fully turning from our sin. Read John 15:10-11.

Which of the following activities is the precursor to "complete joy"?
☐ Bible study   ☐ worship   ☐ obedience   ☐ faith   ☐ reverence

Nothing equals the moment you sense the return of the joy of His salvation, but we must have the willing spirit to cooperate in His marvelous work.

Verse 13: "Then I will teach transgressors your ways, and sinners will turn back to you." What happens after God has created a pure heart in a repentant sinner, renewed his spirit, and restored the joy of His salvation? No more willing and effective evangelist and teacher exists than one who is humbled, cleansed, renewed, and restored. God will never have to goad this person to witness. Her life will have eternal impact.

Thank You, merciful God, for the words You placed in the heart and on the pen of a broken king. Thank You most of all for forgiveness. May we never be able to resist.

As a repentant sinner who has experienced the misery of broken fellowship with God and reveled in the freshness of forgiveness, I would like to conclude with two verses that mean the world to me. Read them aloud if you have the opportunity. May they be a blessing to you too.

> Who is a God like you, who pardons sin and forgives the transgression of the remnant of his inheritance? You do not stay angry forever but delight to show mercy. You will again have compassion on us; you will tread our sins underfoot and hurl all our iniquities into the depths of the sea (Mic. 7:18-19).

David's entire purpose in writing Psalm 51 was to ask for mercy. Did God grant his request? I have a hunch that He was delighted.

In Psalm 32:1-2, "blessed" (Hebrew *asherey*) means "O, the _sheer_ _happiness_ of."[1]

Five Fabulous Facts to _feel_ _happy_ About

1 Pete 2:24

1. I am _forgiven_. In Psalm 32:1, "forgiven" is the Hebrew *nasa* meaning to _lift up_, "to bear, carry off."[2]

In Psalm 32 note three appearances of the same Hebrew root word (*hata*) for *sin*:

• "Whose *sins* are covered" (v. 1).
• "I acknowledged my *sin*."
• "You forgave the guilt of my *sin*" (v. 5).

See its literal rendering in Judges 20:16. The Greek equivalent is *hamartano*, "to _miss_ the _target / goal_." _mark_

Heb 12:23-24

God's completing or perfecting something or someone was "not merely ending it, but bringing it to perfection or its _destined goal_."[3]

What is the destined goal? _God's glory_ (Isa. 43:7; Rom. 3:23).

James 4:17
John 15:8

We cannot repent of something we cannot face

2. I am _Covered_ (Ps. 32:1,5).

3. I am _righteous_ (Ps. 32:6,11; Rom. 4:1-8).
   Our righteousness is not reckoned according to our _behavior_.
   It is reckoned according to our _belief_ (Abraham)

4. I am _Surrounded_
   • by songs of _deliverance_ (Ps. 32:7)
   • by the LORD's unfailing _love_ (Ps. 32:10)

   John 15:11.
   Zephaniah 3:17.

5. I am a _lesson_ (Ps. 51:12-13). *teach transgressors, Your ways.*

Because I am forgiven by God, I can _celebrate_ _life_.

1. John Eaton, *The Psalms* (New York: Continnuum International Publishing Group, 2003), 148.
2. Warren Baker, gen. ed., *The Complete Word Study Dictionary OT* (Chattanooga, TN: AMG Publishers, 1994), #5375.
3. Spiros Zodhiates, gen. ed., *The Complete Word Study Dictionary NT* (Chattanooga, TN: AMG Publishers, 1992), #5055.

The Unrelenting Sword

Day 1
Family Secrets

Day 2
Bring Home the Banished

Day 3
An Abandoned Throne

Day 4
Traitors and Friends

Day 5
If Only

DAY ONE
Family Secrets

TODAY'S TREASURE

"In the course of time, Amnon son of David fell in love with Tamar, the beautiful sister of Absalom son of David." 2 Samuel 13:1

God's Word speaks to virtually every issue plaguing our society. We will see His Word boldly penetrate the heart of the family this week. As Nathan's prophecy regarding David's sin comes to pass, turmoil escalates and David's responses reveal he was a far more effective king than father. We have volumes to learn about family dynamics and the cost of ignoring family problems.

I want to warn you. This week's material may prick some wounds or surface some old scars, especially if you've ever had serious family problems. Let's be honest. Who hasn't? Deep healing awaits us if we face our hurts. Let's courageously learn from David's mistakes and maybe from some of our own. God's desire is to restore us no matter which side of a family calamity we're on. Keep that in mind all week. God is both merciful and just.

By heaping sin on sin and refusing to repent for a year, David dreadfully increased the discipline he received. Week 8 comes crashing in like a tidal wave with the fulfillment of Nathan's prophecy. Begin today with a reminder of the prophecy in 2 Samuel 12:10.

What would happen to David because he had despised God and taken the wife of Uriah to be his own?

The sword would never depart from your house.

We have a sobering reminder—God is faithful even when His promise is judgment. Ask God to give you a teachable spirit. Read 2 Samuel 13:1-22.

Identify the children of David listed in verses 1 and 2 and any information you learn about them.

Amnon   2 Sam 3 V2 - first born - Ahinoan
Absolom   V 3. third son - Maacah.
Tamar   sister of Absalom

People often say, "You can learn a lot about a person just by looking at his friends." What can you learn about Amnon by looking at his friend Jonadab?

3: 3   Jonadab was a very shrewd man.
Schemer

"Now, therefore, the sword will never depart from your house, because you despised me and took the wife of Uriah the Hittite to be your own."
2 SAMUEL 12:10

171

Which of the following describe Tamar's attempts to reason with Amnon?
- ☐ She reminded him of his betrothal to another woman.
- ☑ She said his actions would be considered wicked in Israel.
- ☑ She asked him to consider the disgrace she would suffer.
- ☐ She told him she would have to tell their father.
- ☑ She suggested that he ask David for her hand in marriage.

Why do you think Amnon's love turned so quickly to hate?

repulsion of the victim of his crime.

Why was Tamar wearing a richly ornamented robe?

V18. This was the kind of garment the virgin daughters of the king wore.

In the margin describe the reactions of the three individuals to the crime against Tamar in verses 19-22.

Tamar

mourned, wept. desolate

Absalom

comforting & taking care of Tamar. Silent hatred of Amnon.

David

furious - did not do anything.

These verses are replete with tragedy. The focus was a beautiful young virgin daughter of the king, no doubt awaiting the man she would one day marry. The events in chapter 13 are scandalous even by today's standards and as painful as the horrid descriptions of rapes we read in a big city paper.

The tragic irony of her dress touches my heart. The richly ornamented robe was her cloak of dignity and honor. She ripped the fabric of her robe as surely as Amnon had ripped the fabric of her honor. His crime against her was heinous. I am acutely aware that many who read these words have been victims of rape. I deeply desire to handle this subject with tenderness and reverence. I have asked God to pour His Spirit through me so that I will neither be untrue to Him or to you.

Our first reaction is to assign appropriate responsibility. All wrong, fault, and blame for the rape belongs to the perpetrator—Amnon. Strangely, but typically, Tamar also fell victim to all three men surrounding this event. Consider Amnon, Absalom, and David's roles in Tamar's life.

Amnon was David's firstborn. Ironically, his name means "trustworthy" and "faithful."[1] Obviously he was neither. We see the immediate evidence of a father's influence on his son. In a nation where polygamy was forbidden, Amnon had watched his father take one wife after another. As far as Amnon could see, his father never wanted anything he did not ultimately get. Interesting, Bathsheba and Tamar were described by the same adjective in our first introductions to each of them.

According to 2 Samuel 11:2; 13:1, both women were ... *beautiful*

Like his father, Amnon saw something beautiful and determined to have it. He gave no consideration to the other party involved. Only his lust mattered. He literally became sin-sick to the point of stopping at nothing to satisfy his appetite. Tamar pled with him to spare her disgrace and his reputation, but "he refused to listen."

I found one of the most sickening moments in the tragic events to be Amnon's immediate reaction. Amnon hated her with intense hatred.

Read Genesis 16:1-6. What comparison can you make between Sarai's reaction to the sin she had sown and Amnon's reaction to his sin?

Sarah mistreated Hagar.

We humans often practice a kind of blame shifting. When we have done something sinful and shameful, <u>we blame our actions on someone else</u>—often the <u>victim of our behavior.</u> Ultimately, Sarai treated Hagar just the way Amnon treated Tamar centuries later. Did you notice in 2 Samuel 13:17 that Amnon "called his personal servant"? Amnon had to know that servants talk. He did everything possible to increase Tamar's feeling of shame and disgrace.

In the story of Hagar and Sarai, God did not ignore Hagar's pain. In her rejection she discovered that God is *El Roi*—the God who sees (Gen. 16:13). Surely God was just as faithful to Tamar as she mourned before Him, completely innocent of any sin. He did not look away for an instant. Tamar lived the rest of her life in desolation, but ultimately God will replace her tattered robe and cover her with finest white linen, and she will stand before Him once again the virgin daughter of a king.

We can also be assured that God will deal appropriately with <u>Amnon.</u> We see <u>no sign of repentance.</u> When he sees the face of the righteous Judge, he may utter words like those in Revelation 6:16, "They called to the mountains and rocks, 'Fall on us and hide us from the face of him who sits on the throne and from the wrath of the Lamb!' "

Absalom was Tamar's brother. Both Absalom and David reacted inappropriately toward Tamar and the crime she suffered. Absalom obviously discovered his sister in extreme distress. He guessed the nature of the crime against her from the tearing of the virgin's robe. No one can doubt Absalom's love for his sister, but his reaction to her could only have added further injury. Countless victims of rape and molestation have been hurt by similar advice. Absalom told her to "<u>be quiet</u>" and not "<u>take this thing to heart</u>" (v. 20).

> When we have done something sinful and shameful, we blame our actions on someone else.

cover up, ignore.

What was Absalom advising Tamar to do? Respond in the margin.

Perhaps you have been the victim of shame in some way. If so, I offer you company today. I've been there too. When I was a small child, someone I should have been able to trust violated God-drawn boundaries and victimized me. The ramifications in my life have been almost inestimable.

Friends and family members of victims often ask me what they can possibly say to their hurting loved one. I know from my own experience that the most important thing anyone can say to a victim of a shame-breeding crime is, "I am so sorry. I love you, and I support you." We often think we need to come up with answers when another has been hurt. Sometimes the words of comforters are well-meaning but hurtful.

Have you ever experienced someone giving well-meaning advice or answers when you needed love and support? ☐ yes ☐ no   If so, what about their words added to rather than took away from your pain?

Simple words like "I love you" and "I support you" work best for those of us who are not counselors. In case you've been a victim of shame and no one has ever said these words before: I am so sorry.

    Absalom's advice to Tamar was to keep the secret and pretend nothing happened. Unfortunately, he took his own advice. He never said a word to Amnon, either good or bad. But his hatred for him would finally cause him to lose control. You see, overwhelming feelings cannot be stuffed. They invariably turn inward, take the person prisoner, then often force a break-out with tragic consequences.

Can you remember a time in your life when you had to remain silent on an overwhelming issue? ☐ yes ☐ no   If so, what emotions did your silence evoke in you? Write about it in the margin.

Take a look at David's own words in Psalm 39:1-3 as he described an attempt to keep his mouth shut when he was overwhelmed with emotion. Describe the impact of silence on him.

 V2 my anguish increased,
my heart grew hot within me, the fire burned.

David's very next words in Psalm 39:4 were "Show me, O Lord." Pour out your heart to God when emotions threaten to overtake you, and ask Him what to do next. He will provide positive outlets for painful emotions.

    Absalom was wrong to tell Tamar to be quiet and not take it to heart. The shame was crushing her to pieces. He minimized the significance of the terrible crime against her. She was invited to live with him, but she was not invited to be honest with him. She was left desolate—like the living dead.

    David was Tamar's father. Absalom's immediate assumption of Amnon's guilt speaks volumes. Amnon's lack of character was common knowledge. David should have dealt with Amnon before disaster struck. Then after the crime, David still refused to do anything. If only David had applied the wisdom of Psalm 39 to this tragedy, things would have been so different. How did David react (2 Sam. 13:21)? We see just one description: He was furious. What did he do about the crime? Absolutely nothing.

Why didn't David take control of his family tragedy? I believe the enemy may have been working on David just as he works on us when we blow it. Satan uses sin and failure against us so that even after sincere repentance we often remain disabled. He whispers questions in our ears like, "How dare you expect obedience from your children after what you've done? How dare you walk into church again? You hypocrite."

Two wrongs don't make a right. If we blow it as a parent, spouse, servant, employee, or leader, we should fall before God in complete repentance and ask Him what we must do to cooperate with restoration. Then we should follow Him in utmost obedience. Restoration does not mean you can no longer stand for the truth because you fell. Restoration means you must stand.

v8 Do not gloat over me, my enemy! Though I have fallen, I will rise. Though I sit in darkness, the Lord will be my light.

Micah 7:8-9 are two of my favorite verses. Write your own personal paraphrase of the verses in the margin.

v9 .... He will bring me out into the light; I will see all his righteousness

David allowed his failure to disable him to lead his household in righteousness. He had been forgiven by God but he chose not to live like a forgiven person. He allowed his own sense of guilt to handicap him as a parent.

Do you see how crippling our unwillingness to fully accept the Lord's forgiveness can be? ☑ yes ☐ no   Why do you think God can forgive us but we often have difficulty fully accepting His forgiveness?

David and his family would have been better off had he never fallen at all, but he could not change the past. He could, however, learn from his mistakes, become zealous for righteousness in his life and household, and affect the present with God on his side.

"Be ye angry and sin not" (Eph. 4:26, KJV) does not mean "be angry and do nothing." God created anger. It energizes us to respond when something is wrong. David needed to channel his anger and respond to the crime committed in his household. No weaker house exists than one that lacks appropriate authority. Lack of authority is a breeding ground for untold recklessness and sin. Just ask Tamar.

Has your outlook on victims changed at all as a result of what we've learned from Tamar's tragedy? ☐ yes ☐ no If so, how?

No excuses for wrong deeds & attitudes.

I pray you continue to allow God to bring you victory in vulnerable areas. God is faithful. He has miraculously escorted many women just like Tamar through their grief. I can't explain it, but I've seen it with my own eyes.

DAY 2

Bring Home the Banished

TODAY'S TREASURE

"Like water spilled on the ground, which cannot be recovered, so we must die. But God does not take away life; instead, he devises ways so that a banished person may not remain estranged from him." 2 Samuel 14:14

After the intensity of previous lessons, the words of 2 Samuel 14:14 are like summer showers on parched land. May it motivate us through some difficult passages ahead. Our present lesson will require more reading than usual. Ask God to keep you focused. Pray that He will speak to you through His Word.

Read 2 Samuel 13:23-39. Reflect on your previous lesson. Two years had passed since Amnon's crime against Tamar. Think creatively.

In the margin describe what you think might have been going on during those years in the minds of the people listed.

Tamar
hopeless, no future

Amnon
thinks he won't be punished.

Absalom
Schemed, festered hate.

David
unable to act due to his own sin

What evidence could you offer to support the idea that Absalom was counting on his father's unwillingness to attend his celebration?
The king & his officials are invited.

Did you note the false first report David received and that Jonadab was the one who told the king not to be concerned? How do you suppose Jonadab knew that only Amnon was dead?
Amnon was his friend.

How was Jonadab identified in 2 Samuel 13:3?
Shrewd.

Based on verse 32, why do you think the "shrewd" Jonadab might have played both sides of the conflict between Amnon and Absalom?
wants influence - power.

When they returned, what was the condition of David's sons?
wailing loudly

Check the statements in the margin that accurately describe the conclusion of the events of 2 Samuel 13.

☐ Absalom returned with his brothers.

☑ Absalom fled to Geshur and stayed for three years.

☑ David longed to go to Absalom.

☐ David disowned Absalom.

☐ David was inconsolable over Amnon's death.

Two years passed. Bitterness multiplied in Absalom's heart. That's the nature of bitterness. It never stays in its cage. Absalom must have watched and waited to see if his father would call Amnon to account for his crime. His father didn't.

Absalom waited for an opportunity. He devised an elaborate scheme to summon Amnon to his house. The time of sheep shearing was a festive occasion with huge family celebrations. Absalom seized the opportunity, counting on his father to continue in distancing himself from family obligations and celebrations. When David refused to come, Absalom requested Amnon's presence in his place, assuming no one would be suspicious. Customarily, the oldest son represented his father in the father's absence.

David may have been suspicious since he questioned Absalom's choice, but he may have concluded no grounds existed to refuse Amnon the right to attend the celebration. David sent Amnon and the rest of his sons—never to see his eldest again. You may have noticed Absalom did not take the sword to Amnon himself, but, like his father, involved subordinates in the crime. Irony rings from the mouth of a coward who shoves others into action with the words, "Be strong and brave" (v. 28).

Jonadab reared his ugly head in another scandalous scheme. He would never have known Absalom's plans had he not become his confidant. I wonder if he ever told Absalom that he was the one who devised the scheme against Tamar. Not likely. The tragedy ends with one son dead, one son missing, and a father grief stricken. David had two responses toward Absalom after Amnon's death: He mourned for him and longed for him. How odd. Remember when David became furious over Amnon's sin but did nothing? He had the appropriate feelings but inappropriate actions. Once again David *felt* the right thing and *did* the wrong thing. See for yourself. Read 2 Samuel 14:1-33.

Why do you think Joab devised a method somewhat like a parable to get through to David?

It was not easy/possible to speak directly to David about Absalom's murder of Amnon

You've had an opportunity to see today's treasure in context. What does God devise ways to do?

He devises ways so that a banished person may not remain estranged from him

Which of the following statements best reflects your responses toward David's actions in verse 24?

☑ I feel sorry for Absalom.   ☑ David's actions make me mad.

☑ I feel sorry for David.   ☐ Absalom got what he deserved.

☐ I don't blame David; I probably would have done the same thing.

☐ Other:

How long did Absalom live in Jerusalem "without seeing the king's face"?
☐ 3 years   ☐ 1 year   ☑ 2 years   ☐ 5 years

Cousin Joab refused to come when Absalom summoned, but Absalom finally got his attention by setting his field on fire. I think I've seen some children use the same method. Wise parents engage before some form of arson occurs.

Was the meeting between David and Absalom what you expected or did you imagine their reunion differently? Explain in the margin.

Very little detail about what happened, nothing about what I imag[...]

We've just taken a look at the complications of family dynamics. What in the world was David doing? His heart was too complex for us to risk conjecture, yet one thing is obvious. Again he refused to take action regarding his family.

Have you ever experienced the frustration of someone close to you refusing to take responsibility? ☐ yes ☐ no   If so, describe some of the things you felt or experienced.

Joab had obviously witnessed David's irresponsibility toward Absalom for as long as he intended. He devised a plan to capture David's attention. Through a concocted story of a woman and her prodigal son, Joab convinced David to summon Absalom. I believe Joab used this method because he had seen God use a similar approach through Nathan once before (2 Sam. 12:1-7).

We sometimes resist seeing the sin in our own lives. When the preacher uses an illustration of someone else's sin, we're often ready to judge just like David. Then the blade of conviction slices our hearts and the Holy Spirit says, "You are that person." Twice the method worked to penetrate David's heart. More than twice God has used this approach to penetrate mine.

David granted Joab's request and let him summon Absalom. Joab was so thrilled, he "fell face to the ground … and he blessed the king" (v. 22). Joab joyfully hastened to bring the young man home, no doubt picturing the emotional reunion of father and son—only to be met with these words from the king: "He must go to his own house; he must not see my face" (v. 24).

I'm so grateful God will not call us to the heavenly Jerusalem and say, "She must not see My face." Jesus is preparing us a place in our Father's house where we will see His face. I've waited all my life to see His beautiful face.

David did not respond like the father in Christ's parable—the father who searched the horizon daily for his son to come home. That father, who represents our Heavenly Father, caught a glimpse of his son in the distance and "ran to his son, threw his arms around him and kissed him" (Luke 15:20).

Some things in life are do-overs. God sometimes gives us a second chance to do something right. Some chances never come back around. The chance for David and Absalom to be completely reunited in their hearts would

"In my Father's house are many rooms; if it were not so, I would have told you. I am going there to prepare a place for you."
JOHN 14:2

"No longer will there be any curse. The throne of God and of the Lamb will be in the city, and his servants will serve him. They will see his face, and his name will be on their foreheads."
REVELATION 22:3-4

not come again. By the time David finally received Absalom, his son's heart was cold. Do you find yourself like me, wishing God had told you more about David and Absalom's reunion? I believe God didn't tell us more because there was nothing more to tell. Nothing else happened. The scene had all the right ingredients: Absalom bowing down; the king kissing his son. Only one thing was missing—the heart. The actions of David and his son were generated by custom, not emotion. Fearing his son would do something more than set Joab's field on fire, David summoned Absalom to appease him, not accept him. Absalom sought his father's face to force David to look him in the eye, not to beg forgiveness like the prodigal.

Have you ever had a chance to be reconciled with someone but resisted? ☐ yes ☐ no   If so, for what reasons did you resist?

Did the lack of reconciliation cost you in any way? ☐ yes ☐ no
If so, how? Respond in the margin.

God is never in the wrong when He and one of His children are separated, yet He devises ways so that the banished person may not remain estranged from Him. Never underestimate the significance of timing when it comes to mending. You may not get another chance.

DAY 3
An Abandoned Throne

TODAY'S TREASURE

"Then the king said to Zadok, 'Take the ark of God back into the city. If I find favor in the Lord's eyes, he will bring me back and let me see it and his dwelling place again.'" 2 Samuel 15:25

King David and Absalom finally saw each other face to face. Sadly, however, their reunion was too little too late. Today we will see evidence of Absalom's deep dissatisfaction about his encounter with his father. Their meeting did nothing but fuel his bitterness. The relationship between David and Absalom teaches us an important object lesson: Reuniting and reconciliation can be two very different things.

What do you believe is the difference between reuniting and true reconciliation?

Many couples previously separated have returned to one another to live under the same roof for the sake of the children, finances, religious convictions, or the family business. They may live together the rest of their lives without healing or dealing with the problems. Reuniting is one thing. Reconciliation is another. One difference is the presence or absence of misery. We'll see this precept today. Read 2 Samuel 15:1-12.

What was Absalom trying to accomplish with the people of Israel?

Rebellion against David.
Gaining their admiration & trust.

What evidences do you see that Absalom was trying to present himself as a very approachable alternative to his unapproachable father?

"If only I were appointed judge in the land.

According to verse 10, Absalom sent secret messengers throughout the tribes of Israel to say: "As soon as you hear the sound of the trumpets, then say Absalom is _king in Hebron._ "

Absalom tried not only to steal the hearts of the people but also David's counselor, Ahithophel (v. 12). Why do you think he wanted Ahithophel?

Ahitopel was Bathsheba's grandfather.

Absalom was dissatisfied by his meeting with his father. What was wrong with him? Possibly he suffered from the same thing many adults suffer from today. When Absalom was a child, his daddy was his hero. Plenty of shortcomings existed, but the boy could not see them until one day an emotional bombshell hit home—exploding in the bedroom of the oldest son.

Although people got mad, no one cleaned up the mess. Lives continued to be torn by the shrapnel no one ever swept away. David did not—perhaps could not—live up to Absalom's expectations. The results were devastating. The revenge he had taken on Amnon was not enough. The fact that his father still called him a son was not enough. He still cried out for vengeance and was determined his father would pay.

Obviously, Absalom tried everything he knew—good and bad—to get his father's attention. He could not get to David through his home, so he determined to get to him through the throne.

Absalom had specific reasons for every move he made. Each morning he arrived with a chariot and an entourage of men and horses. He looked impressive as he stood at the gate to the city. Absalom called out to anyone entering the city with a complaint, making them feel important. He was quite an effective politician. I wouldn't be surprised if he kissed a few babies too.

Absalom went to the trouble of working his scheme for one reason: to steal the hearts of the men of Israel. He continued to work through every step of his plan for four years, waiting for the right moment to stage his coup.

Absalom could not get to David through his home, so he determined to get to him through the throne.

Absalom spent two years waiting for David to punish Amnon, three years in hiding after killing Amnon, two years in Jerusalem waiting for David to receive him, and four years working his devious plan of vengeance against his father. Unforgiveness and retaliation stole eleven years of his life. Eleven years is a long time for anyone to seethe and harbor bitterness.

Has anger or bitterness stolen years of your life? ☐ yes ☐ no   If so, estimate how many, if possible. _____

Has your season of bitterness or anger ended? ☐ yes ☐ no   If so, how did it finally end? If not, why do you still feel bitter or angry?

God tells us to forgive those who hurt us, but He never qualifies the command by saying forgive only when someone asks for your forgiveness. He simply says forgive (Luke 6:37). Christ set the perfect example in Luke 23:34.

Had those who crucified Jesus asked for forgiveness? No. Had they admitted their wrong? No. Then why did Christ ask God to forgive them? I believe His purpose was not for His persecutors to be let off the hook but for Christ to disavow bitterness. He chose to continue His painful destiny with the love of the Father in Him. He made no room for unforgiveness.

David had never asked for forgiveness. He had never taken his rightful place of authority over family events. David made plenty of mistakes, but Absalom did not have to follow suit. He could have called on the mercy of God and forgiven David for failing him, even if his father never admitted how wrongly he had handled his family. God would have held David responsible, and Absalom would have been free. Instead, he locked himself in the prison of bitterness where character eroded in the darkness of his soul. We often resist forgiveness by saying, "It's too difficult to forgive." Forgiveness may be excruciating for a moment. Anger and bitterness are excruciating for a lifetime.

> "Jesus said, 'Father, forgive them, for they do not know what they are doing.' And they divided up his clothes by casting lots."
> **LUKE 23:34**

Have you ever resisted forgiving because the person never took responsibility and asked forgiveness? ☐ yes ☐ no   If so, can you see any ways in which your unwillingness to forgive hurt you more than the person who injured you? Write about this in the margin.

Often the people who hurt us don't realize the magnitude of their actions. The people who mocked and crucified Christ had no idea they were dealing with the very fullness of God Himself. The man who hurt me when I was a small child had no idea how much I would suffer for decades to come. Can we muster the courage to say regarding those who hurt us: God forgive them and help me to forgive them?

When we harbor bitterness and refuse to forgive, we become our own persecutors. While we blame the other person, we really continue to injure ourselves. What percentage of Absalom's 11 years of bitterness—and ruined life—would you say was David's responsibility? What percentage of responsibility do you suppose should be assigned to Absalom?

Those who hurt us often have no idea how deeply we will suffer. If we follow Christ's example, we will be free. We can save ourselves a lot of heartache! Learning to forgive even if no one takes responsibility for his or her actions will save us from the kind of misery that ultimately destroyed Absalom.

Absalom may have been miserable, but he was not dumb. If his plan were a chess game, stealing Ahithophel was checkmate. Ahithophel was a highly respected advisor and Bathsheba's grandfather. "And so the conspiracy gained strength" (v. 12). Read 2 Samuel 15:13-37.

What did David do when he heard the news of Absalom's conspiracy?
☑ He fled. ☐ He commissioned his army.
☐ He went to Absalom. ☐ He stood by his throne.

How did the people respond to David's departure (v. 23)?
☐ with jeering ☐ with rejoicing ☑ with weeping ☐ with shouting

According to verse 30, where did David and all the people go?
the Mount of Olives

What was David's prayer concerning Ahithophel?
☐ "O LORD, let him return to my charge."
☐ "O LORD, take the life of my conspirator!"
☐ "O LORD, open his eyes to Absalom's wicked heart!"
☑ "O LORD, turn Ahithophel's counsel into foolishness."

Is this the same David God anointed as His chosen king? The one who conquered the giant? The one God prospered like no other? Did he not know that God gave him the kingdom and only He could take it away? How could he run from his throne? David found himself right in the middle of a cycle of self-appointed failure. Stricken with grief and dressed for mourning, he and his loyal followers trudged the Mount of Olives, where people once worshiped.

There on the Mount of Olives, continuing up to the summit, an amazing thing happened: "David prayed" (v. 31). Little by little, things began to happen. David had run from his throne practically hopeless. "We must flee, or none of us will escape from Absalom" (v. 14). But somewhere on top of that mountain, David got down on his knees and prayed. See his prayer for yourself. God had him write it down. It's Psalm 3.

Read the psalm. In the margin write your impressions of David's heart and state of mind as he wrote these words from God's holy hill.

God did not answer every one of those requests immediately, but He returned enough strength to David for him to begin walking in faith, not fear.

Some years ago I came upon an isolated, abandoned church and found the front door open. The musty smell and mildewed curtain did not keep me from feeling the Spirit of the living God fall on me and the strength of God-fearing forefathers within me. I could almost hear the congregation singing. I received such courage there. It was a precious moment to me.

On the Mount of Olives where people used to worship, David confronted the Spirit of God who had grown accustomed to being honored there. Still hovering—just in case someone might follow in the footsteps of old and worship once more. Someone did.

Many years later Jesus trudged that same path and found strength to walk on to a cross. I wonder if Christ ever thought of David when He prayed on that same mountain. One thing is certain: as He sat on the Mount of Olives on the eve of His crucifixion, He was thinking about us. You don't have to climb a mountain to find strength to fulfill your God-given calling. He's as close as a whisper. He's as close as a prayer.

DAY 4
Traitors and Friends

TODAY'S TREASURE

"Absalom and all the men of Israel said, 'The advice of Hushai the Arkite is better than that of Ahithophel.' For the LORD had determined to frustrate the good advice of Ahithophel in order to bring disaster on Absalom." 2 Samuel 17:14

Begin by praying that God will speak to you through His Word. Today's study will drive us further into the conflict between a refugee king and his embittered son. The conflict in the kingdom rekindled old supporters of Saul who were still nursing grudges against David. Read 2 Samuel 16:1-14.

For the sake of review, identify the following individuals. Look back at 2 Samuel 9 if necessary.

Mephibosheth *Son of Jonathan, crippled.*

Ziba *Servant of Saul's household*

How did Ziba take advantage of David's vulnerability?

Supplied donkeys, food, wine.

Why do you think David might have so readily believed Mephibosheth had betrayed him?

Trusted Ziba

What did David give Ziba?

All that belonged to Mephibosheth.

Shimei son of Gera insulted David in several ways. Check any of the statements that are not accurate descriptions of Shimei's actions.

- ☐ He cursed him.
- ☑ He threw stones at him.
- ☑ He struck David.
- ☐ He told David he got what he deserved.

How did Abishai respond to Shimei's actions?

Wanted to kill him.

Why wouldn't David let Abishai defend him?

the Lord has told him (Shimei) to

Restate David's hope in verse 12 in your own words.

It may be that the Lord will see my distress and repay me w. good.

Have you noticed how mean-spirited people will kick a person when he's down? David had seemed invincible, yet the moment he appeared vulnerable opportunists descended on him like vultures. David had no reason to disbelieve Ziba. If his Absalom, his own flesh and blood, could betray him, why not the adult son he adopted? David had suffered so much betrayal that he assumed no one was beyond turning on him.

Have you ever felt like someone took advantage of you at a time when you were vulnerable? ☐ yes ☐ no   If so, in the margin describe what happened in general terms without mentioning any names.

Nothing makes us as vulnerable as family problems. Personal difficulties may cause us to lack discernment. David told Ziba he would give him everything Mephibosheth owned without confirming Ziba's claims. His vulnerability caused him to believe the worst and respond with haste rather than prudence.

We are wise to be careful about the decisions and assumptions we make when we are stressed. We will tend to react rather than respond. Grief counselors tell those who have recently lost loved ones to avoid making life-altering decisions too quickly. When pain is acute, we often can't discriminate properly between good and bad decisions.

Have you or someone you love ever made a poor or hasty decision at a vulnerable time? ☐ yes ☐ no   If so, in the margin briefly explain.

I can't think of a situation when sound, godly advice is more valuable than times of great vulnerability. David could have used a little advice before he gave Mephibosheth's belongings to Ziba. Unfortunately, Ahithophel, his head counselor, was unavailable. He was busy advising Absalom. No wonder David was vulnerable. On the heels of Ziba's claims about Mephibosheth, David encountered a vile man by the name of Shimei. He was profane and violent. He began to curse David and throw stones at the deposed king. I have a feeling the words hurt more than the stones. The man's actions were wrong, but David feared his words might be right. Through all his ups and downs, victories and failures, we've never seen David walk through this kind of humiliation.

Jesus also walked the road of humiliation. People spat on Him and slapped Him in the face. Unlike David, He was completely innocent. He could have summoned the armies of heaven or ordered the earth to quake, yet He was the One "who for the joy set before him endured the cross, scorning its shame, and sat down at the right hand of the throne of God" (Heb. 12:2).

With just a word or two, describe a time you experienced humiliation.

Like Christ, we could be in the middle of God's will and find ourselves on a path of humiliation. Or like David, we could suffer the further humiliation of knowing we chose our own path. God is merciful to still meet us on the humiliating paths of our lives whether or not we chose them through rebellion.

Consider the timing of David's obstacle—just as David was regaining a shred of strength. Coincidental? No way! Just when Satan suspects we are regaining a spark of hope, he hastens to greet us with discouragement and rejection. Notice David's response to Abishai's request to avenge David's persecution: "My son, who is of my own flesh, is trying to take my life. How much more, then, this Benjamite! Leave him alone" (v. 11). I believe David was saying: *My own beloved son has rejected me. There is nothing anyone can do to injure me any more deeply. Let him go ahead. Maybe I deserve it.*

I want to express something to you that I hope you'll receive with your whole heart: We can still cry out to God for help even when we think we're getting what we deserve. God comes to us even when our pain is self-inflicted. Times of humiliation and persecution do not have to be permanent injuries.

Few experiences are more exhausting than keeping your head up through the unjust attacks, but all journeys have an end. Finally, "The king and all the people with him arrived at their destination exhausted. And there he refreshed himself" (v. 14).

We can still cry out to God for help even when we think we're getting what we deserve.

How can you refresh yourself when you've been down a rocky path?

Read 2 Samuel 16:15–17:29. In the margin list the names of everyone who came to David's aid in 2 Samuel 17.

Sometimes when we're down, it's hard to see how many people have come to our aid. We're often so focused on our circumstances we don't realize how many people God sends to encourage us. At times I've cried out, "God, please help me get through this difficult time," or "Please help me meet this deadline."

I am often humbled as God opens my eyes to all He's done and says to my heart, "I was the One who sent Mary Helen to your house with home-baked cookies. I was the One who told Nancy to send you a note of encouragement. I was the One who gave you that good laugh. I've been there all along."

Think of a time when you have been down or in vulnerable circumstances. Who did God send to encourage you?

God was there all along, wasn't He? He was there for David, too. We will have missed the turning point of the conflict between David and Absalom if we miss the importance of God "frustrating" Ahithophel's advice. Absalom's decision not to follow his counsel led to David's upper hand in the battle for the kingdom. Ahithophel was a traitor to his king. Note several parallels between David's betrayer and Christ's betrayer many centuries later. Ahithophel and Judas had several things in common:

- *Both were chosen members of a very important cabinet.* A factor that certainly separates King David from the King of kings is that Christ knew Judas would betray Him, yet Jesus loved him and treated him like His other disciples.
- *Both betrayed their masters and went with the crowd.* In their own ways, both Ahithophel and Judas defected from what they believed to be a losing team to sign up with the obvious winners. We're so tempted to think numbers mean power. What a lesson to be learned. Don't let the enemy make you think you're on a losing team. Remember, looks can be very deceiving. Ahithophel would testify from the grave if he could. Don't let Satan tempt you to betray the One who promised victory because it looks like the bigger team is winning. When the final judgment comes and the few who took the narrow road oppose the masses who followed the wide, safety will not be in numbers.
- *The last parallel between Ahithophel and Judas is their tragic end.* Note in the margin verses what happened to both betrayers.

"When Ahithophel saw that his advice had not been followed, he saddled his donkey and set out for his house in his hometown. He put his house in order and then hanged himself. So he died and was buried in his father's tomb."
2 SAMUEL 17:23

"So Judas threw the money into the temple and left. Then he went away and hanged himself."
MATTHEW 27:5

As we conclude, consider one last question. Why did Ahithophel betray David while Hushai remained faithful? Hushai risked exposure and death by entering the household of the enemy. He helped buy time for his king by "counseling" and deceiving Absalom so that David could strengthen his forces. Why did Hushai respond so differently to a leader who appeared to be on his way out? First Chronicles 27:33 offers a beautiful explanation.

Fill in the blanks from 1 Chronicles 27:33. Ahithophel was the king's
counselor. Hushai the Arkite was the king's _friend_.

You and I have a "friend who sticks closer than a brother" (Prov. 18:24) for "Greater love has no one than this, that he lay down his life for his friends" (John 15:13). No matter what happens, no matter who rejects you or humiliates you, He will never betray you. Stay faithful, believer. You are on the winning team. The King of all kings will return and take His rightful throne.

DAY 5
If Only

TODAY'S TREASURE

"As he [David] went, he said: 'O my son Absalom! My son, my son Absalom! If only I had died instead of you—O Absalom, my son, my son!'"
2 Samuel 18:33

We've seen an emotional match involving two opponents torn between love and hate. Today we see one go down tragically. We can't change the story. We can only agree to be changed through it. Read 2 Samuel 18:1-18.

Why do you think David might have wanted to lead the battle himself?

To inspire his army or to keep Absalom safe.

Why didn't David's men want him to go to battle?

V3: You are worth 10,000 of us.

What were David's specific instructions to Joab (v. 5)?

Be gentle with the young man Absalom for my sake.

What strange accident happened to Absalom?

His hair got caught in the large oak tree.

How does the soldier represent a direct contrast to Joab in verses 10-14?

Obedient to the king's command

Why do you think Joab killed Absalom even though he had been commanded to spare him?

What things did Joab and his men do with Absalom's body?
- ☑ threw it in a pit in the forest
- ☐ took it back to David
- ☐ burned it
- ☐ other:

According to verse 18, what had Absalom done during his lifetime?

Erected a pillar in the King's Valley as a monument to himself.

At one time Absalom was a handsome and compassionate man. He loved his sister deeply, grieving the shame Amnon heaped on her. He made a place for his desolate sister in his own home. He named his daughter Tamar in her honor. He tried to do the right things for Tamar, but he ended up doing all the wrong things for himself.

Absalom wasn't the first nor the last person to confront the cold, hard fact that life isn't fair. Some have experienced more harshness than others. For example, a couple in my area recently discovered their eleven-year-old son missing from their home, only to learn that one of their close family friends had kidnapped and murdered him for money. No doubt you know someone who has faced—or is now facing—tragedy.

What have you or someone you care about experienced that you consider the harshest evidence of life's unfairness?

Have you been able to come to grips with it in any way? ☐ yes ☐ no

Life is not fair, but God is. He will ultimately settle all scores and make all wrongs right. God would have eventually taken care of Amnon, but Absalom could not wait. He decided to take care of Amnon himself.

The real issue for us is not whether or not life is fair. The real issue is "How will I respond to the difficult and painful events that occur in my life?" Ultimately our response to difficulty becomes far more important than the hardship itself. The rape of Tamar seems to have launched Absalom on his path of destruction, but his response to the rape was the key. He had the choice to respond in wisdom or in bitterness.

My older daughter was always relatively easy to discipline. When she was a little girl and misbehaved, all I had to do was walk toward the drawer that held a flimsy plastic spatula and she would sweetly say, "I feel better!" Though she could not state the situation clearly, she chose to respond to discipline in the least painful way. "I feel better."

One day a good friend of mine grabbed that same spatula and spanked her little boy for repeatedly disobeying her. The son wasn't hurt, but he was as mad as a hornet. Amanda stood right next to him while his mother paddled him and continued to ask, "Do you feel better?" If looks could kill, my precious angel would have been dead! He finally screamed, "No, I not feel better!"

Those words could apply to Absalom. He didn't feel better after Amnon was in the grave. He didn't feel better when David let him return to Jerusalem without punishment. He didn't feel better after he was summoned to the king's quarters and reunited with his father. After stealing the hearts of his father's people, he still didn't feel any better. Absalom ultimately possessed as little self-control as the brother he despised—and his lack of self-control killed him.

Another figure came to my mind as I thought about Absalom's tragic end. His name was Samson and he also lived outside the restraints of self-control all of his adult life. He finally went too far, but he didn't realize he was caught until it was too late. "He … thought, 'I'll go out as before and shake myself free.' But he did not know that the LORD had left him" (Judg. 16:20).

We can only shake ourselves free so many times. If we keep flirting with disaster, we're finally going to get trapped. Whatever the issue, unrestrained passions will ultimately catch up with us. Samson learned the hard way. So did Absalom. Can you imagine the thoughts going through the head of that beautiful but troubled young man as he struggled to set himself free?

The picture of his death was the picture of his life: the noose of bitterness choking the captive's cry. In the end, those close enough to hear him choking no longer cared. Like departing words on a tombstone, we read Absalom's eulogy in verse 18: "Absalom had taken a pillar and erected it in the King's Valley as a monument to himself." At first glance, the verse seems to fit the chapter like a square peg in a round hole. At second glance, the passage relates perfectly to the verse before it.

> Absalom ultimately possessed as little self-control as the brother he despised.

What did the soldiers do after they threw Absalom's body in a big pit?

piled a large heap of rocks over him

Let's do a little research. Check the context of these two Scriptures and record the circumstances under which stones were heaped.

Joshua 4:5-9 *to serve as a memorial that the Jordan was opened for the ark to pass through.*

Joshua 7:20-26 *Achan stoned to death & large pile of rocks. a reminder of the consequences of disobedience & covetousness*

The people of Israel often set up stones as a memorial of a never-to-be-forgotten event. The piles of stones taught lessons—either good or bad. The rocks over the bodies of Achan and Absalom did not just keep wild animals away; they served as a traitor's reminder.

I see great irony in the fact that the record of Absalom's grave and the account of the monument he erected to himself appear together in Scripture. The verses demonstrate that Absalom's death as a traitor remains far more memorable than his self-absorbed life. Through bitterness Absalom's heart became as hard and cold as the pillar he raised. Even though David committed many sins and was unfair to others, his heart did not grow cold.

Read 2 Samuel 18:19-33. Why do you think Ahimaaz ended up lying to David after he had been so anxious to carry the news (v. 29)?

David's concern about Absalom safety.

What did David say when he realized Absalom was dead?

If only I had died instead of you.

I wanted you to write the last words of chapter 18 so that your own hand and heart could experience the repetition of the words, "O Absalom, my son, my son!" The words put chills up a parent's spine, don't they? Suddenly, a heart of tragically suppressed love exploded. Tears he should have cried long ago poured from his eyes. Words he should have said the moment he first saw his prodigal finally burst from his lips: "O my son, Absalom! My son, my son Absalom!" He did not speak about him. He spoke right to him, as if his voice would carry to the depths of the pit where the body lay.

"If only I had died instead of you!"

Death would have been far easier than life without him. What grieving parent hasn't cried exactly those same words? Felt those exact emotions? And where was God when David lost his son? Where was He when a king's own countrymen pierced his son? Where was He when the blood poured forth? The same place He was when He lost His own Son. Thank you for opening your heart to this week's study.

Please try not to miss our next session as we invite God to bring us an extra measure of healing. You are greatly loved.

[handwritten left margin: Not to know neither how you feel.]

Review 2 Samuel 13:20-22.

- "Be quiet now, my sister. … Don't take this thing to __heart__."
- "Tamar lived in her brother Absalom's house, a __desolate__ woman." *[handwritten: to stir... devac... sdit... spec...]*
- "When King David heard all this, he was __furious__."
- "Absalom never said a word to Amnon, either good or bad; he __hated__ Amnon."

[handwritten left margin: Hate kills forgiveness / peace / takes up the love space / 1 John 4:20 / withhold affection / big chasm between / David's emotions / & his deeds]

Two years later: Absalom killed Amnon. Absalom fled to Geshur and remained for three years.

- "The spirit of the king __longed__ to go to Absalom" (2 Sam. 13:39).

Review 2 Samuel 14:21-24.

- "He must go to his own house; he must not __see my face__."

Two years later, after getting Joab's attention, Absalom finally saw his father. The gesture came too late. He spent four years systematically undermining his father's authority and then attempted to overthrow the throne in battle.

[handwritten: Total of 11 years.]

Review 2 Samuel 18:12,31-33.

- "__Protect__ the young man Absalom for my sake" (2 Sam. 18:12).
- "O my son Absalom! My son, my son Absalom!
  __If only I__ had died instead of you—
  O Absalom, my son, my son!"

[handwritten: Absalom 3X / my son 5X]

A Corporate Lesson on Family _Calamity_

1. It is no _respecter_ of _persons_, race, gender.

2. It's _never_ _uncomplicated_.
   sort out what is real & what we have imagined, blame & shame
   2 Sam 13:1, 15

3. It often _involves_ _consequences_.
   victimization,

See Hebrews 12:5-13; Psalm 103:10.

> "Wherefore straighten out the limp hands and the paralyzed knees and
> make straight paths for your feet in order that the lame thing may not
> get turned wrong but rather _be_ _cured_"
> (Heb.12:12-13).[1]

consequences go into discipline ↓ to teach/train healed.

4. It doesn't have to be _irreparable_.
   to forgive & to ask forgiveness humility.

5. If the relationship is irreparable, the individual _need_ _not_ _be_.
   See Psalm 8:3-5.

> "God sets the _lonely_ in _families_, he
> leads forth the prisoners with singing; but the rebellious live
> in a sun-scorched land" (Ps. 68:6).

honor - dignity crowned.
We do not get treated by God like what we deserve.
We have our dignity from God - His image.

1. Richard C. H. Lenski, _The Interpretation of the Epistle to the Hebrews and the Epistle of James_ (Minneapolis, MN: Augsburg Fortress Publishing, 2008), 441.

Back Where He Belonged

Day 1

Crossing the Jordan

Day 2

Unfinished Business

Day 3

The Unwelcomed Sight of an Old Enemy

Day 4

A Great Celebration

Day 5

A Hand Withdrawn

DAY 1
Crossing the Jordan

TODAY'S TREASURE

"He won over the hearts of all the men of Judah as though they were one man. They sent word to the king, 'Return, you and all your men.'"
2 Samuel 19:14

Week 8 ended with Absalom's death and David's broken heart. The father's grief nearly consumed him. Divided loyalties left God's nation in an upheaval. Week 9 ushers David back to the throne where he belonged. No one will hand him his throne. He will take it back with exhausting tenacity.

We see a long season of conflict and crisis take its toll on David, but we also encounter heroes God raised to aid him. Years of turmoil and final exhaustion did not extinguish David's praises. He leads us to a fresh discovery of God's mercy in peculiar circumstances. David's reign remained eventful throughout his 40-year rule. In the later years, he faced more struggles and challenges. Today we concentrate on a chapter of Scripture bulging with information and significant encounters. We will consider each portion with a certain amount of generality and brevity to cover all the bases. Take a moment for prayer and begin the first reading. Read 2 Samuel 19:1-14.

Based on verse 2, how do you believe David's men felt about him?

for the whole army the victory that day was turned into mourning.

What do you think of Joab's method of motivating David?

tough love? Self serving.

Do you think Joab may have had a personal reason for not wanting to see David mourning? If so, what was the reason?

He killed Absalom + disobeyed David.

God's nation would not split into a Northern Kingdom (Israel) and a Southern Kingdom (Judah) until after the death of Solomon. Yet the tribe of Judah already functioned in many ways as a separate people. David realized the tribes of Israel were in a quandary because they had alienated their king and pledged allegiance to a leader who was now dead. David responded by appealing to his own tribe, Judah, suggesting they lead the way for Israel in restoring the throne to its rightful king. He would receive his people back without punishing the general population, but he intended to make some changes.

- ☐ David appointed Solomon as his right-hand man.
- ☑ David vowed to replace Joab as army commander with Amasa.
- ☐ David placed the tribe of Judah in authority over the tribes of Israel.
- ☐ David punished Amasa for Israel's betrayal.

One major change is listed in verse 13. Check the change in the margin.

How did the people of Judah accept David's message (v. 14)?

He won over the hearts of the men of Judah

The next time I suffer a painful loss, remind me not to call someone like Joab for a sympathetic ear. Nothing is more natural than grieving a devastating loss, but David was met by immediate condemnation from Joab.

Job also suffered a terrible loss and could have used comforters other than the friends who came. His good friend Bildad had the nerve to say, "When your children sinned against him, he gave them over to the penalty of their sin" (Job 8:4). Then his friend Zophar said, "You will surely forget your trouble, recalling it only as waters gone by" (Job 11:16). In other words, "You'll get over it." Some friends, weren't they?

A good rule when a friend is grieving might be to offer hugs and say little. Joab did not confront King David as a friend, however. He approached him as commander over the king's armies. Joab had the best interest of his soldiers in mind and not the emotional well-being of a mourning father. He had seen many lives stolen in battle. If we give Joab the benefit of the doubt, we could see a shred of humanity in his desire to see David cease mourning. If we don't, we can assume his vehement resistance to David's grief showed his guilt for having disobeyed David's order to spare Absalom. Joab was the man who thrust the javelins into Absalom's heart.

Even if Joab's heart was wrong, David concluded his advice was right. He returned to the business of the kingdom, but he decided to replace Joab with Amasa. David realized his army had fought in his behalf, and he must not have them return in shame. He got up and took his seat in the gateway. "When the men were told … they all came before him" (2 Sam. 19:8). The words represented a pivotal moment—the king became accessible once more. It had been a long time, far too long. My heart aches as I consider how different things might have been had David never made himself so distant from the people.

My father-in-law has kept a yellowed newspaper article in his wallet for decades. The article describes the worst event in his life: a fire that engulfed the garage of his home while his two tiny sons played with a gasoline can. The article ends with the chilling words, "The father rushed into the garage to rescue his sons. It was too late for Duke. But it was not too late for Keith."

How different my life would be had it been too late for Keith—my husband. It was too late for Absalom, but it was not too late for David. He had a chance to do the right thing, and he did it. David was back—in his heart—if not yet on his throne. "He won over the hearts of all the men of Judah as though they were one man" (v. 14).

We've looked at David from many angles at this point in our study. In the margin write four or five adjectives that describe David.

Let's continue reading about the return to Jerusalem. We are about to meet David's first welcoming party. Read 2 Samuel 19:15-30.

Why did the men of Judah come to Gilgal (v. 15)? *1 Sam 7:16 Samuel judged Israel thre. 1 Sam 13:4. Strategic place*

Compare 2 Samuel 19:21 to 2 Samuel 16:9. Abishai was obviously itching for a chance to kill Shimei! David responded to Abishai's intentions the same way each time: "What do you and I have in common, you sons of Zeruiah?" (v. 22).

What do you think David meant by this expression? *He is the king & they are subordinates.*

In verses 24-30, do you see any evidence suggesting Mephibosheth's loyalty to David and his innocence in Ziba's former claims? If so, what is the evidence? *M. is not interested in gaining land for himself.*

One of two reasons may have been at the heart of David's order for the land to be split between Ziba and Mephibosheth. Either David was attempting to end the rivalry as simply as possible or he was testing Mephibosheth's heart.

David may have been employing the same wisdom his son Solomon later applied between two women fighting over a child (1 Kings 3:24-26). When Solomon suggested the child be cut in half and divided between them, the true mother emerged, ready to sacrifice her own position to spare her son. Likewise, Mephibosheth's integrity emerged as he responded, in effect, "Let Ziba have everything as long as I have you back safely." Mephibosheth's response was wise and an example of humility and gratefulness.

No doubt, the encounter between David and Mephibosheth was a priceless example of authentic restoration. Ironically, the son of his own blood was never reconciled to David; but his adopted son, inspired by love and loyalty, escorted the king back to his throne. I cannot help but notice an astonishing parallel. God's own beloved nation, His chosen ones, His natural descendants, refused to be reconciled to Him through Christ, yet the adopted sons—the church—accepted Him, loved Him, remained loyal to Him, and will escort Him to His rightful throne. (See Zech. 14:4,5,9 in the margin.)

The point where the parallel ends is perhaps the point of greatest celebration. Absalom was never reconciled to his father on this earth, but the apostle Paul suggested that Israel will be reconciled to her God (Rom. 11:25-27). Somehow God intends to heal His wayward people.

This promise does not mean that Jews will be saved apart from Jesus Christ. Romans 9:6 warns that "Not all who are descended from Israel are Israel." But the promises of Scripture encourage me to believe that Israel will one day take her rightful place among the nations. God's natural-born children

"On that day his feet will stand on the Mount of Olives, east of Jerusalem, and the Mount of Olives will be split in two from east to west. ... Then the LORD my God will come, and all the holy ones with him. ...The LORD will be king over the whole earth. On that day there will be one LORD, and his name the only name."

ZECHARIAH 14:4-5,9

and the church, His adopted children, will one day gather as His family in heaven before the throne of God (see Rom. 8–11).

I will never forget having a family picture taken at Thanksgiving after Keith's young cousin, Michael, came to stay with us. He wanted to be considered part of a real family so badly, and since he stayed with us seven years, he certainly qualified. I framed a new family picture with him smack in the middle of it. He jumped up and down and exclaimed, "It's the whole Moore family, and not one of us is missing!" We had covered our house with his pictures, but I never realized how much the ones taken before he came had bothered him. One day God may take a family portrait in heaven. All of God's children—the natural born of Israel and the adopted sons and daughters, the church—will be there and not one of us will be missing. Read 2 Samuel 19:31-43. Reconsider the tender scene between David and Barzillai.

Why did David want Barzillai to stay with him in Jerusalem?

to repay him for his help.

In one sentence, why did Barzillai refuse David's offer?

he would be more of a burden than being able to enjoy the pleasure of the king's kingdom.

Based on your impressions of verses 41-43, what was the problem between the men of Israel and the men of Judah?

rivalry.

The nineteenth chapter of 2 Samuel ends with business as usual. The king crossed the Jordan with an entourage escorting him back to his throne, and before he could dry off his feet, his folks were in a fight. How typical! Welcome home, David.

Have you ever finally resolved yourself to a former relationship, job, or situation only to discover things had not changed much? ☐ yes ☐ no If so, when was it?

How did you feel?

Did you hang in there in spite of it all? ☐ yes ☐ no   If so, what motivated you to continue in reconciliation or resolution? Respond in the margin.

Returning to a former relationship or position isn't always easy. Going home isn't always fun, especially when infighting awaits you. The smoke David was seeing between Israel and Judah was coming from a fire that had only begun to blaze. Going home was not going to be easy, but it was his destiny. Across the Jordan River was David's promised land. He had been chosen by God to perform a difficult task. Doing the right thing is rarely the easy thing. It was too late for Absalom. It was not too late for David. It's not too late for you.

DAY 2
Unfinished Business

TODAY'S TREASURE

"They buried the bones of Saul and his son Jonathan in the tomb of Saul's father Kish, at Zela in Benjamin, and did everything the king commanded. After that, God answered prayer in behalf of the land."
2 Samuel 21:14

On day 1 we ushered a prodigal king back across the Jordan to his throne to face quarreling tribes. David had ample business to settle as he returned to his post. Reclaiming a kingdom is no small matter. We read in history books gory accounts of kingdoms reestablished after mutiny, but somehow we are unsettled about the vivid accounts in the Word of God. Remember, the Bible is the ultimate history book. God tells it like it is. And like it was.

Expect God to speak to you today. He is far too practical to include in His Word accounts that cannot teach, rebuke, correct, or train in righteousness (2 Tim. 3:16). I sincerely hope you will find the encounters in this lesson and the next interesting enough to keep you focused. Sometimes God speaks in black and white. Other times, as in the following, He speaks in living color.

Read 2 Samuel 20:1-26. Use your imagination for a moment as you consider Sheba, son of Bicri. Imagine the kind of man who could incite an army of men to follow him and desert their king.

Why did Joab kill Amasa? (See 2 Sam. 19:13.) Choose answer in margin.

Why did Amasa's body have to be moved?

the army stopped

How did the woman of Abel Beth Maacah prove herself wise?

She realized Sheba was the problem

We can't seem to get rid of Joab, can we? We might as well accept him as a permanent figure whether or not we like him. David should have known Joab was not going to clean out his desk and resign peaceably. He forced his way back into his former position by killing Amasa, the man David had chosen to replace him. Another fact makes Joab's actions against Amasa considerably more heinous. Read 1 Chronicles 2:16-17 carefully.

- ☐ Amasa had plans to betray David.
- ☑ David had given Amasa Joab's position.
- ☐ Amasa had violated David's orders.
- ☐ The families of Amasa and Joab were enemies for generations.

199

What was the relationship between Amasa and Joab?

causing

> "Amasa lay wallowing in his blood in the middle of the road, and the man saw that all the troops came to a halt there. When he realized that everyone who came up to Amasa stopped, he dragged him from the road into a field and threw a garment over him."
>
> **2 SAMUEL 20:12**

Power was so important to Joab that he did not stop at spilling his own family's blood. I was a little amused over Joab's words in verse 20 of 2 Samuel 20: "Far be it from me to swallow up or destroy." He probably sold beach front property in the wilderness as a side job.

Joab meant to cause Amasa's death but not to cause a traffic jam. We may have witnessed the first reference to rubber-necking in Scripture. What is it about our human nature that draws us to the morose? Aren't we just as guilty as others? Don't our eyes fall almost automatically on the captions depicting violence and death as we glance over the front page of the paper? We've almost grown accustomed to reading articles describing crimes witnessed by people who refused to help. I sat in amazement not long ago over an article describing a woman who was beaten and thrown from a bridge while many watched.

Why do you think people are unwilling to get involved when they see someone in need or when they witness a crime? Respond in margin.

Have you known of a situation where someone was in trouble and no one came to the person's aid? ☐ yes ☐ no

As the plot thickened in the twentieth chapter, one woman was willing to become more than a spectator to imminent disaster, and an entire city was spared. Just when we're about to throw up our hands over the unwillingness of people to get involved and help, out steps an authentic hero. Let's allow her a moment's glory. We don't even know her name. She wasn't looking for recognition. She was looking for her city's salvation. An entire village could have perished because one person was such a troublemaker.

Do you know someone who risked involvement in a community need or personal need and made a significant difference? ☐ yes ☐ no   If so, in the margin describe the situation.

I know a woman whose son was openly pursued by a sexual predator teaching at the university he attended. The professor had targeted numerous other students, but no one was willing to confront him. Her son's meeker personality could have made him easy prey, so she became a woman with a mission to protect him. She tried to enlist her husband's support. He did not want to get involved. Because it was a local Christian college, she tried to enlist her pastor's support. He did not want to get involved either. She finally approached the Dean of Students and an investigation ensued. Many people came forward and mountains of evidence emerged. The professor never again pursued another student on that campus. The woman's son now credits his mother for having snatched him and others from the jaws of a ferocious lion.

Read 2 Samuel 21:1-14. From the responses in the margin choose why a famine fell on the land for three years.

What did God do after the Gibeonites were repaid and David had the bones of Saul and Jonathan moved to the tomb of his father (v. 14)?

God answered prayer.

> ☑ Saul had put the Gibeonites to death.
> ☐ The tribes of Israel were divided.
> ☐ David disobeyed God.

Many years later the people of Israel were suffering the ill effects of a king who was rebellious to God. God was holding the nation of Israel to an old vow made with the Gibeonites generations prior to David's reign. (Read Joshua 9:1-21.) The Gibeonites tricked Joshua into making a treaty of peace with them—a treaty God never intended but did expect Israel to honor.

God meant for His people to be good for their word. He still does. Surely one reason is so observers might come to believe He is good for His.

Israel had to keep their agreement with the Gibeonites even though they should never have entered it. Saul broke the agreement with the probable aid of his sons and tried to annihilate a people innocent of their father's sins. Ironically, Saul's sons were brought to account for their father's sins.

God considers vows extremely important. Countless men and women have broken marriage vows by claiming their marriage was a mistake. Maybe they were like the Israelites who did not inquire of the Lord and were sorry later, but a vow is still a very serious thing. Others have vowed to honor their mates, but although they still live under the same roof, honor moved out long ago. We don't live in a society that supports long-term vows, but we live under the heavenly authority who does. I can hardly remember an early vow I made to God that I didn't grievously break. I am still scarred from foolish decisions I've made and promises I've broken. God, on the other hand, has never broken a single vow. He promises that when we truly repent, He forgives. Praise His merciful name! Rather than continue in disobedience, God provides two responses to broken vows: *repent* and *recommit*.

I wish I had kept every vow from the very beginning; but I am so thankful that God allowed me numerous opportunities to seek forgiveness and restoration and to recommit my life. I don't find myself in the ditch nearly as often these days, but any victory along the way has been His grace overcoming my frailty. He is so much better than He has to be.

> "It is better not to vow than to make a vow and not fulfill it. Do not let your mouth lead you into sin. And do not protest to the temple messenger, 'My vow was a mistake.'"
> **ECCLESIASTES 5:5-6**

Do you have a vow to God that could use a fresh dose of recommitment? ☐ yes ☐ no   If so, in the margin write a prayer of commitment to God. Ask His help in fulfilling your vow.

The Israelites recommitted themselves to the vow they made by satisfying the demands of the Gibeonites. David gave the Gibeonites what they asked and the famine ended. The first drops of rain fell from the skies bringing the sweet smell of water on parched land.

As rain drenched her hair, a grieving mother gathered her sackcloth and returned home. The mental image of a mother guarding her sons' bodies from predators was obviously more than David could shake. The image reawakened old pictures from years past that disturbed him so deeply—the exposed bodies of Saul and his dear friend Jonathan (1 Sam. 31). Their remains were not where they belonged. The king also had unfinished business left waiting.

David did not send a soldier for their bones. He went for them himself. He gathered them, brought them back, and "They buried the bones of Saul and his son Jonathan in the tomb of Saul's father Kish, at Zela in Benjamin, and did everything the king commanded" (2 Sam. 21:14). Obedience has amazing effects: "After that, God answered prayer in behalf of the land."

Do you happen to have any unfinished business in your life? old scores that need to be settled Christ's way? chapters that need to be completed? ends that need to be rewritten? books that need to be closed?

Christ has led us to a warfare far more effective than guns and tanks. We have weapons of grace, mercy, love, and the Sword of the Spirit which is the Word of God. Anybody need your forgiveness? your acceptance? your release? It's time for some old battles to end. Just like the Israelites, we will suffer in ways that seem totally unrelated when we allow matters to continue unsettled and outside the will of God. Rebellion inevitably leads to famine in our relationship to God. A new beginning is as close as the fresh smell of rain.

DAY 3

The Unwelcomed Sight of an Old Enemy

TODAY'S TREASURE

"Once again there was a battle between the Philistines and Israel. David went down with his men to fight against the Philistines and he became exhausted." 2 Samuel 21:15

King David brought the bones of Saul and Jonathan from Jabesh Gilead to bury them in the family tomb. His tasks were overwhelming. He returned to Jerusalem and realized he must take back his throne—rather than receive it from cheerful givers. The business of politics and inevitable battles must have seemed insurmountable. One last enemy arose before he could take a breath and proclaim a victory. One very familiar enemy. One very persistent enemy. We'll meet this enemy again in our first reading. Read 2 Samuel 21:15-22.

In the margin fill in the blanks according to verse 15.

What did Abishai do for David? *Saved D. from Ishbi-Benob*

Why did David's men insist he not accompany them to battle anymore?

So that the lamp of Israel will not be extinguished

How many battles with the Philistines are mentioned in verses 15-22?

4

Let's not overlook some of the riches in these few verses! Verse 15 begins, "Once again there was a battle." The next thing we know "David … became exhausted." I am so thankful God chose to tell us David knew about exhaustion in battle. I need to know that others have experienced the weariness of fighting the same old enemy over and over. The original word for *exhausted* in Hebrew is *uwph*. The word even sounds like something you might say at a glimpse of an old enemy. *Uwph* means "to cover, to fly, faint, flee away."[1] It is the overwhelming desire to run and hide.

When was the last time you wanted to run and hide?

Few things make us want to flee more than the prospect of fighting an old battle. The moment that old enemy reappears, we want to run into the nearest forest and never come out. Have you ever noticed that Satan always chooses just the right time to haunt you through an old enemy? When you haven't had enough rest, when things have been emotional and turbulent, when you're completely vulnerable—that's when the enemy strikes.

Satan is the counterfeit god of perfect timing. He's watching for just the right moment to pull the rug out from under us, but even that rug is under God's feet. And He always has victory in mind. He will never allow Satan to discourage you without a plan to lead you to victory. Consider this carefully: We may not always follow Christ to victory, but He is always leading.

In the margin or on a card for you to memorize, write 2 Corinthians 2:14.

One of the most important truths we can apply from David's ongoing battles with the Philistines is that God will always lead us to victory, but He will lead us His way. God led David to victory in all four of the battles in 2 Samuel 21:15-22, but He brought the victory to David through someone else.

Just like us, I'm sure David's preference would have been for God to make him the hero and leave others in awe over his great strength. God had other plans. He saved David all right, but He purposely made him dependent on others. Several wonderful reasons might exist for the method God used.

"Once again there was a battle between the ___Philistines___ *and* ___Israel___. *David went down with his men to fight against the Philistines and he became* ___exhausted___."

To shed some light on them, I am going to ask you to do something we rarely practice in our study. I want you to look ahead. Your second reading involves a list of names that relate to our lesson today. Read 2 Samuel 23:8-39.

According to verse 8, who are all these men?

David's mighty warriors.

How tired did Eleazar become as he stood his ground against the Philistines (v. 10)? *his hand got tired & froze to the swo*

Why wouldn't David drink the water his mighty men drew for him?

Is it not the blood of men who went @ the risk of their li

How many mighty men did David have in all (v. 39)?

God purposely brought victory to David through someone else on many occasions. Consider a few reasons why God might have used this method.

1. For the sake of the people. Israel did not need David to be like a god to them. He could not deal with being put on that kind of pedestal or subjected to that kind of pressure. He was bound to disappoint them. When it comes to hero worship, the line between love and hate is very fine! How many close followers have turned against their leaders? God will never allow any of us to be the only one through whom He appears to be working mightily.

2. For the sake of King David. Remember what happened when David was so exalted that he became disconnected from his people? Remember how isolated he became? Remember what happened when he thought he'd risen above the normal duties of a king and stayed behind when other kings went off to war? That's when the nightmare began.

God protected David by not always letting him be the hero. God extended David a wonderful gift. He gave David some heroes instead—a few men who commanded his respect. He humbled David and made him depend on them. None of us will escape this important life lesson. God will teach us dependency. God will allow us to become exhausted and force us to receive help.

Philippians 2:3-4 *V3 Do nothing out of selfish ambition — value others above yourse*

Read the Scriptures in the margin and describe how God may have been teaching David the same truths later expressed in these verses by allowing him to depend on others.

V4 not looking to your own interests but ... to the interests of others

1 Corinthians 12:21

The eye cannot say to the hand "I don't need you
head
feet

3. For the sake of the men he empowered. People can easily be discouraged if they perceive God works mightily through others but never works through them. God does not play favorites. Anyone who cries out to Him, He answers. Anyone who surrenders to His call, He uses.

Ministry to the individual is as mighty an act of God as is ministry to the masses. We'd be mistaken to conclude that God is honored more by a speaker to hundreds than a homemaker praying with a neighbor to receive Christ or a mom singing "Jesus Loves Me" with her preschooler. Every faithful servant displays the mighty work of God. Each is a hero in His sight.

Don't cringe. God has heroes. If you don't believe it, check Hebrews 11. You'll only find part of the list, however, because it just keeps getting longer and longer in heaven. The name of every surrendered person who endures by faith and not by sight is on it. No doubt some of your heroes are on that list. You may be surprised to find your name listed there as well.

What other characteristics do you consider marks of a hero of the faith?

Having heroes of the faith is perfectly appropriate for you. In fact, I am saddened at the thought of anyone who cannot name a living hero. We can let one person's failure tempt us to believe no one is genuine. Don't let Satan make you cynical. If you can't name a single hero in the faith, you may have already allowed Satan to sow a seed of cynicism in you. Remember, heroes aren't perfect. They simply live to serve and honor God.

Write a brief prayer asking God to keep you from cynicism and help you see the heroism in others from the least to the greatest deeds.

In my neighborhood I have a friend in the faith I admire deeply. She has joyfully ushered more of our neighbors to a place of receiving Christ than anyone I have ever known. She is responsible for countless women coming to love the Scriptures. If she meets someone who can't afford to buy a Bible study workbook, she buys it for her. I remember when she enlisted three different women into Bible study from a health club. They didn't know how to get to the church so she picked them up and brought them. God's Word is changing their lives—all because of one obedient minister of the gospel. I can hardly hold back the tears as I celebrate her faithfulness with you. She is one of my heroes. And I know she's one of God's.

Through David and Eleazar (whose hand grew tired and froze to the sword) God is reminding us that heroes get tired too. Getting weary is no shame. The shame comes in refusing to accept the victory through another when God supplies a hero. A hero accepts help. Remember, genuine martyrs are never self-appointed. Our God is so faithful, isn't He? His ways are so much higher than ours. Who would ever guess that He could use things like exhaustion to take our minds off ourselves and cause us to esteem another?

Use the space in the margin to name or describe a few of your heroes; then take time to thank God for them.

DAY 4

A Great Celebration

TODAY'S TREASURE

"He brought me to a spacious place; he rescued me because he delighted in me." 2 Samuel 22:20

Nothing is more appropriate than celebrating a victory God sovereignly and majestically won for us. Today we get to experience the sheer pleasure of attending a celebration. Anyone who has ever experienced victory in Jesus is invited to attend. Someone else just wouldn't understand. Begin your reading today with just one verse. Read 2 Samuel 22:1.

How did David present these words to the Lord?

Sang a song

In the margin check the occasions when David presented these words to the Lord.

☑ when the Lord delivered him from the hand of all his enemies
☐ when the Lord delivered him from Absalom
☑ when the Lord delivered him from the hand of Saul
☐ when the Lord delivered him from the pit of despair

Wouldn't you love to have heard David sing? Just wait until you see the lyrics. Before you do, I want you to think about what motivated David to sing the words. Sometimes God puts a new song in our mouths—a hymn of praise to our God. Other times, He brings us back to an old song, one that fell from our lips many years ago and has gathered a film of dust only a fresh breath could blow away. No doubt about it, sometimes God wants to hear an old song from a new heart. This was the case for David.

The first verse of 2 Samuel 22 tells us David remembered the words he had sung many years before after God delivered him from the hand of Saul. Why had his recent victory over the Philistines rekindled the remembrance of his victory over Saul? I believe there might have been several similarities:

1. Both conflicts seemed they would never end.

2. Both conflicts sapped his strength. David vividly described how he felt about being encircled by an enemy over and over. You don't have to be a poet or a song writer to describe how you feel in pictorial terms. In our previous lesson, we talked about exhaustion. Read Psalm 22:14-15,19.

In the margin try to describe a time when you've been exhausted after a long battle. Use figurative language to draw comparisons. You can do it. Give it a try.

3. Both conflicts caused him to rely on another's strength. Decades wedged their way between the solos of this one song. How different the sound of the same singer's voice—so young and daring when first he sang. Now the voice was old, but suddenly, unexpectedly filled with the passion of a young warrior.

I believe the words we are about to read comprise the testimony of an old man with a fresh passion. Praise God, we need never get too old to experience a young passion. Please participate willingly and expectantly in the following exercises. Our purpose today is to take part in David's celebration. The exercises will help you experience the psalm, the psalmist, and the Savior he praised. You will be writing most of the commentary. These words will mean one thing to me and another thing to you. May we ascribe to God His right to teach them and apply them to us individually. Read the questions below before you read 2 Samuel 22:1-51. This will enable you to identify some of the answers as you go.

1. List every single name, object, or role by which David referred to God:

V2: rock, fortress, deliverer
3: " shield, horn, stronghold, refuge, savior

Consider the various themes of the chapter by searching for the answers to the following questions. Answer the questions according to your understanding. Don't worry about whether or not another's list is like yours. Feel free to search the text with the understanding God gives you. Use extra paper if necessary.

2. Which verses and phrases describe God in such a way that you are awed by Him? List the verse and an identifying phrase.
V 8 – 17. God's power, anger demonstrated in storm, earthquakes, natural disasters.

3. Which verses and phrases describe how God readies His warrior(s) for battle?
V 20 , 33 – 37

4. Which verses and phrases testify that God blesses the obedient?
V 25, 26, 31

5. Which verses and phrases acknowledge God's Word?
V 31, 23

6. Which verses and phrases remind you that God hears the cries of His children?
V 4, 7

7. To which one verse can you most readily relate? Tell why.

V1 – 3 (17), 20, 29, 31, 47, 50

David's life continually challenges us to answer questions such as: Am I becoming more and more committed to God? Do I have an increasing awareness that He is my rock, my fortress, and my deliverer? Addressing God personally and confidently comes from having a history with Him. You will notice in 2 Samuel 22 that David is serving us a slice of his personal history with God.

Are you actively building a history with God? Can you readily say that the two of you have done lots of living together since your salvation? Have you allowed Him to reveal Himself to you in the many experiences of life?

Imagine a book recording the history between you and God—things you have been through together, seasons you've experienced. You don't have to know Him long to have some kind of history with God.

What would be the title of the book?

List the name of five chapters. Have fun with this exercise in small group.

Chapter 1

Chapter 2

Chapter 3

Chapter 4

Chapter 5

If you are a Christian but you've attempted a life of self-sufficiency, you may not be able to relate to having a close personal relationship with God. Claiming Him personally is the most precious right of any believer. Look at the revolutionary news the risen Lord told Mary Magdalene: "Go … to my brothers and tell them, 'I am returning to my Father and your Father, to my God and your God' " (John 20:17). Blessed Calvary, cheated grave that made Christ's God my very own. Glory in the cross!

The Book of 2 Samuel is not the only place David's words of victory are found. Turn to Psalm 18 and glance through the chapter. You'll find an almost identical set of verses to those God placed in 2 Samuel 22. One of the exceptions is too precious to miss.

Write verse 1 of Psalm 18.

I love you, Lord, my strength.

"I love you, O Lord." No demands. No despair. Just I love you. The words might seem more fitting as the grand finale rather than the opening line. Their sudden appearance suggests they were words that could not wait. The psalmist considered his delivered estate and his Father's stubborn love, and he burst forth with the words: "I love you, O Lord."

The One who delivered David from his enemies was no distant deity. He was the object of the psalmist's deepest emotions, the One with whom he shared authentic relationship. David deeply loved God. David was a man after God's own heart because his desire was also the sheer pleasure of the Father. The Father's deepest desire is to be loved—genuinely loved—by His child.

If 2 Samuel 22 and Psalm 18 compel us to see one thing, it is that God is a personal God we each can call our own.

- He is my Strength when I am weak.
- He is my Rock when I am slipping.
- He is my Deliverer when I am trapped.
- He is my Fortress when I am crumbling.
- He is my Refuge when I am pursued.
- He is my Shield when I am exposed.
- He is my Lord when life spins out of control.

A heart that makes Him its own—one which can state "He is mine"—is a heart that cannot help but love. I love you. I wonder if you hear those words often. I wonder if you say those words often. Saying those words can be difficult when you've rarely heard them or rarely believed them. Whether they come easy to you or lodge in your throat, I ask you to conclude this lesson by considering the following as specifically as you can.

When has God shielded you from what appeared to be imminent harm? Name one particular time.

Tell Him He is your Shield. You do not need a lot of words. Just acknowledge Him by this title.

When has He been your Deliverer?

Tell Him He is your Deliverer.

When has He been a Refuge when you felt like everyone needed more from you than you could give?

Tell Him He is your Refuge. Now tell Him you love Him.

Do you have anyone in your life to whom you've never been able to express your genuine love? As a gift to God, a sacrifice of praise, call or write that person to tell him or her—just for practice. Then listen ever so carefully for the applause of love's Author.

DAY 5

A Hand Withdrawn

TODAY'S TREASURE

"The king replied to Araunah, 'No, I insist on paying you for it. I will not sacrifice to the LORD my God burnt offerings that cost me nothing.'"
2 Samuel 24:24

Today will be our most involved lesson. You will do a tremendous amount of research to understand an easily misunderstood event in David's history. This journey in Scripture will be worth the end result if you'll stick with it.

Satan always seeks to make us believe God is unfair or unkind. In this task, the adversary particularly likes to use a few difficult-to-understand events recorded in Scripture. The passage we study today may be confusing and unsettling to us if we don't keep one thought in mind. We do not know every fact about every event in Scripture. We don't always have the explanations for certain events and acts of God. He is sovereign. He owes us no explanation. He is also obligated to teach us to walk by faith and not by sight. When Scripture records an event or judgment of God that seems cruel or unfair, we need to respond in the following two ways:

• *Acknowledge that His ways are higher than ours.* We do not have all the information nor the understanding. We have no idea the depth of evil God may have seen in human hearts that necessitated such serious judgment.

• *Acknowledge what we do know about God.* Anytime you are overwhelmed by what you do not know or understand about God, consider what you do know about Him. Your heart and mind will be quieted, and you will be able to walk in faith. Begin our first reading. We will use this method to learn to handle these kinds of difficulties in the future. Read 2 Samuel 24:1-17.

In verse 1, God's anger was directed to _Israel_.

What options did God give David?
3 years of famine
3 months of fleeing
3 days of plague

What happened when the angel stretched out his hand to destroy Jerusalem?

the Lord relented.

At what exact location did the angel stop the plague?

the threshing floor of Araunah

We have the perfect opportunity to employ the method of Bible study I suggested prior to our first reading assignment—to measure what you don't know or understand by what you do. I see at least two occurrences in today's references that Satan could twist to cause doubt or dismay in the reader: (1) God's role in David's sin, and (2) punishment that appears to exceed the crime.

Let's consider the first point. The first verse of chapter 24 says, "He [God] incited David against them, saying, 'Go and take a census of Israel and Judah.'" A brief look at this one verse may cause us to wonder why God would ask David to do something and then kill 70,000 people as a result.

Just as God included four Gospels to tell the story of Christ, He recorded many of the occurrences of David's reign in both 2 Samuel and 1 Chronicles. We can understand passages or events by comparing these parallel accounts.

First Chronicles 21:1 sheds a little light on what happened to David. What does this verse add to what you learned in 2 Samuel 24:1?

Satan rose up against Israel a incited David.

Who enticed David to sin—God or Satan? As we confront something we do not know, consider what we do know.

How do the following Scriptures shed light on the issue?

James 1:13 *When tempted no one should say "God is tempting me" for God cannot be tempted by evil, nor does he tempt anyone.*

According to 1 Corinthians 10:13, what makes us vulnerable to temptation? *what is common to mankind. he will also provide a way out.*

From these two verses we know that God does not tempt us. He may allow us to be tempted to test, prove, or help us to grow, but He is definitely not the tempter. In our temptation He always makes a way of escape. How do we explain the activity of God in David's sin? God's obvious role had to be somewhat like His role in the suffering of Job. Read Job 1:9-12; 2:1-6.

How would you describe God's position in the confrontation between Satan and Job?

We can be assured that God did not tempt David to sin and then judge him harshly for it. God has no sin; therefore, He is incapable of enticing one to sin. He did, however, allow David to be tempted because He saw something in David's heart that needed to be exposed. The Disciple's Study Bible suggests that God allowed Satan to tempt David by giving him the idea of a military census, which Joab knew was contrary to faith in God.[2] In light of 1 Corinthians 10:13-14, Joab's plea was David's "way out."

Now consider the second matter that Satan, as the author of confusion and doubt, may use—the punishment seemed to exceed the crime. If we are not careful to study the text, 70,000 men seemed to die solely as a result of David's sin. Although David's actions no doubt displeased God and caused judgment, 2 Samuel 24:1 clearly states the anger of the Lord burned against Israel. Let's apply our method once again. What is the first thing we do not know? We do not know why God's anger burned against Israel. What can we know in order to shed light on Israel's action that angered God?

1. *The promise of God's blessing or cursing.* Skim Deuteronomy 28:1-24.

In general, what would happen to Israel as a direct result of obedience?

Blessed - politically, economically, spiritually

In general, what would happen as a direct result of disobedience?

Cursed

Based on Deuteronomy 28, what can you conclude about the nature of Israel's sin against God that angered Him in 2 Samuel 24:1?

disobedience

2. *The tenderness of God.* Read Exodus 33:1-17.

Glance back at Exodus 32. What had been Israel's sin?

idolatry of the golden calf.

In Exodus 32:25-30, what happened to those who were not for the Lord?

killed by the Levites (3000)

In Exodus 33:3-5, what did God tell Moses and the people of Israel He would not do because they were a stiff-necked people?

- ☐ bless them
- ☐ deliver them
- ☐ provide for them
- ☑ go with them

Why did God allow His presence to go with them after all?

God responded to Moses' intercession.

Now look at Exodus 33:11. How would you describe God's relationship with Moses—the kind of relationship He desires with His people?

- ☐ angry and distant
- ☐ harsh and judgmental
- ☑ close and intimate
- ☐ other: *face to face, as one speaks to a friend*

We don't know what Israel had done to make God so angry in 2 Samuel 24, but we do know that His judgment was consistent with that which He had promised for rebellion against His commands. Somehow Israel had severely disobeyed God. Several scholars suggest God may have been judging Israel for their quickness to desert David, God's sovereign choice, and follow Absalom. In effect, they would have been overruling God's authority and judgment. In Scripture you virtually never see God's hand move in a major act of judgment except over blatant and continued rebellion with an unwillingness to repent.

Why, then, was David also wrong? I'd like to suggest three possible reasons David was involved in the anger of God toward Israel.

1. David deserted the throne God had given him and did not trust God to fight his battles for him. Earlier David trusted God to direct his battles and to fight them for him. This time David ignored God and depended on human resources and wisdom.

2. David did not stand in the gap and intercede for the sins of his nation as Moses did. God revoked a portion of His judgment on Israel as a direct result of the humility and intercession of Moses. David saw the evil ways of his nation and did not intercede nor take any responsibility. David finally arrived at a place to cry out on behalf of the people, but not until the angel threatened his own area.

3. David had wrong motives for taking the census. He fell to the temptation of counting his fighting men either out of the sin of pride, distrust, or both. Anyway, David's heart was wrong toward God. God had proved Himself many times in the life of this king. David had no grounds for pride or distrust.

Based on 2 Samuel 24 and 1 Chronicles 21, David and the people of Israel shared the responsibility for the judgment handed down to them. In the heart of this difficult account of anger and judgment is something vital you must not miss—God's mercy.

Reread 2 Samuel 24:15-16. Exactly when did God grieve? When the angel stretched out his hand to destroy Jerusalem. Exactly where was the angel of the Lord at the time? The threshing floor of Araunah the Jebusite. Read further so you may revel in the special significance of this threshing floor and the mercy God poured out at this place. Read 2 Samuel 24:18-25.

What did Gad tell David to do on the threshing floor (v. 18)?

build an altar to the Lord.

What reason did David give Araunah for building the altar (v. 21)?

that the plague on the people may be stopped.

When Araunah offered to give it to David, how did David respond?
"No, I insist upon paying you for it. I will not sacrifice to the LORD my God burnt offerings that *cost me nothing*" (v. 24).

According to 1 Chronicles 21:27–22:1, what else was to happen on this exact location?

☐ The Messiah would appear.
☐ The glory of the Lord would appear.
☑ The house of God, or the temple, would be built.
☐ The crucifixion would take place.

According to 2 Chronicles 3:1, the temple, thus the threshing floor, was located on Mount ___Moriah___.

The exact location of the threshing floor of Araunah the Jebusite was the most vital place in Israel's history. Scripture says God grieved when the angel reached the threshing floor of Araunah the Jebusite and stretched out his hand to destroy Jerusalem. The Hebrew word for grieve in this passage is *nacham*, meaning "to draw breath forcibly, pant, breathe strongly; to groan; to be sorry; to pity; to grieve; to have compassion, to comfort oneself." *Nacham* carries the idea of breathing deeply as "a physical display of one's feeling, usually sorrow, compassion, or comfort."[3] The word was used once before in 2 Samuel 12:24 in which it means "being consoled over the death of an infant child."[4]

When the angel of the Lord stretched out his hand at the threshing floor of Araunah the Jebusite, God seemed to cry. He "panted" in grief somewhat like one "being consoled over the death of an infant child." I want to suggest that the primary reason God grieved as if over the death of a child at that exact location was related to an event that took place on that soil many years before. Read Genesis 22:1-2 then skim the remainder of the chapter.

What event does this pivotal chapter record? *Sacrifice of Isaac.*

Where did this event take place (v. 2)? *the region of Moriah.*

God did not coincidentally grieve at this exact spot generations later during David's reign then coincidentally direct an altar, and ultimately the temple of God, to be built there as well. Each occurrence was based on the vivid lesson God taught about substitutionary death at the same location. Look at the similarities.

The altar. God commanded that an altar for sacrifice be built by both Abraham and David—and ultimately by Solomon—on the same spot. Something at that location obviously represented sacrifice and substitution.

The timing. Genesis 22:10-12 tells us that when Abraham reached out his hand and took the knife to slay his son, God intervened and stopped him. God then presented a sacrifice in his place. Consider the timing during David's reign: 1 Chronicles 21:16 tells us "David looked up and saw the angel of the LORD standing between heaven and earth, with a drawn sword in his hand extended over Jerusalem." Of the same event, 2 Samuel 24:16 says, "When the angel stretched out his hand to destroy Jerusalem, the LORD was grieved because of the calamity and said to the angel who was afflicting the people, 'Enough: Withdraw your hand.' The angel of the LORD was then at the threshing floor of Araunah the Jebusite."

In both cases, the moment God saw a sword raised to destroy life at this location, He intervened and accepted substitutionary sacrifices. That both of these events happened at the same place and at the moment a sword was being drawn is no accident. When the angel of the Lord drew his sword at the threshing floor of Araunah the Jebusite, I believe God remembered a father who was willing in obedience to take the life of his dearly loved son. I believe God not only cried over the memory of Abraham and Isaac but over the gospel they foretold—"For God so loved the world, that he gave his only begotten Son, that whosoever believeth in him should not perish, but have everlasting life" (John 3:16, KJV).

The day Abraham offered Isaac pictured the cross as the ultimate altar of sacrifice and the substitutionary death of the unblemished Lamb as the perfect sacrifice. Many years later, during David's reign, God saw the angel raise his sword over the lives of His people at that same location and He grieved and said "Enough!" Why? Because when God saw the threshing floor at Mount Moriah, He saw mercy. Mercy that would finally be complete on Calvary when God would look on the suffering of His Son and be satisfied (Isa. 53:11).

The legacy of sacrifice on Mount Moriah would continue from Abraham to David to Solomon because access to God is forever based on sacrifice and mercy. No wonder the New Testament bursts upon the page with a record of the genealogy of Jesus Christ the son of David, the son of Abraham! The intersection of covenants old and new falls squarely in the shadow of an ageless cross.

As we conclude we must meditate for a moment on David's words as Araunah offered him the threshing floor free of charge. He said, "I will not sacrifice to the LORD my God burnt offerings that cost me nothing."

Mount Moriah did not represent a cheap offering. The sacrifice depicted on that mountain throughout the ages was costly. Abraham's sacrifice cost him dearly. God's sacrifice cost Him severely. The chastened king's sacrifice was costly as well. At the threshing floor of Araunah, the cost of sacrifice was counted—and God wept.

When faced in Scripture with something you don't understand and God seems cruel, never forget how God identifies Himself. "Then the LORD came down in the cloud and stood there with him and proclaimed his name, the LORD. And he passed in front of Moses, proclaiming, 'The LORD, the LORD, the compassionate and gracious God, slow to anger, abounding in love and faithfulness'" (Ex. 34:6).

When you don't know *why*, a personal history with God will tell you *who*.

The New King James Version arranges David's descriptions like this:

"Now these are the last words of David.
Thus says David the ___son___ of Jesse;
Thus says the ___man___ raised up on high,
The ___anointed___ of the God of Jacob,
And the sweet ___psalmist___ of Israel" (2 Sam. 23:1).

1. The son of Jesse
   All spirituality begins with ___biology___ *regular*.

2. The man raised up on high
   "The two Hebrew words reflected in this translation, *huqam 'al*, have a
   ___gorgeous___ ___strangeness___ as
   compacted idiom."[1] Compare 2 Samuel 22:36.

   Robert Alter.

   lifted up by the lofty One already high.

   Eph 2:6
   2 Sam 22.
   John 1:14

2 Sam 23; 3 + 4

Leadership was meant to grow the people that are being led.

Ver 1: to rule — to govern — mashal

v3: God of Israel. Gen 32: 24-32.

3. The anointed of the God of Jacob *— supplanter, deceiver, cheater, √ insecure!*

   This title refs to God as "the one who *transforms*
   twisted human material."[2] "May the LORD answer you when you are in
   trouble; may the God of Jacob *make you secure*!"
   (Ps. 20:1, NET).

   • The Hebrew word *Mashach* is the root word of *Messiah* and *-y: Christos*
     means "anointed one."

   • This anointing was nothing less than the anointing of the divine royal
     lineage (2 Sam. 23:1). (See 1 Sam. 2:10; 2 Sam. 23:5.)

2 Sam 7: 28-29   *Hannah sees a king. — begins the narrative of 1 + 2 Samuel.*

Luke 1: 31-33

Mary identified w/ Hannah

4. The sweet psalmist of Israel
   "Yahweh's *breath spoke* through me, His word was
   upon my tongue" (2 Sam. 23:2, The Anchor Bible).

2 Peter 2:21

   "God does not go to all the trouble of revealing *reality* so that
   we can stand around as *spectators* and look at it."[3]

Read 2 Samuel 22:4-17.

   Note "He drew me out" (Hebrew *Masha*). *→ Moses*

1. Robert Alter, *The David Story* (New York: W. W. Norton & Company, 1999), 345.
2. Joyce G. Baldwin, *1 and 2 Samuel: An Introduction and Commentary* (Downers Grove, IL: IVP Academic, 2008), 291.
3. Eugene H. Peterson, *First and Second Samuel* (Louisville, KY: Westminster John Knox Press, 1999), 250.

The Final Years and Settled Fears

Day 1
A Breath of Life

Day 2
A New King

Day 3
Wholehearted Devotion

Day 4
Praises of the Great Assembly

Day 5
A Resting Place

DAY 1
A Breath of Life

TODAY'S TREASURE

"When King David was old and well advanced in years, he could not keep warm even when they put covers over him." 1 Kings 1:1

We made it, Sister! I'm so proud of you for sticking it out and sad to see it end. Week 10 ushers us to the final years of David's life. Our protagonist is old and frail. God made the life of David literally an open book—one that teaches until the very last page. David had mounds of work to do before he could rest. A new king had to be prepared and presented before the people. Preparations had to be made for the temple. David often neglected his parental duties, but we'll see him rising to the occasion as father and counselor to the new king.

God graced us with the accounts of David's final years in the beginning of 1 Kings and the ending of 1 Chronicles. We do not know the exact order of events because the books record different activities without an explanation of their order. Therefore, we will concentrate on events and subjects addressed rather than the chronological order. Nine weeks ago we began in the Book of 1 Samuel when David was a young, innocent shepherd. Last week concluded our lengthy look at 2 Samuel. Our first reading assignment this week introduces us to the historical record in 1 Kings. Read 1 Kings 1:1-27.

Identify the statements in the margin as either true or false.

What impact on Adonijah do you think David's lack of discipline had?

✓ Adonijah was the son of David born after Absalom.

✗ Bathsheba was Adonijah's mother.

✗ Adonijah wanted to take Joab's place and command the army.

✓ Adonijah wanted to be king.

✓ David had never questioned Adonijah's behavior.

Nathan was the prophet God used to confront the sin between David and Bathsheba. He also warned Bathsheba about Adonijah's plans, which probably would have resulted in their deaths. Nathan showed himself to be a true prophet of God. He could both confront sin and lovingly care for sinners.

What conclusions can you draw concerning Nathan's character from these two events?

honest, loyal

I am saddened by the initial words of 1 Kings: "When King David was old and well advanced in years." The words suggest the inevitable to us. One of the most well-documented lives in history was hastening to an end. Perhaps more

difficult to consider are the words that followed: "He could not keep warm even when they put covers over him." Our David? the one who killed a lion and a bear? who thundered the ground with the frame of an overgrown Philistine? who made caves his bed and stole the spear of a savage king? the one who conquered nations and called on the might of heaven? I am almost shocked by his sudden mortality. As he lay chilled beneath the weight of heavy blankets, we realize his humanity and his frailty.

By the standards of his day, David was not an extremely old man. He was approaching his death at a far younger age than the patriarchs who preceded him. Perhaps his 70 years of active living could easily compare to 100 years of simply being alive. He had known virtually every extremity of the human experience—unparalleled success, unabashed rebellion, unashamed mourning, and uninhibited celebration. Life rarely free of extremity can be life rarely free of anxiety. It takes its toll.

Do you ever feel your life has been a frazzled string of highs and lows? I've lived so much of my life in the extremes. I seem to find myself in the valley or on the mountain as often as in between. Sometimes I feel like I'm doing the splits with one foot low and the other high. The most memorable of all is when my earthly circumstances are in the valley while my awareness of God takes me to the mountain. Some years ago God led me to express on paper my responses to the extremities of life. I'd like to share these words with you.

> *Satisfy me not with the lesser of You*
> *Find me no solace in shadows of the True*
> *No ordinary measure of extraordinary means*
> *The depth, the length, the breadth of You*
> *And nothing in between.*
> *Etch these words upon my heart, knowing all the while*
> *No ordinary roadblocks plague extraordinary miles*
> *Your power as my portion, Your glory as my fare*
> *Take me to extremities,*
> *But meet me fully there.*

Do those words mean anything to you? Jot your thoughts in the margin.

David lived most of his life in the extremes, but he met God at every venture. I want my life to be like his. I don't want to make every mistake he made. Goodness knows I've made enough on my own. But I do want to meet God at every high, every low, and every stop in between. Don't you?

David's roller-coaster ride was nearing an end. The psalms prove he had discovered God at every curve. His tumultuous journey left him weak and chilled. The fourth son of David took quick advantage of his father's failing health and followed in the footsteps of his deceased half brother Absalom. Adonijah did not count on Bathsheba's words to warn David about his plan.

After a long absence from Scripture, the prophet Nathan reentered the scene. I am touched by his support of David and the union with Bathsheba after acknowledgment of their grave sin. Nathan knew Bathsheba was the key to restoring decision-making strength to the king. I wonder if Bathsheba was a sight for David's tired eyes. To the exclusion of all good judgment, she captivated his attention on a moonlit roof many years before. Now after the passage of decades, I imagine he found her beautiful once more.

Need has a way of breathing fresh life into a soul, if just for a moment. We will see David, who seemed chilled with the onset of death, assume swift control, perform the will of God, and meet the desires of his queen's heart. Whether on his sickbed or on his throne, David was indeed still king.

David's brief refreshment reminds me of someone very dear to me. My family watched helplessly as our mother approached the age of 70 with rapidly failing health. I watched her pace slow dramatically. I despised the doses of pain that continued to invade in her body. Then my older sister announced that she was expecting a baby. Mother, the eternal optimist, responded with firm resolve: "Well, I may as well forget getting old. We've got a baby coming. I've got work to do." And work she did. Eight months later a beautiful red-headed baby boy named Joshua came into our lives. My mother, who just months before was aging rapidly, kept him virtually every weekday of his young life. She didn't just keep him. She rocked him, sang to him, kissed his plump little cheeks, read to him, took pictures of him, called his mom with every new accomplishment, kept a journal about him, and added continually to his adorable vocabulary.

I called my mother right after Joshua's first birthday and almost cried as I said, "Thank you, Mother, for giving him the sweetest gift in all the world—an enormous amount of time and attention." My mother responded with a broken voice, "Are you kidding? He practically brought me back to life."

We lost the matriarch of our family to cancer before Joshua made it to kindergarten. We miss her so much; but in a wonderful way, we'll glimpse her in him for the rest of his life. All because she was needed once again.

That's what Bathsheba did for David. She called on him for something only he could do, and the need breathed enough life into his soul to finish the task. We will see David live no longer than his last few responsibilities lasted. We will allow his final contributions to God's chosen nation to capture our attentions for the remainder of our journey.

Have you seen someone receive a fresh breath of life like David? like my mother? ☐ yes ☐ no   If so, what happened to revive him or her? Margin.

I'm thankful David enjoyed a brief reprieve from his sickbed. I was not ready to part with him yet. Were you? Deep within the aging king we can still see glimpses of a heart after God's own. May God deal tenderly with us as we approach our study's conclusion.

> Need has a way of breathing fresh life into a soul, if just for a moment.

DAY 2

A New King

TODAY'S TREASURE

"King David said ... 'Take your lord's servants with you and set Solomon my son on my own mule and take him down to Gihon. There have Zadok the priest and Nathan the prophet anoint him king over Israel. Blow the trumpet and shout, "Long live King Solomon!"'" 1 Kings 1:32,33-34.

Bathsheba captured David's full attention with the threat to Solomon's succession. Then Nathan confirmed Bathsheba's claims. Apparently she stepped out of the room so Nathan could have full access to the king. Our Scripture reading begins today with David summoning Bathsheba back into his private quarters. Read 1 Kings 1:28-53.

What did David promise Bathsheba (vv. 29-30)?

Solomon your son will be king after me

David could easily have issued the orders without Bathsheba being present, but he summoned his queen so that he could make an oath to her. The words were addressed directly to Bathsheba, intimating that this was a matter not only between king and queen, but between husband and wife—father and mother.

What words did Bathsheba say to David as she "bowed low with her face to the ground" (v. 31)?

May my lord King David live forever.

These words were customarily proclaimed by anyone fortunate enough to receive the audience of an ancient Eastern king, but I wonder if they fell from her mouth with peculiar emotion as she bowed before King David. I believe Bathsheba's words were far more than custom. She bowed low with her face to the ground, perhaps wondering if the next time she would assume such posture would be before her son. "May my lord King David live forever!"

Zadok – *priest*

Nathan – *prophet*

Benaiah
(2 Sam. 20:23; 23:20)

*Valiant fighter
– army commander*

David purposely called three men to escort Solomon to his rightful place of authority. In the margin note their roles or positions.

The margin statements are directions David gave to Zadok, Nathan, and Benaiah. Place them in proper order by numbering them 1 to 4.

A prophet, priest, and warrior were chosen to confirm the new king. For the nation to be strong, all four areas of authority needed to be present: prophet, priest, warrior, and king. Interestingly, our Lord and Savior Jesus Christ will ultimately fill every one of those positions. All authority has been given to Christ (Matt. 28:18). Under one Head, all nations will finally be unified.

2 — Have Zadok and Nathan anoint Solomon king over Israel.

3 — Blow the trumpet and shout, "Long live King Solomon!"

1 — Set Solomon on my mule and take him to Gihon.

4 — Seat Solomon on David's throne.

How did the people react to the sound of the trumpet announcing the anointing of Solomon? How did David respond?

"Long live King Solomon"
"Praise be to the Lord, the God of Israel, who has allowed my eyes to see a successor on my throne today."

Why do you think Adonijah took hold of the horns of the altar of sacrifice when he realized Solomon had been anointed king of Israel?

fear of Solomon, protection from God @ the altar.

We've seen many pivotal points in David's life over the last 10 weeks. Now we come to one of the most significant. I can't help but wonder what emotions filled Bathsheba. The crown would be taken from her husband and placed on the head of her son. Did she feel sadness and joy? mourning and celebration? Bathsheba wanted nothing more than for Solomon to receive the crown, but was she prepared for David to have to lose it for Solomon to gain it?

Have you ever been torn between two people? ☐ yes ☐ no   If so, what were the circumstances? How did you feel? Respond in the margin.

Being wife and mother can sometimes feel like two exclusive roles tearing one woman in half. No doubt, Bathsheba experienced those feelings. Her husband assured her Solomon would be king. He was true to his word. Next we focus on the steps taken to bring Solomon to the throne of his father.

David issued specific commands regarding Solomon's rise to power. He sent the primary prophet and priest to anoint him. In addition, he sent his most trustworthy warrior and his army to protect Solomon. They were to put Solomon on King David's mule and escort him. Customarily, a king rode on a mule to signify his intent to be a servant to the people. The mule was often dressed with a wreath of flowers around its neck or a royal drape over its back.

Solomon surely knew he would one day be king. He knew the time would come, but I wonder if he knew what it would be like. Did a servant girl tell him three dignitaries were at the door to speak to him? Or did he hear the bray of the mule? We simply read that Zadok, Nathan, Benaiah, the Kerethites, and the Pelethites went down and put Solomon on King David's mule. Picture the scene as Solomon took the ride of his life. David specifically commanded the men to escort Solomon to Gihon.

Two springs supplied Jerusalem's water: En Rogel and the Gihon spring.
What was happening at the En Rogel spring (1 Kings 1:9)? Reply in margin.

Mt. Moriah
Temple
Mount

• Gihon Spring

City of David

En Rogel Spring
•

The Gihon spring was directly east of the city wall. The ancient Hebrew people believed God's glory and authority would come from the east. The Gihon spring did not provide a steady flow, but "gushes out at irregular intervals, twice a day in the dry season to four or five times in the rainy season."[1] Even the name was significant. The name *Gihon* comes from a Hebrew word which means "a bursting forth."[2] A new king was bursting on the scene to supply the nation of Israel with security and authority.

Zadok took the horn of oil from the sacred tent and anointed Solomon. Was this the same horn tipped by the hand of Samuel over the head of a young shepherd boy? What other horn would have had a place in the sacred tent?

Solomon was not like Absalom and Adonijah, handsome and obvious choices for a king. Solomon may not have been the natural choice in the eyes of men. He was not the oldest of the sons of David, but Solomon represented God's divine mercy. He was the embodiment of second chances. He was the innocence that came from guilt. He was God's choice as history would prove.

I find such security in God's consistency. He is always merciful. Jesus never would have become flesh to dwell among us if not for man's scandalous sin. Jesus certainly did not display the image of the king Israel was expecting, yet He was the embodiment of second chances. He took our guilt on His innocent shoulders and became sin for us, so we could become the righteousness of God in Him (2 Cor. 5:21). Why? Because we were God's choice.

Do you have difficulty accepting yourself as God's good choice?
☐ yes ☐ no In the margin describe why or why not.

When David received the news from his royal officials "the king bowed in worship on his bed and said, 'Praise be to the LORD' " (vv. 47-48). This verse records the last time God used the word "king" in the Book of 1 Kings in reference to His beloved David. God chose to pen this last reference to King David in a sentence eternally linked to two responses. First, worship. Too weak to move to the floor, David fell on his face right where he was. And second, praise. "Praise be to the LORD, the God of Israel, who has allowed my eyes to see a successor on my throne today" (v. 48).

David's rule ended just as it officially began. His stiffened body bowed before God on his final day as king, with the same abandon he demonstrated when he danced through the streets of Jerusalem. Was it not he who said, "Bless the LORD, O my soul: and all that is within me, bless his holy name" (Ps. 103:1, KJV)? With all that was within him he once danced. On that last day as king, he bowed to worship. David's actions were often contradictory, but one consistency he wove throughout his life and reign—he was a man of worship, a man after God's own heart.

DAY 3
Wholehearted Devotion

TODAY'S TREASURE

"My son Solomon, acknowledge the God of your father, and serve him with wholehearted devotion and with a willing mind, for the LORD searches every heart and understands every motive behind the thoughts." 1 Chronicles 28:9

We greet day 3 with a new king. Historians generally agree that David lived between one and two years after Solomon assumed his reign. God allowed David the strength to prepare the new king for public coronation.

The first order of business for the new king was building a house for the Name of the Lord. First Chronicles records the extensive preparations David made before his death (1 Chron. 22:5). We will turn our attentions momentarily away from the less detailed account in 1 Kings. We have a number of chapters to overview today so our questions will be more general in nature. Ask God to help you understand the activities that led to the firmly established throne of King Solomon. Read 1 Chronicles 22. Review 1 Chronicles 21:22-30.

To what location was David referring when he said, "The house of the LORD God is to be here" (1 Chron. 22:1)?

The threshing floor of Araunan

According to 1 Chronicles 22:5, why did David make preparations for the house to be built for the Lord? Check your answer in the margin.

How would you characterize Solomon's reign based on the prophecy God gave David in verses 9 and 10?

Peace & rest

What order did David issue in verse 17? *to help Solomon*
All the leaders in Israel

To what did David tell Solomon and the leaders of Israel to devote their hearts and souls?

to seeking the Lord your God.

In verses 14-16, David shared with Solomon all that had been gathered for the building of the sanctuary and all who had been commissioned to help. I find his words so pertinent and applicable to us today: "Now begin the work, and the LORD be with you" (v. 16). In other words, "I've set aside everything you

☐ He had no confidence in Solomon.
☐ Solomon asked him to make the preparations.
☑ Solomon was young and inexperienced.
☐ David wanted to be involved in the building of the temple.

will need. You have all the support your task will require. Now get started." I remember my mother often giving her children instructions that we received with moans, complaints, and questions. She'd finally say, "I've already told you. Now, get busy." Her words, like David's, were wise and practical. God provides what we need. Now we need to get busy.

Ephesians 2:10

How do the two margin references suggest our need to "get busy"? Based on a comparison of these two verses, how has God prepared us for the good works He ordained for us?

2 Timothy 3:16-17

God's plans are to prosper us, to give us hope and a future (Jer. 29:11). The Word of God and Christ's indwelling Spirit equip us to fulfill the works preordained for us in God's perfect plan. As my mom would say, Get busy!

Some of David's most important words ever appear in 1 Chronicles 22:19. "Now devote your heart and soul to seeking the Lord your God." The Hebrew word for *devote* is *nathan*. It means "to give, place, add, send forth. *Nathan* indicates … fastening something in place."[3] I especially love the idea this wonderful definition expresses in the word *fastening*. David told Solomon and the leaders of Israel to fasten their hearts to seeking the Lord.

To what is your heart fastened? To what is your heart most attached?

In the Book of Matthew, Christ simplified the process of finding our hearts and their attachments. He said, "For where your treasure is, there your heart will be also" (Matt. 6:21). Our hearts are attached to our treasure. So the question becomes, What is our treasure? Little awakens us to what we've treasured like turmoil and suffering. We find out quickly what our priorities have been.

Job's priorities were tested unlike any who had lived before him. He suffered incomparable loss. The only thing more shocking than his loss was his ultimate gain. Nothing accidental surrounded his bounce back. He bounced back because his heart was fastened to pleasing God. Read Job 23:12.

What was Job's treasure and how much did he treasure it? In margin.

No wonder God brought Job forth as gold (Job 23:10). The aged David had also learned a few things about priorities. He knew what he was talking about when he told the leaders of Israel to devote their hearts and souls to seeking the Lord. David knew that little would influence Solomon's success more than being surrounded by leaders whose hearts were devoted to seeking the Lord.

First Chronicles 23–27 document the organization of Solomon's kingdom under David's commands. These five chapters bridge David's two proclamations and chronicle the appointment of the Levites and priests to serve God in the temple, the singers to lead His praises, and the army to protect the people.

David appointed four thousand people to praise the Lord with musical instruments. Can you imagine an orchestra of four thousand? God Himself gave David the words: "Praise him with the sounding of the trumpet, praise him with the harp and lyre, praise him with tambourine and dancing, praise him with the strings and flute, praise him with the clash of cymbals, praise him with resounding cymbals. Let everything that has breath praise the LORD" (Ps. 150:3-6). "Four thousand are to praise the LORD with the musical instruments I have provided for that purpose" (1 Chron. 23:5). Read 1 Chronicles 28.

Who chose Solomon as king (v. 6)?

Read each of the margin statements. Check each specific command David issued Solomon in verse 9.

David gave Solomon the plans for the temple, but who had given the plans to David (v. 12)?

the H. S.

☐ Subdue your enemies quickly.
☑ Serve God with wholehearted devotion.
☑ Serve God with a willing mind.
☐ Delegate authority among trusted leaders.

Today's lesson concludes with our attention on David's strong and specific words to Solomon in verse 9: "And you, my son Solomon, acknowledge the God of your father, and serve him with wholehearted devotion and with a willing mind, for the LORD searches every heart and understands every motive behind the thoughts." His words to Solomon are pertinent to us in every area of potential success.

David gave his son three vital directives we would be wise to obey:

1. Acknowledge God. Acknowledging God first thing every morning transforms our day. I try to begin my day by reconfirming His authority over me and submitting to Him as Lord in advance of my daily circumstances. The words of Joshua 24:15 comprise the best possible morning challenge: "Choose for yourselves this day whom you will serve." When I begin my day without settling the matter of authority, I am usually a train wreck by noon. Remember, any day not surrendered to the Spirit of God will automatically default to the flesh (Gal. 5:16-17). Spiritual living does not come naturally—sin does. The first step to victory is acknowledging the authority of God in our lives.

How do you acknowledge God in your life?

2. Serve Him with wholehearted devotion. The Hebrew word for wholehearted is *shalem* and is elsewhere used in reference to "unhewn, untouched stones."[4] Notice something quite interesting about the temple God commanded Solomon to build. First Kings 6:7 tells us, "In building the temple, only blocks dressed at the quarry were used, and no hammer, chisel or any other iron tool

"Give me an undivided heart, that I may fear your name."

was heard at the temple site while it was being built." Do you see the significance? No stone could be cut in the temple. The uncut stones represented the kind of devotion God was demanding from His nation—*Shalem*, wholehearted devotion, uncut hearts. David was used of God to describe *shalem* perfectly in Psalm 86:11: "Teach me your way, O Lord, and I will walk in your truth; give me an undivided heart, that I may fear your name."

Do you have a divided heart? Does God have a piece of your heart, but the rest belongs to you? Or someone else? If you've given your heart wholly to God, perhaps you remember a time when your heart was divided. Choose a specific time in your life. Divide the heart below into sections. Label each section according to the divisions you had at that time. As an example, I have labeled my heart at the age of 19.

My divided heart caused me significant pain. Did yours? ☐ yes ☐ no
If so, write about it in the margin.

A divided heart places our entire lives in jeopardy. Only God can be totally trusted with our hearts. He doesn't demand our complete devotion to feed His ego but to provide for our safety. God uses an undivided heart to keep us out of trouble. David learned the price of a divided heart the hard way. He lived with the repercussions for the rest of his life. Let's just take his word for it and surrender now. Never forget, God's commands are for our good.

3. Serve Him with a willing spirit. The Hebrew term for *willing* in this reference is *chaphets*, which means "to find pleasure in, take delight in, be pleased with, have an affection for; to desire; to choose; to bend, bow. The main meaning is to feel a strong positive attraction for something, to like someone or something very much."[5] Do you see what God is saying? He wants us to serve Him and honor Him because we want to. Because it pleases us. Because we choose to. You see, the Lord searches every heart and understands every motive behind the thoughts. Hear the beat of His tender heart as He says, "Choose Me because you delight in Me."

Many motives exist for serving God other than pleasure and delight. What are a few other reasons a person might serve God?

God wants us to serve Him with a willing spirit, one that would choose no other way. Right now you may be frustrated because serving and knowing God is not your greatest pleasure. You may be able to instantly acknowledge a divided heart. Your question may be, How can I change the way I feel? You can't. But God can. I know it from personal experience. Give Him your heart—your whole heart. Give Him permission to change it. The words of Deuteronomy 30:6 have changed my life and my heart.

Read Deuteronomy 30:6. Then turn the verse into a personal prayer for a heart wholly devoted to God.

We will never be men and women after God's own heart with half-hearted devotion. A heart wholly devoted to God is a heart like His. Any old heart will do. Any whole heart will do.

DAY 4

Praises of the Great Assembly

TODAY'S TREASURE

"Yours, O LORD, is the greatness and the power and the glory and the majesty and the splendor, for everything in heaven and earth is yours."
1 Chronicles 29:11

Today we see the conclusion of David's address to the assembly. Notice he formally and publicly acknowledged God's sovereignty over Israel. He finalized plans and preparations for the temple. He lifted prayers for a new king. David's final duties toward his beloved nation teach us new truths and recapture some of the most important lessons from the life of the shepherd king.

We can only imagine the emotions that flooded David's heart. In 1 Chronicles 29:1 he reminded the people: "My son Solomon, the one whom God has chosen, is young and inexperienced." David was looking at a young man bursting with energy, full of plans, rehearsing promises—a young man childishly confident he would never do certain things and would always do others.

Solomon lacked nothing but age and experience—a lack that probably scared his father half to death. Looking at a son full of dreams, David dared not say, "This will be the most difficult thing you have ever done." He could not explain how lonely Solomon would be at the top, the exhaustion of too much responsibility, or the boredom of too much power and too few friends. Chances are good he would not have heard David anyway. He had too many stars in his eyes and accolades in his ears.

So David looked at the whole assembly and basically said, "Give him a hand. He's going to need it." Let's join the colossal assembly now and hear the conclusion of David's address to the nation of Israel. Read 1 Chronicles 29:1-9.

What do you think motivated the leaders to give so freely?

David's example

According to verse 9, why did the people rejoice?

the willing response of their leaders - giving whole hearted & freely.

Never underestimate the power of a positive example. David could not motivate the leaders of Israel to give freely and wholeheartedly to the Lord unless he gave. He could force them, but the willing spirit God desired would be forfeited. Their cheerful giving would be motivated by his own; therefore, he had to give more than what belonged to the kingdom. The third verse clearly tells us, "I now give my personal treasures of gold and silver for the temple of my God, over and above everything I have provided for this holy temple."

David gave what was his. What belonged to him. That which was personal. The people overwhelmingly responded. Do we give that which is personal? Does our monetary giving come from our hearts, not just our checkbooks? Does the giving of our time flow from rejoicing, not resentment? God delights in the giving of our personal treasures—and others are motivated by our example. I love the way verse 9 captures the electricity of the moment: "The people rejoiced at the willing response of their leaders, for they had given freely and wholeheartedly to the Lord. David the king also rejoiced greatly." What a glorious moment! I can't think of much that spurs the hearts of the people of God like the wholehearted devotion of their leaders. When leadership is sold out to God, the followers become willing to sell out.

In Exodus 35 God asked for freewill offerings, or personal offerings given from the heart, for the building of the tabernacle. Why did God want offerings from the heart for the construction of His dwelling places?

Has a leader in your life ever motivated you to give your time, talents, gifts, or treasures by his or her own example? ☐ yes ☐ no   If so, who was he or she, and how has the example affected you?

Read 1 Chronicles 29:10-20. Consider verses 10-13 carefully. Condense in one sentence what you believe David was saying.

God is the Almighty

Read the margin statements and check each one that reflects David's words to God in verse 14.

In verse 17 David acknowledged the importance of integrity to God. What does the word *integrity* mean to you?

What two things did David request from God in verse 18? *keep this desire in the hearts of your people forever*
keep their hearts loyal to you.

David both told Solomon to serve God with wholehearted devotion and asked God to give Solomon wholehearted devotion (1 Chron. 28:9; 29:19). Whole-hearted devotion is obviously a joint work between God and the individual.

In the margin explain your understanding of the joint work of God and man in establishing a wholehearted devotion toward God.

When David said, "Praise the LORD your God," what did the people do (v. 20)? The passage reminds us that God does not demand our praises to make Him feel more like God. He is completely God. All the attention of the earth's inhabitants could never make Him a bigger, greater God. May we never forget the awesome benefits of authentic praise. God desires our praises for many reasons, but I believe among the most vital are these two.

1. Praise reminds us who He is. When I am overwhelmed and wonder if God can see me through, He often calls on me to rehearse out loud—before His ears and mine—some of His many virtues:

- His wonders in the lives of those recorded in the Word
- His wonders in my own life
- His wonders in the lives of those I know

I proclaim out loud His greatness and His power and His glory. Then when I consider my need compared to His strength and bounty, I can proclaim with confidence the words of the prophet Jeremiah.

Write the prophet's words in Jeremiah 32:17.

2. Praise reminds us who we are. Praise is an exercise in perspective. Notice David's words in verse 14 of 1 Chronicles 29, "But who am I?" Authentic praise works every time. Things seem to fall right in perspective. I don't believe we can praise and worship long without ending up with a heart freshly humbled.

☐ God honors our offerings whether or not we want to give.

☐ Giving to God is an awesome privilege.

☐ To withhold from God is to provoke His wrath.

☑ Everything we give to God comes from His own hand.

231

Read Psalm 8:1-4. What caused David to gain a fresh perspective?

Perspective invariably accompanies praise. Hearts prone to praise will keep our perspective on the timeless might and power of God. Without an active praise life, our perspective of God gets turned upside down.

In Isaiah 29:16 God described how wrong our perceptions can be. In the margin restate the verse in your own words.

Isaiah 29:13 holds the key to role confusion and is one of the most important Scripture references in our study. "These people come near to me with their mouth and honor me with their lips, but their hearts are far from me." A study of King David is invariably a study about the heart. As our study comes to a close, we want to know everything we can about having a heart like God's.

We discussed divided hearts yesterday. Today reminds us again of faraway hearts. A heart far from God tends to think it's in charge, demanding its own way. A faraway heart is the opposite of everything Paul writes about love in 1 Corinthians 13. A faraway heart has lost its perspective. Worst of all, a faraway heart can never be a heart like His, the kind of heart God searches for to show Himself strong (2 Chron. 16:9, KJV).

Long after we have closed the last page of this study, I pray we will continue to keep our hearts in check. Surely David's life has taught us to watch over our hearts with all diligence (Prov. 4:23, NASB).

Right now, I ask you to make a personal commitment. Spend a few moments reflecting on what you've learned in the last 10 weeks. Pray for the Holy Spirit to remind you of specific truths about the heart. Our study has shown us the very best of a man's heart and the very worst. David's heart was the origin of his greatest delight and his gravest disaster.

What have you learned about your heart through your journey with David? Try to name both positive elements and negative elements you've learned about the heart.

POSITIVE	NEGATIVE

In light of all we've learned together, do you see the extreme importance of watching over your heart and giving it wholly to the One who both created and loves you? If so, write a prayer of commitment, naming specific ways you will commit to keeping your heart in check. Have courage in your prayer. Let's ask God to uncover every impurity in our hearts as they first develop. Remember, a little discomfort and humiliation in the privacy of our relationship with God is far better than the ultimate exposure of a heart out of control.

Write your prayer below. Use the margin if you need more space.

David reminded us that everything we can offer God comes from His own hand. Even our passion for God comes from Him (Deut. 30:6). He told us to delight ourselves in Him. He is the only One who can supply us with delight (Ps. 37:4). He told us to serve Him with our spiritual gifts. We receive our gifts from Him. Everything we give to God we must first get from God!

Passionate hearts and genuine praises are invariably contagious. David's overflow caused a tidal wave of praise. In 1 Chronicles 29:20, when David called the whole assembly to praise the Lord their God, "they bowed low and fell prostrate before the LORD and the king." Scripture records many instances in which the Hebrew people wandered from God and rebelled against His perfect plan. Joyfully, the Word of God also records refreshing instances in which they rightly responded to the awesomeness of God. The wonderful chapter we've considered today chronicles one of those precious moments—a contagion of praise. David and his people were overwhelmed with the privilege of giving: "But who am I, and who are my people, that we should be able to give as generously as this?" (v. 14). The enormity of what they had been able to give represented the enormity of what they had been given. And they fell on their faces.

Surely time stood still in David's mind as the people fell prostrate before the Lord and before the king. Close your eyes for a moment and picture the scene. Keep the picture like a snapshot in your memory. We've waited 10 weeks to witness an entire kingdom in unity before God. As we compare verses 9 and 20, we know that David was the one to whom Scripture referred as king. All the people fell before the Lord and His beloved David, God's first choice, a man after His own heart. So there David stood, a man of many years and experiences. His legs trembled with illness and age. His heart blazed with emotion. The streets of the city of God were paved with praises, blanketed with the prostrate bodies of all who called Jehovah their God. Praise His name, it won't be the last time. We'll gather with every tribe, tongue, and nation and finally give the Lord the praise He is due.

DAY 5

A Resting Place

TODAY'S TREASURE

"David son of Jesse was king over all Israel. He ruled over Israel forty years—seven in Hebron and thirty-three in Jerusalem. He died at a good old age, having enjoyed long life, wealth and honor. His son Solomon succeeded him as king." 1 Chronicles 29:26-28

How will I ever express to you my gratitude for your desire and discipline to see this lengthy study to completion? I approach you with fresh tears today, praying the truths we've acquired through the last 10 weeks have been sewn into our spirits forever. May the very mention of the psalmist's name spark familiar thoughts and draw portraits in our minds for the rest of our lives. May we remember the heights of his praise and the depths of his sin and be moved appropriately by each.

David has been a worthy subject for our study. The last words of 1 Chronicles read, "As for the events of King David's reign, from beginning to end, they are written in the records of Samuel the seer, the records of Nathan the prophet and the records of Gad the seer, together with the details of his reign and power, and the circumstances that surrounded him and Israel and the kingdoms of all the other lands."

Indeed, our God gave no insignificant space to the chronicles of David's life. He was the object of much love and continues to be the object of much learning. May our final day of study be no exception. Read 1 Chronicles 29:21-25.

How would you describe the mood of the people the day following David's public address?

V22. ate & drank w. great joy

How did the people of Israel respond to their new king?

acknowledged a 2nd time & anointed him
V23 obeyed him

How did Solomon's kingdom compare to David's based on verse 25?

even more royal splendar.

In Psalm 69:16 David wrote: "Answer me, O LORD, out of the goodness of your love." As his life came to its end, we see how God graciously answered. In Psalm 51 David begged forgiveness. Solomon was the tangible evidence of

David's pardon, for of him Scripture says: "The LORD loved him" (2 Sam. 12:24). Just as the contrite father had asked, the Word says of Solomon, "He prospered and all Israel obeyed him" (1 Chron. 29:23). And "All the officers and mighty men, as well as all of King David's sons, pledged their submission to King Solomon" (v. 24).

The unrelenting sword was finally at rest. David's house was in order. God had given a weary man strength and helped him prepare a family and a nation for life in his absence. Surely as he bowed on his sickbed, David had prayed the words of Psalm 71:9.

Do not cast me away when I am old, do not forsake me when my strength is gone

Please write Psalm 71:9 in the margin.

God did not cast David away. God did not forsake him when he was old. The God whose faithfulness endures to all generations completed the good work He started in a shepherd. Now the work was finally finished. The empty grave pled to be filled, the warrior to cease fighting. His thoughts must have been like those of the writer of the 102nd Psalm: "For my days vanish like smoke; my bones burn like glowing embers. My heart is blighted and withered like grass; I forget to eat my food. Because of my loud groaning, I am reduced to skin and bones" (vv. 3-5).

David had no reason to resist death's call. He had lived the length of his days. His throne was filled. It was fitting that his grave be filled as well. He had turned over his crown and joyfully dedicated his personal riches to the building of the temple. He was too old to conquer kingdoms, too sick to fill a sling, too frail to feast on the fatted calf. But that which he treasured most was never so dear to him and never so real. Scholars generally agree that the words of Psalm 71 were written in David's old age as he confronted his hastening death.

Read Psalm 71:14. What would David always have that no one could take from him? *hope & praise*

Read Psalm 71:20 carefully. What hope did David have as the cords of death encompassed him? *you will restore my life again*

He had hope of the blessed resurrection, just as we do. Not just an empty wish, but an anxious and certain expectation. From his proclamation of hope came Psalm 71:22.

What instruments did David speak of using to praise God (Ps. 71:22)?

harp & lyre

Did David speak in the psalm of his commitment to praise God in his final days, or did he speak of his expectation for coming resurrection? I think of David in both situations. I picture the aged king praising God. Once more his fingers wrapped around the strings of his harp, his hands no longer the calloused young hands of a hearty shepherd boy. Bent with age, slowed with time, David's fingers brushed across the strings. His voice, once wavering with adolescence, now wavered with age.

No sweeter voice can be heard than the one which flows, however unevenly, from the sincere heart of the aged. No longer did David's voice resound with the richness that had once awed a tormented Saul. Resigned to the will of the Father, in perfect harmony with God's plan for his life, he sang a final song of hope. The One who would take him to the depths of the earth would bring him up. So he departed this life with two magnificent treasures: peace with his family and hope in his resurrection.

"Then David rested with his fathers and was buried in the City of David" (1 Kings 2:10). The eyes that had peeked into the heart of God now closed in death. The earthly life of one of the most passionate and controversial figures ever to grace this planet ended. The deadly silence must have lasted only long enough for Bathsheba to place her ear close to his mouth and her hand on his heart. The faint rise and fall of his chest had ceased.

No doubt the silence gave way to wails of grief. Trumpets carried the news. A kind of mourning peculiar to the Hebrew nation filled the days that followed. The very instruments commissioned by David for the dedication of the temple ironically may have first played his funeral dirge. Multitudes heaped ashes on their heads and draped sackcloth on their bodies. After an intense period of national mourning with visits from foreign dignitaries, life continued—just as it has the audacity to do after we've lost a loved one.

Life went on, but forever marked by the life of God's chosen king. God sovereignly chose to chisel David's reign into a kingdom that would last forever. As we close our study, carefully read the words of Jeremiah 33:14-22.

How certain is the covenant God made with David?

V17; David will never fail to have a man to sit on the of the house of Israel

How do you know God's covenant with David has never been broken?

Jesus is the king that sits on the throne of Israel

Read Luke 2:4-7. Summarize the content of the verses.

Joseph belonged to the house of David

Write Luke 1:32.

He will be great and will be called the Son of the Most High. The Lord God will give him the throne of father

The distant grandson David wrote about in Psalm 110 was no surprise to David. God whispered these truths in his spirit and caused him to write them down for all eternity.

Please read David's words in Psalm 110 aloud—hopefully with a fresh revelation of their significance. What did David call Christ in verse 1?

my Lord

Indeed, one unexpected day the clouds will roll back and the King of all kings will burst through the sky. "On that day his feet will stand on the Mount of Olives, east of Jerusalem, and the Mount of Olives will be split in two from east to west. ... Then the LORD my God will come, and all the holy ones with him. On that day there will be no light, no cold nor frost. It will be a unique day, without daytime or nighttime—a day known to the LORD. ... The LORD will be king over the whole earth. On that day there will be one LORD, and his name the only name" (Zech. 14:4,5-7,9).

Christ Jesus will sit on the throne of David in the city of Jerusalem and hope will give birth to certainty. We will join the one who said, "You turned my wailing into dancing; you removed my sackcloth and clothed me with joy, that my heart may sing to you and not be silent. O LORD my God, I will give you thanks forever" (Ps. 30:11-12). With David, we will sing to the One and only One who is worthy!

That day there just might be one who can't seem to stop singing. Oh, yes, I believe David will dance once more down the streets of Jerusalem—this time without an eye to despise him. Oblivious to anyone but God, the focus of his affections, the passion of his heart. David will dance his way to that same familiar throne, but this time it will be occupied by another. No one above Him. None beside Him. David will see the Lord high and lifted up and His train will fill the temple. David will fall before the One who sits on the throne, take the crown from his own head, and cast it at His feet. He'll lift his eyes to the King of all kings and with the passions of an entire nation gathered in one heart, he will cry, "Worthy!"

Surely God the Father will look with great affection upon the pair.
All wrongs made right. All faith now sight.
He'll search the soul of a shepherd boy once more
And perhaps He will remark
How very much he has
A heart like His.

What is the most significant way God has spoken to you through *David*?

viewer guide | session eleven

[handwritten margin notes:]
2 metaphors
shepherd
table

each referencing
a relationship of
intimacy & care.

Completeness of God's
Communion.

1. The _____shepherd_____ and the _____sheep_____

2. The _____Host_____ and the _____guests_____

"In his imagination, he goes back to the _____sunny_____ _____days_____ of his _____youth_____ … The Old Testament belief in God … powerfully draws together in a _____single_____ integrated reflection thoughts of the _____past_____, the _____present_____ and the _____future_____."[1]

[handwritten:] What is a need? What is a greed?

PART 1
[handwritten:] Yahweh - timeless.

The Lord Is My Shepherd *[handwritten:] Talking about God.*

- He _____takes_____ _____care_____ of me.

- He _____restores_____ my soul. A more literal rendering of "He restores" is: "He causes to _____come_____ _____back_____."[2]

[handwritten margin notes:]
Act 13:36 - served
God's purpose in his
own generation.

Phil 2:13
according to his
purpose.

- He _____guides_____ me down the right path. *[handwritten:] - rightness.(not right)*

- He is _____with_____ _____me_____. *Salmawet* combines two words: *sel* (_____shadow_____) and *mawet* (_____death_____). "Together these words express the superlative—in this case, something like 'the _____shadowiest_____ of all shadows.'"[3]

[handwritten top margin] to commune w. God - to feast at His table.

PART 2 *[handwritten: Talking to God]*

___You___, Lord, Are My ___Host___.

[handwritten right: Is. 25:6]

- "You prepare a table before me." *Prepare* also means ___arrange___ *[handwritten: , display]*
  We're probably not reading too much into Psalm 23:5 to see
  " ___Eucharistic___ ___overtones___ ."[4]

  [handwritten: Ex 24 8-11 (circled) Luke 22:14-20 NB.]

- "in the ___presence___ of my enemies"

- "You anoint my head with oil; my cup ___overflows___ ." *[handwritten: I am the cup.]*

- "Surely goodness and love will follow me." *Radaf* means ___pursue___ ,
  ___chase___ . "*Pursue* is used outside of its normal context in an
  ironic manner." The verb used here is "often used to describe the
  ___hostile___ ___actions___ of enemies."[5]

  [handwritten right: David had often been chased / pursued. God's love & goodness is faster than the enemy.]

- "I will dwell in the ___house___ of the LORD ___forever___ "

[handwritten: Heb. 4:16 - grace & mercy.] *[handwritten: Ps 27:4]*

1. Artur Weiser, *The Psalms* (Philadelphia: Westminster Press, 1962), 228.
2. Samuel Terrien, *The Psalms* (Grand Rapids, MI: William B. Eerdmans Publishing Co., 2003), 239.
3. Jamie Grant, "Psalms" in the *NIV Application Commentary* (Grand Rapids, MI: Zondervan, 2009), 434.
4. Robert Dorn, Leander Keck, J. McCann, Carol Newsom, *New Interpreters Bible Commentary*, Vol. 4 (Nashville, TN: Abingdon Press, 1996), 770.
5. Scripture quoted by permission. Quotations designated (NET) are from the NET Bible® copyright ©1996-2006 by Biblical Studies Press, L.L.C. *http://bible.org* All rights reserved.

Endnotes

Week 1

1. Robert Alter, *The David Story* (New York: W. W. Norton & Co., 2000), ix.
2. Spiros Zodhiates, gen. ed., *The Complete Word Study Dictionary: New-Testament* (Chattanooga, TN: AMG Publishers, 1992), 1091.
3. Trent C. Butler et al., eds., *Holman Bible Dictionary* (Nashville: Holman Bible Publishers, 1991), 774.
4. Warren Baker, gen. ed., *The Complete Word Study Dictionary: Old-Testament* (Chattanooga, TN: AMG Publishers, 1992), 2363.
5. Ibid., 2306.

Week 2

1. Baker, 2306.
2. John Dryden, "The Hind and the Panther," *The Poetical Works of John Dryden*, Cambridge Edition, ed. George R. Noyes (Boston: Houghton Mifflin Company, 1909), 236.
3. Baker, 2318.
4. Ibid., 105.
5. James Strong, *Strong's Exhaustive Concordance* (Grand Rapids, MI: Baker Book House, 1982), 95.

Week 3

1. Butler, 21.

Week 4

1. Zodhiates, 483.
2. Baker, 2300.
3. Ibid., 2355.

Week 6

1. Zodhiates, 1295.
2. Adam Clarke, *Clarke's Commentary on the Whole Bible* [online] n.d. [cited 30 July 2010]. Available from the Internet: *http://www.studylight.org/com/acc/view.cgi?book=2sa&chapter=008*
3. Baker, 2360.
4. Butler, 946.

Week 7

1. Baker, 2326.
2. Alan Redpath, *The Making of a Man of God* (Grand Rapids, MI: Fleming H. Revell, 1962), 197.
3. Baker, 19.
4. Ibid., 2337.
5. Ibid., 2306.

Week 8

1. Butler, 45.

Week 9

1. Baker, 86.
2. *The Disciple's Study Bible* (Nashville: Holman Bible Publishers, 1988), 390.
3. Baker, 2239.
4. Ibid. 2340.

Week 10

1. Butler, 774.
2. Ibid.
3. Baker, 2344.
4, Ibid., 2375.
5. Ibid., 2317.